Law, Governance and Technology Series

Volume 26

The *Law-Governance and Technology Series* is intended to attract manuscripts arising from an interdisciplinary approach in law, artificial intelligence and information technologies. The idea is to bridge the gap between research in IT law and IT-applications for lawyers developing a unifying techno-legal perspective. The series will welcome proposals that have a fairly specific focus on problems or projects that will lead to innovative research charting the course for new interdisciplinary developments in law, legal theory, and law and society research as well as in computer technologies, artificial intelligence and cognitive sciences. In broad strokes, manuscripts for this series may be mainly located in the fields of the Internet law (data protection, intellectual property, Internet rights, etc.), Computational models of the legal contents and legal reasoning, Legal Information Retrieval, Electronic Data Discovery, Collaborative Tools (e.g. Online Dispute Resolution platforms), Metadata and XML Technologies (for Semantic Web Services), Technologies in Courtrooms and Judicial Offices (E-Court), Technologies for Governments and Administrations (E-Government), Legal Multimedia, and Legal Electronic Institutions (Multi-Agent Systems and Artificial Societies).

More information about this series at http://www.springer.com/series/8808

Nicola Lucchi

The Impact of Science and Technology on the Rights of the Individual

Springer

Nicola Lucchi
Department of Law
Jönköping University International Business School
Jönköping, Sweden

ISSN 2352-1902 ISSN 2352-1910 (electronic)
Law, Governance and Technology Series
ISBN 978-3-319-30437-3 ISBN 978-3-319-30439-7 (eBook)
DOI 10.1007/978-3-319-30439-7

Library of Congress Control Number: 2016942542

Printed on acid-free paper

This Springer imprint is published by Springer Nature
The registered company is Springer International Publishing AG Switzerland

Foreword

Advances in information technology and biosciences have undoubtedly provided for a better information infrastructure and quality of life for many people, but at the same time they brought with them a number of new challenging regulatory issues. The legal response to these developments has been a subject of global controversies and litigations in numerous courts and still remains an unresolved issue. In addition, a relatively new phenomenon is occurring in the field of scientific and technology regulation: constitutional provisions in general and fundamental rights in particular are increasingly considered by courts as a measurement for determining potential threats and impacts deriving from scientific and technology issues. This increasing trend is quite evident not only from the growing scholarly works highlighting the human rights dimension on techno-scientific aspects but also from a relevant and expanding number of international documents "laying down principles to guide and regulate technological development that are openly based upon human rights norms".[1]

This book investigates the conflict between technology, scientific advances and fundamental rights principles proposing alternative strategies and best practices for accessing and using informational assets.

Based on these premises, the manuscript aims to offer a critical and comparative analysis of the impact of science and technology on the rights of the individuals considering alternative regulatory regimes for digital and information goods. This is an increasingly complex area of regulation with a specifically global dimension and involving problems which cannot be resolved at the level of individual states. In this

[1] See Roger Brownsword and Morag Goodwin, Law and Technologies of the Twenty-First Century 226 (2012). Among these relevant documents, see e.g. some recent reports issued by different Special Rapporteurs appointed by the United Nations Human Rights Council. See United Nations General Assembly, Human Rights Council, Report of the Special Rapporteur in the Field of Cultural Rights: The Right to Enjoy the Benefits of Scientific Progress and its Applications, Farida Shaheed, U.N. Doc. UA/HRC/20/26 (14 May 2012); United Nations General Assembly, Human Rights Council, Commission on Human Rights, Report by the Special Rapporteur on the Promotion and Protection of the Right to Freedom of Opinion and Expression, Frank La Rue, U.N. Doc. A/HRC/17/27 (16 May 2011).

context, the book aspires to identify and design a map of the changing nature of law and rights in the face of emerging issues in science and technology, discerning when rights are under stress and when they must be reasserted.[2] To achieve this goal, it covers a wide variety of issues – both theoretical and practical – exploring emerging controversies at the crossroads of law, science and technology ranging from patent implications in the area of personalized or precision medicine, to copyright and free speech issues arising on the Internet, to legal and ethical concerns surrounding new discoveries in the biosciences. In this scenario, the main objective of the book is to seek a better understanding of the role of law in the global regulation of innovative technologies. The overall approach will be to seek provocative parallels and analogies between the regulative rules of technologies for the biological and communicative fields: the so-called "meta-technologies of information".[3] This objective will be achieved through a case-based analysis on the global strategies for accessing and using essential public knowledge assets in the knowledge-based society and in the life sciences in general. Drawing upon comparative and case study material, the research also analyses the functional relationship between modern communication technologies, legislative reforms in the area of digital communications, biomedical innovations and their implications on individual rights and democratic principles. These are serious and sensitive issues which can have challenging consequences on global public health, biomedical ethics, freedom of speech, media freedom and media pluralism.

In addressing these thought-provoking questions, the book investigates ethical, legal and security aspects resulting from emerging technologies and regulatory policies. The law's intersection with science and technology is – in fact – representative of many challenging problems that are part of the EU legal order: tension between "rights" and "regulations" on the one hand, and between national heterogeneity and European harmonization on the other hand. These are two fruitful paths of investigation that make the manuscript an interesting contribution to a number of crucial legal and theoretical aspects within a range of different regulatory spheres: global, European and national. The manuscript looks at these issues in the context of European and North American jurisdictions.

The book is based on research projects undertaken over the past three years and conducted under the sponsorship of various research institutions.

Jönköping
April 2016

Nicola Lucchi

[2] See Sheila Jasanoff, Rewriting Life, Reframing Rights, in Reframing Rights: Bioconstitutionalism and the Genetic Age 1, 9 (Sheila Jasanoff ed., 2011).

[3] See Biotechnology and Communication: The Meta-technologies of Information 3, (Sandra Braman ed., 2004).

Preface

The rapid pace of scientific discoveries and the development of new technologies are creating new legal dilemmas intensifying calls for legislative solutions. At the centre of these dilemmas, there is often a tension between respecting the rights of the individual and the rights of the community. The impact of these innovations can also influence human behaviours, legal constraints and cultural values. At the same time, technological and scientific developments have also drawn attention to the necessity for new rights to be acknowledged or even old ones reinterpreted.

The question of the "new rights" has become a perennial theme. It is the result of a taxonomic trend that goes a long way back. This question has produced several classifications of "rights" ranging from those that distinguish between "negative" freedom and "positive" rights to those supporting the opposition between liberal rights and social rights or between rights with or without a cost, or even the periodization of the different "generations" of rights. Apparently, the emergence of new rights claims belongs to the last of these generations. This phenomenon greatly increased with the development of new technologies, especially in the area of biotech innovations and telecommunications. These technologies – in fact – interact with law, generating discussions for new rights claims or conflicts with existing rights.

In considering this vexed question, classifications and distinctions should be used to better understand the characteristics of the objects to which new and existing rights can be applied. But the different classifications of rights seem to operate in the opposite direction: in fact these classifications do not make clear, but often misrepresent the reality of rights, placing them in frameworks shaped by ideological sclerosis.

As noted by Forsthoff,[1] the rule of law does not arise from the liberal demand to protect the rights of individuals from the aggression of the public authorities, but it stems primarily from the need for individuals to find protection in the public power by the dominance of private individuals who hold economic and social power. *Homo homini lupus* is the Hobbesian condition from which the law of the state must take individuals to safety: this is also the reason why Thomas Hobbes is considered

[1] Ernst Forsthof, Der Staat der Industriegesellschaft (1971).

the "true father of the liberal constitutional state".[2] It is not surprising that the civil and the other national codifications anticipate the constitutionalization of the public institutions: the first request made to the enlightened sovereign by those who fear the predominant power of the stronger, was the legal regulation of the relationships between private parties.

If we look at the current challenge hinged on the recognition of new rights, the problem of the distinction between rights with a cost and rights that cost nothing has been successfully demystified by Holmes and Sunstein,[3] which have highlighted their deeply ideological nature. Holmes and Sunstein's main criticism concerning this distinction is that both these types of rights involve some degree of expenditure by the government. Therefore, all legal rights have costs (both economic and non-economic). Consequently, one of the key problems in deciding what rights individuals should have, is to consider whether they are worth those costs. Under such conditions, the claim of a new right involves considering whether a limitation of other conflicting right or interest is an equitable and reasonable solution.

The theme of the recognition of new rights is currently mostly related to the tangled jungle of "claims" that are being made in the areas of biological and life science, healthcare and information technology. Consider – for example – the categories of rights related to the sphere of biolaw, specifically all those rights claims related to the so-called life sciences or the care of the health of the human being. Along these lines, there is much talk over the reproductive health right, the right to a particular kind of treatment, the right to die with dignity, the right to refuse medical treatment, the right to have a healthy child, the prenatal eugenic right, the rights of the embryo and of the right to abortion, etc. Around the undefined concept of human dignity – often framed under the category of human rights – any kind of "right" generally associated with the phenomenon of globalization and multiculturalism can take shape. In the same way, there is an extensive catalog of "rights" claimable in relation to the development of the Internet and the digital communication technologies: it is here suffice to mention the right to access to knowledge, the right to communicate and the right to access the Internet.

In this context, it is hard to say to what extent the new phenomena that occur in social relationships or in the world of technology can really change the structure of the old rights, or whether they are simply a new perspective in which to view them. However, there is a trend that I see growing in the scientific literature on the issue of "new rights": it is a sort of parthenogenesis of new disciplines, namely the multiplication of new fields and subjects of specific study related to "new rights" and the technologies connected to them. At the same time, the need clearly emerges to study these issues entering the gray area between legal, and scientific or technological knowledge. In addition, the study on "new rights" often requires extensive encounter with scientific data, technological standards, and medical protocols, etc. All these aspects move the attention to factors and information that are not associated with some specific national domains but rather encourage the expansion of this type

[2] Carl Schmitt, The Leviathan in the State Theory of Thomas Hobbes: Meaning and Failure of a Political Symbol 71 (Schwab and Hilfstein trans., 1996).

[3] See Stephen Holmes & Cass R. Sunstein, The Cost of Rights: Why Liberty Depends on Taxes (1999).

of investigation to a cross-border dimension, rather than comparative. The resolution of these issues is increasingly losing relations to the laws of individual states while their treatment is becoming more connected to legislative or jurisprudential answers capable of circulating across different borders.

In this fragmented and complex environment, this book tries to highlight the connections between these various points indicating some of the most recent trends in science and technology policy and their interconnection with individual rights exploring controversies surrounding the creation of new rights claims.

Working with rights is a tricky business. The problem is that the recognition of new rights is a zero-sum game, because every progress in the acknowledgment of a new right often implies a step back of another right. For example, it may happen that to pay the price is the right of another individual (the right to fence off my land produces the limitation of the right of movement of other individuals) or a general interest (the right to carry arms reduces the safety of the community). In addition, in the human rights area admitting a new fundamental right would create downside risks connected to an over-extension of human rights protection. The paradox at the center of the human rights discourse is that the uncontrolled proliferation "of new rights would be much more likely to contribute to a serious devaluation of the human rights currency than to enrich significantly the overall coverage provided by existing rights".[4] In other words, an excessive and uncontrolled proliferation of new rights claims can lead to the erosion of their importance and credibility as well as of the effectiveness of their protection and enforcement.

Any limitation to the enjoyment of a right is justified only on the basis of the need to safeguard rights of other individuals or collective interests. The method of balancing different conflicting values is part of the intrinsic nature of rights, at least in a pluralist constitutional order in which there are no absolute rights or "non-negotiable values". The balancing exercise includes the assessment of the reasonableness of the limits and of the proportionality between the compression of a right and the advantage secured to a competing right or interest. This is increasingly recognized as a constitutional dilemma, and courts and legislatures are more and more called upon to consider these questions.

When we look at a limitation of a right – without considering the category to which it belongs – the questions are always the same: Is this limitation reasonable? What is the competing interest? Is the competing interest appreciable? Is the competing interest proportionate to the sacrifice required? These are the questions we should ask whenever a claim for a new right is made. The merit of this book is to go hunting for these conflicting interests and competing values, making interesting discoveries and finding interesting patterns.

Professor of Constitutional Law Roberto Bin
University of Ferrara
Italy

[4] See Philip Alston, Conjuring Up New Human Rights: A Proposal for Quality Control, 78 American Journal of International Law 607, 614 (1984).

Acknowledgements

This work constitutes the final, comprehensive and exhaustive outcome of previous studies essentially based on a project entitled "The Global Governance of Access to Knowledge: An Interdisciplinary and Comparative Research" undertaken and conducted under the sponsorship of a EU Marie Curie Post-doctoral Fellowship at the Université catholique de Louvain (Belgium) funded by the Marie Curie Actions of the European Commission. The work performed during the fellowship was an opportunity to explore and evaluate the concrete and potential consequences of bio and digital technologies on the global intellectual property regime and the tensions between exclusive private rights, individual legal rights and essential public knowledge assets. The research was then further developed and implemented at Jönköping University International Business School (Sweden) where I am currently tenured as an associate professor in law.

Writing this book helped me to put together two topics about which I am passionate, working on emerging scientific and technological developments and their associated regulatory implications. It also allowed me to revisit, implement, combine and refine ideas described in some of my earlier works. In order to complement this objective, the investigation seeks not only to develop the analytical and theoretical apparatus further, but also to review the current research frontline and stimulate cross-disciplinary approaches. On this terrain, the book extensively discusses cross-cutting research conducted and published by a broad range of scholars and civil rights activists, who pursue diverse methodologies. Extensive citations supplement this controversial debate within the body of research that focuses on these issues. This means that some sections of this book are heavily footnoted. My intention is for this book to assist readers by also providing a compilation and reference resources.

A number of the ideas and arguments in this book were first presented, discussed and tested out in the following public research seminars and conferences: Biotech Innovations & Individual's Rights Conference, University of Ferrara, Ferrara (20–21 January 2011, Italy); the conference on the "Impact of Biotechnological Innovations on Human Society", University of Trento, Trento (17 and 18 May 2012, Italy); the 5th International Conference on Information law and ethics, Ionian

University, Corfu (29–30 June 2012, Greece); the research seminar held at Jonkoping International Business School, Jonkoping (19 June 2012, Sweden); the 1st Global Thematic IASC Conference on the Knowledge Commons, Université catholique de Louvain, Louvain-la-Neuve (12–14th September 2012, Belgium); the Intellectual Property and Human Rights Conference and Roundtable Discussion, American University Washington College of Law, Washington DC (21–22 February, 2013, USA); the Italian-Spanish conference on constitutional law on "The new guiding principles for protection of individual rights", University of Bologna – Real Colegio de España en Bologna, Bologna (3–4 May 2012, Italy); the Workshop on Biodiversity governance and social innovations: taking the legal, governance and epistemological agenda forward- 7th to 9th of October 2013 – Université catholique de Louvain, Collège Thomas More, Louvain-la-Neuve (Belgium); the 22th Biennial Conference of the Italian Association of Comparative Law University of Salerno, Salerno, May 30–June 1, 2013 (Italy); the conference on Pluralism in the Age of Internet – European University Institute – Florence School of Regulation, Florence (8 November 2013 – Italy); XXI International Conference in Law and the Human Genome, May 14, 2014 – Universidad de Deusto & Universidad del País Vasco, Bilbao (May 14, 2014, Spain); IXth AIDC-IACL World Congress on "Constitutional Challenges: Global and Local", Oslo (16–20 June 2014 – Norway); Sixth Annual Conference on Innovation and Communications Law – University of Leeds, Leeds (2–3 July 2014 – England); 2nd Thematic Conference on Knowledge Commons: Governing Pooled Knowledge Resources, NYU School of Law, New York (5–7 September, 2014, USA).

I have benefited greatly from the comments of participants at all these meetings. They are too numerous to mention here, but without their helpful criticism and valuable insights this work would not have been completed in such an inspiring way.

So many people have helped, guided and inspired me during this research study. First of all, for his invaluable and constructive guidance on my Marie Curie project and his generous support of my work, I am most grateful to Tom Dedeurwaerdere. I have learned much from him and I am really indebted for his fruitful collaboration, valuable advice and inspiration to my research activity. I am also grateful for his trust and constant encouragement. Tom and all my former colleagues at the Université catholique de Louvain have been wonderfully supportive of my work. I am then especially grateful to all the friends and colleagues that read, criticized, discussed or suggested improvements to parts and topics of the manuscript during the long course of its composition: Fulya Batur, Marco Bassini, Filippo Benelli, Iñigo de Miguel Beriain, Roberto Bin, Enrico Bonadio, Carlos María Romeo Casabona, Ricardo Chueca, Brendan Coolsaet, Tom Dedeurwaerdere, Carla Faralli, Mathieu Guillermin, Guido Margutti, Giuseppe Mazziotti, Sylvie Nérisson, Mart Ots, Simone Penasa, Oreste Pollicino, Monroe Price, Arul George Scaria, Silvia Schiavo, Carol-Ann Soames, Paolo Sommaggio, Lars-Göran Sund, Stefan Verhulst, Paolo Veronesi and Eric Welch.

For suggestions on how improve some sections of the manuscript, I am finally grateful to the comments provided by the Springer anonymous referees on the penultimate draft of this book that enabled me to make many valuable final edits and improvements to the manuscript.

This book would not have been possible without the active and generous support of my current home institution – Jonkoping University International Business School – and the wonderful people with whom I have now the privilege of working.

I express my gratitude to all these people, but all errors and omissions remain my own.

Contents

List of Abbreviations

ACLU	American Civil Liberties Union
ACTA	Anti-Counterfeiting Trade Agreement
CDA	Communications Decency Act
CJEU	Court of Justice of the European Union
DNA	Deoxy-ribo-Nucleic Acid
ECHR	European Court of Human Rights
EFPIA	European Federation of Pharmaceutical Industries and Associations
EPO	European Patent Office
EUCFR	European Union Charter of Fundamental Rights
EST	Expressed Sequence Tag
GR	Genetic Resource
HADOPI	Haute Autorité pour la Diffusion des Oeuvres et la Protection des Droits sur l'Internet
IP	Intellectual Property
IPR	Intellectual Property Right
ISP	Internet Service Provider
JPO	Japan Patent Office
OECD	Organization for Economic Cooperation and Developement
RNA	Ribo-Nucleic Acid
USC	United States Code
USPO	United States Patent Office
WIPO	World Intellectual Porperty Organization
WTO	World Trade Organization

Journal Title Abbreviations

Alb. L.J.	Albany Law Journal of Science & Technology
Alb. L. Rev.	Albany Law Review
Am. J. Comp. L.	American Journal of Comparative Law
Am J. Int'l L.	American Journal of International Law
Am. U. L. Rev.	American University Law Review
Ann. Surv. Int'l & Comp. L.	Annual Survey of International & Comparative Law
Berkeley J. Int'l L.	Berkeley Journal of International Law
Berkeley Tech. L. J.	Berkeley Technology Law Journal
B.C. Int'l & Comp. L. Rev.	Boston College International and Comparative Law Review
B.C. J.L. & Soc. Just.	Boston College Journal of Law and Social Justice
Brook. L. Rev.	Brooklyn Law Review
Brook. J. Int'l L.	Brooklyn Journal of International Law
Buffalo L. Rev.	Buffalo Law Review
B.U. J. Sci. & Tech. L.	Boston University Journal of Science & Technology Law
B.U. L. Rev.	Boston University Law Review
Cal. L. Rev.	California Law Review
Cardozo Arts & Ent. L.J.	Cardozo Arts & Entertainment Law Journal
Cardozo J. Int'l & Comp. L	Cardozo Journal of International & Comparative Law
Cardozo L. Rev.	Cardozo Law Review
Case W. Res.	Case Western Reserve Law Review
Chi.-Kent J. Int'l & Comp. L.	Chicago-Kent Journal of International and Comparative Law
Chi.-Kent L. Rev.	Chicago-Kent Law Review
Civ. Rts. L.J.	Civil Rights Law Journal

Col. Law	The Colorado Lawer
Colum. Hum. Rts. L. Rev.	Columbia Human Rights Law Review
Colum. J. Envtl. L.	Columbia Journal of Environmental Law
Colum. J. Eur. L.	Columbia Journal of European Law
Colum. J. Transnat'l L.	Columbia Journal of Transnational Law
Colum. L. Rev.	Columbia Law Review
Colum.-VLA J. L. & Arts	Columbia Journal of Law & the Arts
Common Mkt. L. Rev	Common Market Law Review
Comp. Law Rev. Int'l	Computer Law Review International
Contr. e Impr.	Contratto e Impresa
Cornell Int'l L. J.	Cornell International Law Journal
Cornell L. Rev.	Cornell Law Review
Cyber. Law	Cyberspace Lawer
Dir. Aut.	Il Diritto di Autore
Dir. Inf.	Diritto dell'Informazione e dell'Informatica
Dir. Pubbl. Comp. Eur.	Diritto Pubblico Comparato ed Europeo
Duke J. Comp. & Int'l L.	Duke Journal of Comparative & International Law
Duke J. Const. L. & Pub. Pol'y	Duke Journal of Constitutional Law & Public Policy
Duke L.J.	Duke Law Journal
Ecology L.Q.	Ecology Law Quarterly
Emory Int'l L. Rev.	Emory International Law Review
Emory L.J.	Emory Law Journal
Ent. L. R.	Entertainment Law Review
Environs Envtl. L. & Pol'y J.	Environs: Environmental Law & Policy Journal
Eur. Hum. Rts L. Rev.	European Human Rights Law Review
Eur. J. Comp. L. & Gov.	European Journal of Comparative Law and Governance
Eur. J. Risk Reg.	European Journal of Risk Regulation
Eur. Intell. Prop. Rev.	European Intellectual Property Review
Fla. L. Rev.	Florida Law Review
Fordham Intell. Prop. Media & Ent. L.J.	Fordham Intellectual Property, Media & Entertainment Law Journal
Fordham Int'l L.J.	Fordham International Law Journal
Fordham L. Rev.	Fordham Law Review
Foro it.	Il Foro Italiano
Genetics Med.	Genetics in Medicine
Geo. Mason L. Rev.	George Mason Law Review
Geo. Wash. L. Rev.	George Washington Law Review
Georgetown L.J.	Georgetown Law Journal

Ga. J. Int'l & Comp. L.	Georgia Journal of International and Comparative Law
Hamline L. Rev.	Hamline Law Review
Harv. Civ. Rts.-Civ. Liberties L. Rev.	Harvard Civil Rights-Civil Liberties Law Review
Harv. Bus. Rev.	Harvard Business Review
Harv. Envtl. L. Rev.	Harvard Environmental Law Review
Harv. Hum. Rts. J.	Harvard Human Rights Journal
Harv. Int'l L.J.	Harvard International Law Journal
Harv. J.L. & Tech	Harvard Journal of Law & Technology
Harv. L. Rev.	Harvard Law Review
Hastings Comm. & Ent. L.J.	Hastings Communications and Entertainment Law Journal
Hastings Int'l & Comp. L. Rev.	Hastings International and Comparative Law Review
Hastings L.J.	Hastings Law Journal
High Tech. L.J.	High Technology Law Journal
Hous. J. Int'l L.	Houston Journal of International Law
Hous. L. Rev.	Houston Law Review
Hum. Rts. L. Rev.	Human Rights Law Review
Hum. Rts. Q.	Human Rights Quarterly
ILSA J. Int'l & Comp. L.	ILSA Journal of International and Comparative Law
Ind. Int'l & Comp. L. Rev.	Indiana International and Comparative Law Review
Ind. J. Global Leg. Stud.	Indiana Journal of Global Legal Studies
Ind. L.J.	Indiana Law Journal
Info. Comm. & Ethics in Soc'y	Journal of Information, Communication & Ethics in Society
Info. & Mgmt.	Information & Management
Info. Sys. J.	Information Systems Journal
Intell. Prop. L. J.	Intellectual Property Law Journal
Intell. Prop. Q.	Intellectual Property Quarterly
Int'l & Comp. L.Q.	International and Comparative Law Quarterly
Int'l Cont. Adv.	International Contract Advisor
Int'l Digital Media & Arts Ass'n J.	International Digital Media and Arts Association Journal
Int. J. Commons	International Journal of the Commons
Int'l J. Comm. L. & Pol'y	International Journal of Communications Law and Policy
Int'l J Const L.	International Journal of Constitutional Law
Int'l Rev. of Indus. Prop. & Copyright L.	International Review of Intellectual Property and Competition Law

Int. J. Law Info Tech.	International Journal of Law & Information Technology
Jama	Journal of the American Medical Association
J. of Comp. Law	The Journal of Comparative Law
J. Copyright Soc'y U.S.A	Journal of the Copyright Society of the U.S.A
J. Copyright Soc'y U.S.A.	Journal of the Copyright Society of the USA
J. Econ. Behav. & Org.	Journal of Economic Behavior and Organization
J. Inst. Theorethical Econ.	Journal of Institutional and Theoretical Economics
J Int'l Media & Ent. L.	Journal of International Media and Entertainment Law
J.L. & Tech.	Journal of Law and Technology
J. Legal Stud.	Journal of Legal Studies
J. Marshall J. Computer & Info. L.	John Marshall Journal of Computer and Information Law
J. Marshall L. Rev.	John Marshall Law Review
J. Pol. Econ.	Journal of Political Economy
J. Telecomm. & High Tech. L.	Journal on Telecommunications and High Technology Law
J. Transnat'l L. & Pol'y	Journal of Transnational Law & Policy
Jurimetrics	Jurimetrics
Law & Contemp. Probs.	Law and Contemporary Problems
Loy. L. Rev.	Loyola Law Review
Loy. L.A. Ent. L.J.	Loyola of Los Angeles Entertainment Law Journal
Loy. L.A. Int'l & Comp. L.J.	Loyola of Los Angeles International and Comparative Law Journal
Loy. L.A. L. Rev.	Loyola of Los Angeles Law Review
Loy. U. Chi. L.J.	Loyola University Chicago Law Journal
Loy. U. Chi. L.J.	Loyola University of Chicago Law Journal
Marq. L. Rev.	Marquette Law Review
Media L. & Pol'y	Media Law & Policy
Mich. L. Rev.	Michigan Law Review
Mich. Telecomm. & Tech. L. Rev.	Michigan Telecommunications and Technology Law Review
Minn. L. Rev.	Minnesota Law Review
Minn. J.L. Sci. & Tech.	Minnesota Journal of Law, Science & Technology
Nat. Biotechnol.	Nature Biotechnology

New Eng. J. Int'l & Comp. L.	New England Journal of International and Comparative Law
N.M. L. Rev.	New Mexico Law Review
N.Y.L. Sch. L. Rev.	New York Law School Law Review
N.Y.U. J. Int'l L. & Pol.	New York University Journal of International Law & Politics
N.Y.U. L. Rev.	New York University Law Review
Nw. J. Int'l Hum. Rts	Northwestern University Journal of International Human Rights.
Nw. U. L. Rev.	Northwestern University Law Review
Penn. L. Rev.	Pennsylvania Law Review
Pub. Und. Sci.	Public Understanding of Science
Queen Mary J. of Intell. Prop.	Queen Mary Journal of Intellectual Property
Rev. Int'l Pol. Econ.	Review of International Political Economy
Rev. Lamy. Dr. Immatériel	Revue Lamy Droit de l'Immatériel
Rich. J.L. & Tech.	Richmond Journal of Law and Technology
Riv. Crit. Dir. Priv.	Rivista Critica di Diritto Privato
Riv. Dir. Civ.	Rivista di Diritto Civile
Riv. Dir. Priv.	Rivista di Diritto Privato
Riv. Dir. Ind.	Rivista di Diritto Industriale
Riv. Trim. Dir. e Proc. Civ.	Rivista Trimestrale di Diritto e Procedura Civile
Rutgers Computer & Tech. L.J.	Rutgers Computer and Technology Law Journal
Rutgers L.J.	Rutgers Law Journal
Rutgers L. Rev.	Rutgers Law Review
San Diego L. Rev.	San Diego Law Review
S. Cal. L. Rev.	Southern California Law Review
Sci. Cult.	Science as Culture
Sci. Publ. Policy	Science and Public Policy
Soc. Stud. Sci.	Social Studies of Science
Stan. J. Int'l L.	Stanford Journal of International Law
Stan. L. Rev.	Stanford Law Review
Stud. Iuris	Studium Iuris
Tex. Int'l L.J.	Texas International Law Journal
Tex. L. Rev.	Texas Law Review
Tex. Tech. L. Rev.	Texas Tech Law Review
Transnat'l L. & Contemp. Probs.	Transnational Law and Contemporary Problems
Trends Genet.	Trends in Genetics
Tul. J. Int'l & Comp. L.	Tulane Journal of International and Comparative Law

Tul. L. Rev.	Tulane Law Review
UCLA Ent. L. Rev.	UCLA Entertainment Law Review
UCLA L. Rev.	UCLA Law Review
U. Chi. Legal F.	University of Chicago Legal Forum
U. Chi. L. Rev.	University of Chicago Law Review
U. Mich. L. Rev.	University of Michigan Law Review
U. Pa. J. Const. L.	University of Pennsylvania Journal of Constitutional Law
U. Pa L. Rev.	University of Pennsylvania Law Review
U.S.F. L. Rev.	University of San Francisco Law Review
U.N.T.S.	United Nations Treaty Series
Vand. J. Transnat'l L.	Vanderbilt Journal of Transnational Law
Vand. L. Rev.	Vanderbilt Law Review
Va. J. Int'l L.	Virginia Journal of International Law
Va. J.L. & Tech.	Virginia Journal of Law and Technology
Vand. J. Ent. & Tech. L.	Vanderbilt Journal of Entertainment & Technology Law
Va. L. Rev.	Virginia Law Review
W. Comp.	World Competition
Wake Forest L. Rev.	Wake Forest Law Review
Wash. & Lee L. Rev.	Washington & Lee Law Review
Wash. L. Rev.	Washington Law Review
Wis. Int'l L.J.	Wisconsin International Law Journal
Wis. L. Rev.	Wisconsin Law Review
Wm. & Mary Bill of Rts. J.	William and Mary Bill of Rights Journal
Wm. & Mary L. Rev.	William and Mary Law Review
Yale Hum. Rts. & Dev. L.J.	Yale Human Rights & Development Law Journal
Yale J. Of Health Pol'y, L. & Ethics	Yale Journal of Health Policy, Law, and Ethics
Yale J. on Reg.	Yale Journal on Regulation
Yale J. Int'l L.	Yale Journal of International Law
Yale J. L. & Tech.	Yale Journal of Law & Technology
Yale L. & Pol'y Rev	Yale Law & Policy Review
Yale L.J.	Yale Law Journal

Chapter 1
Interactions Between Science, Technology and Society: An Introduction

Abstract This introductory chapter aims to explore and understand the way particular scientific and technological developments affect legal values and institutions and how such phenomena can influence scientific and technological regulations. Scientific discoveries and technological innovations are in fact at the root of the progress made in many areas (in the field of information and telecommunications, agriculture, health, education, environment, etc.). Scientific research and technological innovations are also crucial factors in implementing changes in society and in the economy (See generally Cutcliffe SH, Ideas, machines and values: an introduction to science, technology and social studies, 2000). In particular, advances in fields like medicine, biology, chemistry, information technology, and telecommunications have wrought a Copernican revolution into our daily lives. These are fascinating subjects, but they also have many ethical, legal and social implications.

In the following pages, we will firstly clarify essential theoretical and practical concepts for interpreting and understanding the aspects of the investigation. Then, using some practical and illustrative examples, we will try to explain some of the most challenging issues at the intersection of law, science and technology. In particular, we will illustrate the deep interrelation between science, technology and legal protection of individual rights.

1.1 Mapping the New Terrain

Scientific discoveries and technological innovations have generally enhanced the quality of life for individuals. Examples include medical discoveries that improved the quality of life for countless people expanding access to health services and diagnostic tests. This category includes discoveries like the penicillin, the production of some important vaccines or the isolation of DNA. At the same time, huge and rapid advances can also be found in the communication sector. Advancements in communication technologies have facilitated the global distribution of cultural products and information, spreading freedom and democracy throughout the globe. Let us think – for example – about the huge increase in the number, availability, variety and

N. Lucchi, *The Impact of Science and Technology on the Rights of the Individual*, Law, Governance and Technology Series 26,
DOI 10.1007/978-3-319-30439-7_1

changes of traditional media sources (telephones, radio, television broadcasting and motion pictures) up to the more recent revolution brought by the Internet.

Across the development of human history, the invention of new tools and applications have often resulted in profound transformations in society.[1] Our own historical period is characterized by the so called informational "meta-technologies", namely those technologies that have the capacity to radically transform and affect not just their own industry but entire industrial sectors of the global economy[2] constituting an essential element for the development and use of other technologies.[3] Telecommunications and information technologies as well as new biotechnologies originating from development in microbiology and genetic engineering, are both premiere examples of meta-technologies of information. Both these technologies have changed the nature of society expanding "the degrees of freedom with which humans can act in the social and material worlds".[4] In addition, their informational nature is transforming the way we deal with information resources. As with biological information technologies, the progress of digital information technologies in recent years has had significant impact on both individual and collective rights. In particular, these two particular domains share common semantic characteristics as well as a number of economic, cultural, social, and legal features.[5] The shared spaces of these two types of meta-technologies are evident in different areas including – among others – legal, regulatory and technical aspects suggesting a strong convergence between genetic and digital information.

It is precisely in the legal ground that the dimension of these shared spaces for biotechnology and digital information technologies becomes more evident.[6] Their metatechnological nature has provided challenges to the legal process, particularly intellectual property rights issues.[7] Let us consider for example, the relationship between copyright and freedom of expression or the relationship between pharmaceutical patents and the right to health.[8] Biotechnology, like digital technology, obliges us to reassess fundamental questions about the nature of life, the role played by technology in both enhancing and impairing human rights principles, the limits of science and the interferences between the biological and social worlds.

---

[1] See Sandra Braman, Technology, in The Sage Handbook of Media Studies, 123, 124 (John D.H. Downing et al. Eds. 2004).

[2] See Thomas C. Lawton, Technology and the New Diplomacy 6 (1997).

[3] See Jeroen van den Hoven, The Use of Normative Theories in Computer Ethics, in The Cambridge Handbook of Information and Computer Ethics, 59, 60 (Luciano Floridi ed. 2010).

[4] Sandra Braman, Informational Meta-Technologies and International Relations: The Case of Biotechnologies 91, 92, in Information technologies and global politics: The changing scope of power and governance (James N. Rosenau and J.P. Singh, eds. 2002).

[5] See Sandra Braman, The Meta-Technologies of Information, in Biotechnology and Communication: The Meta-Technologies of Information 10 (Sandra Braman ed., 2004).

[6] Sandra Braman, The Meta-Technologies of Information, in Biotechnology and Communication: The Meta-Technologies of Information 3, 4 (Sandra Braman ed., 2004).

[7] Id.

[8] The literature on the subject is wide. For a latest work, see Research Handbook on Human Rights and Intellectual Property (Christophe Geiger ed., 2015).

Considering this multilayered scenario, the aim of this book is to examine the latest trends in science and technology policy exploring ways in which these technologies are used and the impact and the legal consequences of these uses on individuals and society. Accordingly, we want to explore the changing nature of law in the regulation of emerging issues related to the exploitation of informational resources. In particular, recent case law seems to indicate the existence of a problematic balance between the governance of access to different categories of information highlighting the existence of barriers and distortions. In this framework, it seems possible to draw provocative parallels and analogies between the regulative rules of technologies for the biological and communicative fields. This body of decisions provides indirect evidence of a convergence between the question of the use, collection and management of information made by digital technologies and the one than happens in the biological world. The nature of contemporary biotechnology and the enabling role of communication technologies have in common many shared features which can properly demonstrate the link that connects these two apparently far domains. This very deep and meaningful connection appears to have been largely neglected in the previous literature.[9] The ongoing evolution of information and communication technology (and related digital communications) is dramatically and constantly changing the nature and dynamics of communication across the world. This trend has profound implications for the production and distribution of knowledge, culture and information. It is therefore important to examine the potential constraints, opportunities and challenges posed by this process, highlighting areas in which governmental institutions could develop specific regulatory interventions. In other words, it is necessary to investigate and evaluate the efficiency, consciousness and effectiveness of policy interventions offering a detailed analysis of alternative ways to revise existing or developing new regulatory instruments. There is in fact some evidence that information (human and biological) is bringing about a new model of legal regulation. The result of this ongoing process is an exponential increase in the "information intensity" of the different technologies. In this context, it is also necessary to effectively address the consequences of these technological innovations on the way people use and interact in this space as well as the effect it has on their lives. In order to understand these dynamics, we need to examine the inherent regulatory framework as a result of major reforms undertaken at the North American and European Union level. This will also lead us to observe the emergence of a new paradigm of regulation which requires some form of cooperation between public authorities and private actors. In the following pages, we will try to move the research agenda into a new and more convergent dimension showing possible junctions between information technologies and the organic world. The investigation will look at these issues in the context of European and North American jurisdictions.

---

[9] C.f. generally Sandra Braman, Biotechnology and Communication: The Meta-Technologies of Information x (2004).

1.2 Issues and Rights in Scientific and Technological Innovations

Continuing advances in scientific and technological innovations are essential to modern societies. Historically, such developments had improved living conditions in both developed and developing countries. Understanding their function and regulation means defining and clarifying the relationship between science and technology advances and society's ability to benefit from it. Contemporarily, science and technology policies are one of the most important factors that affects economic and social domain of a country.[10] They also constitute one of the most important driving factors behind the recent increased interest of governments and international organizations in seeking transnational collaboration for regulatory solutions.[11] For these reasons, the social, legal, economic, and political issues surrounding the introduction and development of new technologies are having a significant impact on a variety of legal issues. Law has the responsibility to regulate the use and abuse of science and technology and the extent of their application. The advent of a knowledge economy has then coincided – both in Europe and in the United States – with a crisis of public trust in science and technology.[12] There are also increasing demands for more control and regulation of the risks deriving from science-based[13] or technology-based developments.[14] The implications of some of these developments are particularly apparent today. Antagonistic interests to freedom of science, access to scientific knowledge and freedom of expression are emerging distinctly, requiring a careful balance between public and private interests. In this specific perspective, it is essential to consider the dominant transatlantic trends in science and technology policy and regulation, deserving a pointed focus

---

[10] See generally Sheldon Krimsky & Peter Shorett (eds.), Rights and Liberties in the Biotech Age: Why We Need a Genetic Bill of Rights (2005); Barry Bozeman et al. (eds.), Knowledge Flows and Knowledge Collectives: Understanding The Role of Science and Technology Policies in Development (2003).

[11] See Roger Brownsword, Rights, Regulation, and the Technological Revolution (2008).

[12] Ronald E. Leenes et al. (eds.), Constitutional Rights and New Technologies. A Comparative Study (2008);

[13] On this, see generally Human Rights in the Global Information Society (Rikke Frank Jørgensen ed., 2006); Oliver Mills, Biotechnological Inventions. Moral Restraints and Patent Law (2010); Sheila Jasanoff, Science at the Bar. Law, Science and Technology in America (1995); Sheila Jasanoff, Designs on Nature: Science and Democracy in Europe and the United States (2005); Michael Heller, Michael & Rebecca Eisenberg, Can Patents Deter Innovation? The Anticommons in Biomedical Research, 280 Science 698 (1998); Matthew Rimmer, Intellectual Property and Biotechnology. Biological Inventions (2008); Robin Feldman, The Role of Science in Law (2009).

[14] On this, see generally Human Rights in the Global Information Society (Rikke Frank Jørgensen ed., 2006); Natali Helberger, Controlling access to content: regulating conditional access in digital broadcasting (2005); Yochai Benkler, The wealth of networks: how social production transforms markets and freedom (2006); Jack M. Balkin, The Future of Free Expression in a Digital Age, 36 Pepperdine L. Rev. 427 (2009); The Commodification of Information (Niva Elkin-Koren & Neil W. Netanel eds., 2002); Lawrence Lessig, Free Culture: How Big Media Uses Technology and the Law to Lock Down Culture and Control Creativity (2004).

on what happens within the biosciences and digital communication domains. The disruptive nature of contemporary innovations in these two fields "is restructuring the institutions and practices of knowledge production"[15] as well as the specific purpose of intellectual property rights and public policy objectives. Knowledge-based activities are in fact strictly linked with intellectual property protection. A more comprehensive vision of the problem can be formulated and delivered by providing a map of the changing nature of law in the face of emerging issues in science and technology. This will be achieved by investigating the challenges that contemporary governance is facing to promote access to knowledge and information. The impact of science and technology on law can however be declined into several categories or sub-dimensions. For the purpose of this analysis, the accent can be placed on a largely unexplored aspect of the law's interactions with science and technology: the dilemma of reconciling respect for individual rights and liberal principles with other conflicting interests (such as ownership, control and profit). This is a fast-developing and dynamic field of research, which currently needs a more intensive and interdisciplinary investigation.[16] Given the large diversity of scenarios and operating policies, it could be useful to choose and analyze a selection of emblematic cases exploring the likely implications different government policies and legislations could have on individuals. To achieve this objective, we will examine and compare the different regulatory and judicial approaches used to respond to scientific and technological developments. Understanding the dynamics of these regulatory mechanisms is then even more important when considered in the larger framework of global governance. In addition, exploring these questions in a wider European and transatlantic perspective can open up thought-provoking comparative features within these fields.

The United States and the European Union are undoubtedly the two world's leading actors in the fields of science innovations, technology advances and creativity. Despite their extensive differences, they share a common body of fundamental legal principles and values on which the constitutional democratic system of government depends. But the American legal approach to many technology or science related issues significantly differs from the European one, producing reciprocal

---

[15] See Sandra Braman, Biotechnology and Communication: The Meta-Technologies of Information x (2004).

[16] For some of the most recent studies on this, see e.g. Weeramantry, Christopher Gregory (ed.) Human rights and scientific and technological development (1990); Seán Ó Siochrú et al., Assessing Communication Rights: A Handbook 20 (2005); Rikke Frank Jørgensen (ed.) Human Rights in the Global Information Society (2006); Mpaz Sinjela, (ed.) Human Rights and Intellectual Property Rights: Tensions and Convergences (2007); Roger Brownsword, Rights, Regulation, and the Technological Revolution (2008); Robin Feldman, The Role of Science in Law (2009); Thérèse Murphy (ed.) New Technologies and Human Rights (2009); Lisa Horner et al., Information and Communication Technologies and Human Rights (2010); Laurence Helfer and Graeme Austin Human Rights and Intellectual Property: Mapping the Global Interface (2011); Cheryl Ann Bishop, Access to Information as Human Right (2012); Mario Viola De Azevedo Cunha et al., New Technologies and Human Rights: Challenges to Regulation (2013).

obstacles to trade as well as legal concerns impacting the global economy.[17] At the same time the evolution of European science and technology governance is often heavily influenced by American practices and policies.[18] There are two lines along which this investigation can be conducted and they are not exclusive but complementary. In particular, consideration will be given to two main aspects: first, the relevance and impact of computer-mediated communication, its potential on democratization of freedom of expression and the problem of conflicting rights; and second, the debated question of the technological manipulation of life and the boundary of scientific knowledge with regard to the challenging argument of genetic invention patents, their side effects on access to the scientific information and health care opportunities. Both aspects will be investigated from a comparative legal perspective (focusing both on constitutional and international law). The "case based" approach will then permit to evaluate the coherence between the law in the books and the law in action. It will also emerge how problems at the intersection of law, science and technology flow not only from the changing nature of science and technology, but also from the changing nature of law.[19]

1.3 Governing Science and Technology

It is generally recognized that science and technology have shaped modern society, economics, politics, law and culture. They deeply affect the lives of all people and they are now central features of our social and commercial landscape. From the food we eat to the medicines we take, from the information we share and the means of transportation we use, science and technology assume a fundamental role in the everyday life of each individual.[20] Regulatory interventions in the management and control of science and technology may be required for several reasons. Usually they may be associated with the necessity to control health and safety, legal ownership of intellectual property rights, rules for ethical purposes, competition policy and consumer protection.[21] Rapid advances in the area of science and technology and their regulation are frequently presented as adversaries.[22] Actually, the history of science and technology shows that developments in these two fields have always evolved symbiotically with their legal regulation. The real point is that regulation may be

[17] Raymond J. Ahearn, U.S.-EU Trade and Economic Relations: Key Policy Issues for the 112th Congress (2011).

[18] See generally Nicola Lucchi, Digital Media & Intellectual Property (2006).

[19] On this, see generally Robin Feldman, The Role of Science in Law (2009).

[20] See Kleinman, Daniel Lee Democratizations of Science and Technology, in Science, Technology, and Democracy 139, 157 (Daniel Lee Kleinmann ed. 2000).

[21] See Helen Lawton Smith, The Context for Science and Technology Regulation, in The Regulation of Science and Technology 3, 14 (Helen Lawton Smith ed. 2002).

[22] See Jonathan B. Wiener, The regulation of technology, and the technology of regulation, 26 Technology in Society 483, 483 (2004).

responsible for stimulating or inhibiting technological or scientific innovation. Regulation can – in fact – have an impact on the production, ownership, exploitation, access and utilization of scientific and technological advances. For example, the invention of the printing press was a key component of the transformation from the middle Ages to the European Renaissance.[23] But, until the advent of this invention, nobody needed protection against others who might copy their intellectual work. For this reason, the printing revolution also gave also rise to the first copyright laws.[24] Today the Internet is very similar in terms of functionality, purpose and intended usage to the invention of the printing press with the same potential to create substantial transformation in the society and in the regulatory intervention of the State.

Another similar example is provided by the controversy that arose in early 1980 over the possible threats posed by genetic engineering and recombinant DNA research activities.[25] In this case, it was raised the question of citizens' involvement in the regulation of scientific investigation.[26] It soon became clear that to deal adequately with commercial applications of biotechnology it was also necessary to implement proper guidelines and rules. Since that moment, biotech innovations have increasingly advanced into new technologies and modern practices raising several legal, ethical and regulatory issues. In particular, the revolutionary speed of biotech innovations has had a significant impact on the protection of the rights of the individual. Nowadays, the legal regulation of scientific research and scientific investigations impact more and more directly on the freedom of research and therapies as well as on the broad diffusion of scientific knowledge.

The challenge in these areas is to design meaningful theoretical and practical approaches and solutions to the global policy priorities for the upcoming new "Tech-Ade".[27] In particular, a socially responsible and sustainable governance of scientific research and technological innovation – as recently emphasized by the European commission – has become a global political and policy concern faced by both developed and developing countries.[28] It means developing solutions that are

---

[23] See e.g. Elizabeth Eisenstein, The Printing Press as an Agent of Change: Communications and Cultural Transformations in Early-Modern Europe (1979); Gillian Davies, Copyright and the Public Interest 14 (2d ed. 2002).

[24] See Mark Rose, Authors and Owners: The Invention of Copyright (1993).

[25] See Kleinman, Daniel Lee Democratizations of Science and Technology, in Science, Technology, and Democracy 139, 142 (Daniel Lee Kleinmann ed. 2000).

[26] See generally Susan Wright, Molecular politics: developing American and British regulatory policy for genetic engineering (1994); Sheldon Krimsky, Genetic Alchemy: The Social History of the Recombinant DNA Controversy (1982).

[27] See William H. Dutton et al., Freedom of Connection - Freedom of Expression: The Changing Legal and Regulatory Ecology Shaping the Internet (2011); Lisa Horner et al. (eds.), Information and Communication Technologies and Human Rights, (2010); Gaëlle Krikorian & Amy Kapczynski (eds.), Access to Knowledge in the Age of Intellectual Property (2010).

[28] See generally Zaneta Ozolina et al., Ethical and Regulatory Challenges to Science and Research Policy at the Global Level, Expert Group Report, Directorate-General for Research and Innovation of the European Commission (2012).

specifically targeted at overcoming the legal questions posed by science and technology advances. In this respect, it is also important to identify and discuss the limits of legal responses adopted so far. When regulating science and technology, it must be taken in account that research and innovation are not ends in themselves but they are grounded in international human rights law and they are linked to the field of public good such as wildlife, health care, culture, education and knowledge flows.[29] In this debate, there are two opposing view-points. One view clearly support an unrestricted promotion of science and innovation because they are necessary to enhance the economic development, public health, and societal progress of any country. At the same time, others argue that neither science and technology nor the market can be left alone "to operate wholly on their own without societal guidance and regulation".[30]

The global governance of science and technology involves the regulatory function of appropriately standardized set of values and norms. Scientific research and technology policies have recently placed great interests on identifying and prioritizing human rights risks and other potential adverse effects of techno-scientific developments. In this regard, the internal ethical norms and principles of science and technology – although important and useful in many situations – are considered inappropriate when it is necessary to implement responsible and effective directions for strategic research and innovation.[31] In order to create and foster effective responsible practices in research and innovation, it is essential starting from "those anchor points that serve society across the whole spectrum of social institutions and human activities" such as: "human rights and the principles of dignity, freedoms, equality, solidarity, individual rights protection, justice, and sustainability".[32]

In addition, there are various other elements that play significant roles in the structure of science and technology regulation. For example, the progressive discouragement of the national borders – both in economic and legal terms – has been driven by computer technology and scientific discoveries. This situation imposes governments to receive legislative and administrative solutions inspired to criteria and interests that are not only those already recognized by States or defined by their national legislation. It is therefore crucial to map the changing landscape underlining the best practices and actions to be undertaken by policy makers in order to facilitate convergence and to respond to the challenges associated with the global knowledge society and the biotech-economy.

For all these reasons, governing science and technology also implies to consider their public values creating a dialogue between governments, the public and the scientific community about new potential risks connected to their use, application and impact on society.

One of the most pressing problems that scholars currently address is the democratization of science and technology and their compatibility with democratic

[29] Id.

[30] Id., at 7.

[31] Id. at 8 and 51.

[32] Id. at 51.

principles.[33] In general – as argued by Sheila Jasanoff – scientific and technological artifacts "not only influence but also reaffirm social values and institutional practices" providing us the opportunity to deepen our understanding of constitutional rights.[34]

Historically, public access to and contribution in the production of scientific knowledge or in the development of technology has been limited. However, over the past few years, the social and cultural barrier between the public domain and the techno-scientific domain has started to move from the closed position towards the opened.

From a practical perspective, the democratization of science and technology can take many forms. For example, democratization of science and technology is often referred to participation in decision making processes, to the possibility to have access to scientific information, to the control over science and technology related risks or the opportunity for people to understand policy and regulatory issues related to scientific and technological advances. In general, the democratization can be reached through a more informed public participation in questions related to scientific or technological choices and policy regulations. Accordingly, the narrative in the following pages provides an illustration of some of the ways to reconcile the tension between science, technology and democratic principles proposing criteria to be used in evaluating appropriateness of different regulatory approaches. Supporting elements will be captured through the analysis of particular cases and controversies at different levels of government and in different jurisdictions, offering a detailed analysis of alternative ways to revise existing or develop new regulatory interventions.

1.4 Private Ownership of Information: Risks and Vulnerabilities

The governance of scientific and technological innovations is strictly connected with intellectual property protection. The value of the information in question is enormous, but it cannot only be understood in monetary or proprietary terms.

---

[33] See e.g. Malcom L. Goggin, Governing science and technology in a democracy (1986); Andrew Feenberg, Questioning Technology (1999); Alan Irwin, Constructing the Scientific Citizen: Science and Democracy in the Biosciences, 10 Pub. Und. Sci., 18 (2001); Richard Pierre Claude, Science in the service of human rights (2002); Michael Hardt and Antonio Negri, Multitude: War and Democracy in the Age of Empire (2004); Sheila Jasanoff, Science and Citizenship: A New Synergy, 31 Sci. Publ. Policy, 90 (2004); Dominique Pestre, Challenges for the Democratic Management of Technoscience: Governance, Participation and the Political Today, 17 Sci. Cult. 101 (2008); Michel Callon, Pierre Lascoumes, and Yannick Barthe, Acting in an Uncertain World: An Essay on Technical Democracy (2009).

[34] See Sheila Jasanoff, Introduction: Rewriting Life, Reframing Rights, In Reframing Rights. Bioconstitutionalism in the Genetic Age, 1, 13 (Sheila Jasanoff ed. 2011). See also generally Sheila Jasanoff, Science at the Bar: Law, Science and Technology in America (1995).

Intellectual property protection is extremely relevant for business innovation but it is not so significant for basic research, which essentially depends on free access to existing knowledge.[35]

Ownership of physical property can be protected by physical means while ownership of ideas is far less easily protected. In today's society, information is power and its control can be easily abused, intentionally or not. The right to access information can cover information of high value to safeguarding one's right, regardless of who retains the information, particularly in cases where private entities are supported by government through "indirect instruments" to maintain control over information of a primarily public or rights-concerning nature.

With the rise of the networked communications environment and the continuing progress of scientific advances, knowledge has become an increasingly key factor in fostering innovation, growth and health care technology and in sustaining cultural creativity. In addition, the ability of people to acquire, access and control knowledge is strictly related to questions pertaining to the ownership of knowledge. At present, intellectual property rules are the principal tool for controlling the creation, diffusion and use of knowledge and related goods and services. In order to have a market in knowledge, intellectual property protection is considered a fundamental instrument for creators of knowledge securing and maintaining exclusive access rights to knowledge-based products. For example, in the pharmaceutical and biotechnology industry, where development of new products requires substantial investments with long incubation periods, it is generally acknowledged that companies need exclusive right in order to recover research and development costs.

However, the exceptional reinforcement of intellectual property rules in the past two decades has become a major cause of deep concern and conflict based essentially on the tension between the interest in the free flow of information and the fragmentation of knowledge occurred after the development of stronger mechanisms for international protection of intellectual property.[36] Existing measures for global knowledge governance encounter a number of significant challenges ranging from those related to patent eligibility of DNA claims, to the barriers and obstacles posed by intellectual property to information flow, to the issues resulting from the human rights implications of intellectual property policy.

Intellectual property rights have the potential to create scarcity in some category of expression.[37] As already exemplified by some authors:

---

[35] See Helge Hveem & Lelio Iapadre, Global Governance of Knowledge Policies: Summary and Conclusions, in The Global Governance of Knowledge Creation and Diffusion 183 (Helge Hveem & Lelio Iapadre eds., 2011).

[36] On this, see generally Dana Beldiman (ed.), Access to Information and Knowledge: 21st Century Challenges in Intellectual Property and Knowledge Governance (2013) (discussing the need for other conceptual models of knowledge governance); Aurora Plomer, Patents, Human Rights and Access to Science (2015) (highlighting the inherent tensions of patents with access to science and knowledge).

[37] See Laurence R. Helfer & Graeme W. Austin, Human Rights and Intellectual Property 221 (2011). The authors, emphasized how to create markets for these goods, the law intervenes by

> [...] copyright owners can entirely suppress some form of speech by seeking injunctions against those who want to express themselves by means of unauthorized uses of copyright-protected material. Alternatively, if license fees for such uses are required, the cost of particular expression increases, sometimes prohibitively. These actions implicate the right to freedom of expression – a right that is found in many international and regional human rights instruments and domestic constitutions. Limits on access to the manifestations and products of culture and science also implicate other rights and freedoms.[38]

These particular limits and constraints can determine possible adverse effects to individuals experiencing participation restrictions in the "cultural life of the community, to enjoy the arts," to access information and "to share in scientific advancement and its benefits".[39] The rise of this consciousness has become particularly strong today that calls for the urgent deployment of effective global strategies in terms of access and use of essential public knowledge assets. This also includes the adoption of appropriate measures to deal with new technologies and new ways of communicating. There are several concrete examples of the technical difficulties of countries in fulfilling the rights to information and freedom of expression, as well as in balancing intellectual property with the rights to participate in culture and benefit from scientific progress. This challenge has become even more critical because it has been recognized that the right to access information can also serve as an indispensable gateway right to the protection of a bundle of other rights.[40]

1.5 Boundary Problems in Science and Technology

Limitations to individual rights are often a necessary condition for their efficient functioning. This means that often the recognition of rights and freedoms of others is not just a limit, but also a condition for the freedom of all. In addition, individual freedoms are often in conflict. As a consequence, there is always the possibility that some individual might be constrained or impeded in the exercise of his rights by the exercise of someone else's rights. Let us consider, for example, the protection of the environment versus right to property; censorship versus right to expression, freedom of speech versus right to privacy etc. It means that in many cases, this conflict of rights makes necessary the intervention of a court to balance the opposing

creating artificial scarcity though an array of different exclusive legal rights (citing Yochai Benkler's book The Wealth of Networks at 311).

[38] Id. at 221.

[39] Id. at 222. These are all rights set forth in Article 27 of the Universal Declaration of Human Rights (Universal Declaration of Human Rights, G.A. Res. 217A (III), art. 27, U.N. Doc. A/810, Dec. 10, 1948) and in Article 15 of the International Covenant on Economic, Social and Cultural Rights (International Covenant on Economic, Social, and Cultural Rights, art. 15, opened for signature Dec. 16, 1966, 993 U.N.T.S. 3).

[40] See United Nations General Assembly, Human Rights Council, Commission on Human Rights, Report by the Special Rapporteur on the Promotion and Protection of the Right to Freedom of Opinion and Expression, Frank La Rue, U.N. Doc. A/HRC/17/27 (16 May 2011).

interests using impartial criteria. These disputes are normally resolved on a case-by-case basis, according to principles and interpreting criteria set out by legal acts and implemented by case law. Basically, this is exactly the source of conflict underlying, for example, the debate over the relationship between freedom of expression and intellectual property rights.[41]

As pointed out by other authors, on the one side "intellectual property furthers freedom of expression values by encouraging speech"[42]; on the other side "the right to freedom of expression imposes legal and normative limits on the scope of intellectual property rights".[43]

> The first perspective reflects the view that intellectual property – copyright in particular – promotes speech through the incentives it provides to creators and those who invest in the dissemination of creative works.
>
> The second perspective reflects the view that the right to freedom of expression establishes a borderline beyond which intellectual property protection cannot expand.[44]

According to new theories, these two positions, in particular the second one, are interestingly relevant also in the patent environment: as we will see later, freedom of expression concerns "are increasingly providing a platform for questioning […] the migration of patent rights into areas such as computer technology and biotechnology".[45] The biotechnology and genomic revolution provides a rich terrain where to explore the tension between property rights and freedom of expression. As noted above, this phenomenon is particularly prominent and dominant in both Europe and United States. They are not only the largest trading partners, but they are also the biggest incubators of scientific and technological innovation.

In addition, it is interesting to note a growing scholarly literature revealing a convergence between the realm of intellectual property and the realm of fundamental rights.[46] Even if the influence of fundamental rights in the field of technology

---

[41] See e.g. P. Bernt Hugenholtz, Copyright and Freedom of Expression in Europe, in Expanding the Boundaries of Intellectual Property. Innovation Policy for the Knowledge Society 343 (Rochelle Cooper Dreyfuss, Diane Leenheer Zimmerman & Harry First eds., 2001); Christophe Geiger, "Constitutionalising" Intellectual Property Law? The Influence of Fundamental Rights on Intellectual Property in the European Union, 37(4) Int'l Rev. Intell. Prop. & Competition L. 371, 383–390 (2006); Neil Netanel, Copyright's Paradox (2008); Copyright and free speech: comparative and international analyses (Jonathan Griffiths & Uma Suthersanen eds., 2005); Copyright and Freedom of Expression, Proceedings of the ALAI 2006 Study Days, Barcelona 19–20 June 2006 (Raquel Xalabarder ed., 2008).

[42] Laurence R. Helfer & Graeme W. Austin, Human Rights and Intellectual Property, cit., at 222.

[43] Id.

[44] Id.

[45] Id.

[46] For a comprehensive discussion on the issue, see Copyright and Free Speech. Comparative and International Analyses (Jonathan Griffiths & Uma Suthersanen eds. 2006); Human Rights in the Global Information Society (Rikke Frank Jørgensen ed., 2006); Human Rights and Intellectual Property Rights: Tensions and Convergences (Mpazi Sinjela ed., 2007); Intellectual Property and Human Rights, En. ed., (Paul L.C. Torremans ed. 2008); New Technologies and Human Rights (Thérèse Murphy ed. 2009); Giogio Resta, Proprietà Intellettuale e Diritti Fondamentali: Una Relazione Ambigua, in Persona, Derecho y Libertad: Nuevas Perspectivas. Escritos en Homenaje

regulation "is a relatively new phenomenon",[47] stronger intellectual property rights have already shown to affect – in different situations – the realization of people's right.[48] Considered reciprocally independent from each other, intellectual property rights and fundamental rights now reveal increasingly evident points of contact and lines of influence. The conventional view tries to reconcile their relationship "by bringing into play the harmonious idea of mutual strengthening, especially in the sense that the guarantee of intellectual property is in itself the expression of a human right".[49] But today it is clearly evident that the most basic distinction of interest is that of their conflict.[50]

In science and technology policy debate, fundamental rights are increasingly claimed in order to counterbalance the conflicts generated by the expanding boundaries of intellectual property law, "also in respect to goods and services crucial to human development".[51] Case records on the matter are numerous and constitute an

---

al Profesor Carlos Fernández Sessarego 787 (Carlos Alberto Calderón Puertas et al. eds., 2009); Intellectual Property and Human Rights. A Paradox (Willem Grosheide ed., 2010); Louise Bernier, Justice in Genetics: Intellectual Property and Human Rights from a Cosmopolitan Liberal Perspective (2010); Marcelin Tonye Mahop, Intellectual Property, Community Rights and Human Rights (2010); Laurence R. Helfer & Graeme W. Austin, Human Rights and Intellectual Property (2011); Duncam Matthews, Intellectual Property, Human Rights and Development (2011); Frantzeska Papadopoulou, TRIPS and Human Rights, in Intellectual Property Rights in a Fair World Trade System: Proposals for Reform of TRIPS 262 (Annette Kur & Marianne Levin eds., 2011); Research Handbook on Human Rights and Intellectual Property (Christophe Geiger ed., 2015); Aurora Plomer, Patents, Human Rights and Access to Science (2015).

[47] See Roger Brownsword and Morag Goodwin, Law and Technologies of the Twenty-First Century, cit., at 228.

[48] See Philippe Cullet, Human Rights and Intellectual Property Rights in a TRIPS Era, 29 Hum. Rts. Q. 403, 406 (2007).

[49] See Giorgio Resta, The Case Against the Privatization of Knowledge: Some Thoughts on the Myriad Genetics Controversy in Biotech Innovations & Fundamental Rights 34 (Roberto Bin et al. eds, 2011).

[50] On the argument, see e.g. Audrey R. Chapman, The Human Rights Implications of Intellectual Property Protection, 5 J. Int'l Econ. L. 861 (2002) (highlighting how human rights potentially impacted by IP protection, in particular on the right to health); Jakob Cornides, Human Rights and Intellectual Property: Conflict or Convergence?, 7 J. World Intell. Prop. 135 (2004); Peter K. Yu, Reconceptualizing Intellectual Property Interests in a Human Rights Framework, 40 U.C. Davis L. Rev. 1039, 1077 (2007); Laurence R. Helfer, Human Rights and Intellectual Property: Conflict or Coexistence?, in 5 Minn. Int. Prop. Rev. 47 (2003); Id., The New Innovation Frontier? Intellectual Property and the European Court of Human Rights, in 49 Harv. Int. L. J. 1 (2008); Lea Shaver, The Right To Science And Culture, 10 Wis. L. Rev. 121 (2010).

[51] See Resta, The Case Against the Privatization of Knowledge: Some Thoughts on the Myriad Genetics Controversy, cit. at 34. For an insightful discussion of these issues, see also P. Bernt Hugenholtz, Copyright and Freedom of Expression in Europe, in Expanding the Boundaries of Intellectual Property: Innovation Policy for the Knowledge Society 343 (Rochelle Cooper Dreyfuss, Diane Zimmerman & Harry First eds., 2001); Laurence R. Helfer, Regime Shifting: The TRIPS Agreement and New Dynamics of International Intellectual Property Lawmaking, 29 Yale J. Int'l L. 29 (2004); John R Thomas, On Proprietary Rights and Personal Liberties: Constitutional Responses to Post-Industrial Patenting in Death of Patens 110 (Peter Drahos ed., 2005); Christophe Geiger, "Constitutionalising" Intellectual Property Law? The Influence of Fundamental Rights on Intellectual Property in the European Union, 37 Int'l Rev. Intell. Prop. & Comp. L. 371, 382–385

interesting and important point of departure in the interpretation and application of conflicting statutory provisions. Also some recent scholarly works support the idea that "human rights are increasingly seen as a relevant point of departure in considering the legitimacy of the content and consequences of technology regulation".[52] This is visible also "from the increasing number of international documents laying down principles to guide and regulate technological development that are openly based upon human rights norms"[53] as well as from numerous court decisions dealing with fundamental rights in the context of science and technology policy.[54] According to this theoretical approach, the aim of the following chapters is to investigate through concrete examples the linkages between these two levels of value conflicts.

1.6 Science and Technology Advances, Individual Rights, and Areas of Conflict

The protection of individual rights broadly encompasses activities aimed at obtaining full respect for the rights of all individuals in accordance with national and international law. The recognition and protection of individual rights is a *conditio sine qua non* for any democratic and civil society, since they guarantee equality, non-discrimination and protection against the arbitrary exercise of power. This includes the protection of ownership of physical and intellectual property but also the protection of a range of other rights pertaining to health, natural resources, education, free expression, self-determination, and more. The problem is that ownership of physical property can be protected by physical means while ownership of ideas or informational assets is far less easily protected. This is most likely one of

(2006); Id., Fundamental Rights, a Safeguard for the Coherence of Intellectual Property Law?, 35 Int'l Rev. Intell. Prop. & Competition L. 268, 277 (2004); Geertrui Van Overwalle, Human rights' limitations in patent law, in Intellectual Property And Human Rights. A Paradox 236, 243–245 (Willem Grosheide ed., 2010).

[52] See Roger Brownsword and Morag Goodwin, Law and Technologies of the Twenty-First Century, cit., at 225.

[53] Id.

[54] See e.g. The recent decision of the Court of Justice of the European Union in Digital Rights Ireland v Minister for Communications, Marine and Natural Resources. In this case, the Court of Justice held that Directive 2006/24/EC (the Data Retention Directive) - which asked providers of publicly available electronic communications services to retain traffic and location data for a specified period of time - seriously interferes with the right to respect for private life and the protection of personal data under articles 7, 8 and 11 of the EU Charter of Fundamental Rights. See Joined Cases C-293/12 and C-594/12, Digital Rights Ireland and Seitlinger, ECJ, Preliminary Ruling of April 8, 2014. But see also another recent decision of the Court of Justice of the EU in Google Spain SL & Google Inc v Agencia Española de Protección de Datos (AEPD) & Mario Costeja González (C-131/12) May 13, 2014, ECJ. Here the Court argued that the fundamental rights recognized in articles 7 and 8 of the Charter of Fundamental Rights of the European Union are binding rules that take precedence over the over economic interests of search engines' activities.

the reasons behind many conflicts in the area of scientific knowledge and communication technologies.

The question about the appropriate balance between law, science and technology underlies one of the most heated debates in the legal circles and which regularly results in legal dispute before courts of different levels and jurisdictions.[55] This difficulty is partly due to the apparently growing incapacity of legislator to regulate this field or to the lack of effective legislation. Such regulatory problems were already being observed and discussed by several authors but the evidence does not seem to be completely conclusive. More evidence should be gathered in the setting provided by contemporary controversies. The point of the issue – as put by Robin Feldman – is that most of the scholars who consider contemporary problems at the intersection of law, science and technology are used to present the question "in terms of how rapidly scientific information changes and how slowly the legal system responds".[56] At the same time "others describe how the legal system distorts scientific information".[57] Though many acknowledge that these perspectives are absolutely important for understanding the relationship between law, science and technology, there is less agreement as to how "the problems go beyond misinterpretation and misuse" of scientific and technological information.[58] As for the reasons for this observation, we completely agree with the view pointed out by Feldman, according to whom "the core problem at the intersection" of law, science and technology "flow not from the changing nature" of science and technology but also "from the changing nature of law".[59]

However, in addition to these potential obstacles, it is also important to remember that the ground of individual rights and liberties has historically hosted intellectual matches between legal positivists and their adversaries.[60] According to the positivist' theory of legal obligation, the law is a set of rules used to control the behavior of people in society.[61] If a specific case is not covered by a rule, there is no legal obligation until a judge creates a new rule for the future.[62] In other words, a legal right or obligation must directly fall under a legal rule. On the other hand, according to Dworkin, law is not only comprised of rules but also of principles, policies and social standards: "if we treat principles as law we must reject the positivists' first tenet, that the law of a community is distinguished from other social

[55] For some of the seminal works within this field, see Sheila Jasanoff, Science at the Bar: Law, Science, and Technology in America (1995); Robin Feldman, The Role of Science in Law 4 (2009). See also generally Human Rights in the Global Information Society (Rikke Frank Jørgensen ed., 2006).

[56] Robin Feldman, The Role of Science in Law 4 (2009).

[57] Id.

[58] Id.

[59] Id.

[60] See Lorenzo Zucca, Constitutional Dilemmas: Conflicts of Fundamental Legal Rights in Europe and the USA 7 (2007).

[61] Ronald A. Dworkin, Taking Rights Seriously 44 (1978).

[62] Id.

standards by some test in the form of a master rule".[63] In deciding hard cases, for example, judges should decide "by trying to find the best justification they can find, in principles of political morality, for the structure as a whole, from the most profound constitutional rules and arrangements to the details of, for example, the private law of tort or contract".[64] In this context, it may be also complex to recognize the legitimate emissaries of science and to adjust to the message of which they are bearers.[65] Furthermore, the judge and the legislator, when dealing with a scientific or technological issue, can easily be seduced by legal moralism.[66]

These findings, however, do not justify policies that override fundamental legal rights and basic human needs of individuals. Occasionally, fundamental legal rights can be seen by the government as an obstacle to what it wants to do. However, in a "nation of laws" the role of the judiciary is to apply those laws, even when the government perceives such judicial enforcement as inconvenient or excessively costly.[67]

Working on emerging issues at the intersection of law, science and technology, requires also to comply with different regulatory instruments, accommodating conflicting principles and balancing different sets of rules (moral, economic and social). These are exactly the reasons why the question of the conflict of rights can be best explored by looking to the specific areas where tensions may arise.[68] The first key provision in an international agreement that identifies possible areas of conflicts of rights, is found in article 27 of the Universal Declaration of human rights[69] and in article 15 of the International Covenant on Economic, Social and Cultural Rights[70]:

[63] Id.

[64] Ronald A. Dworkin, "Natural" Law Revisited, 34 U. Fla. L. Rev. 165 (1982).

[65] On this see Sheila Jasanoff, Science at the Bar. Law, Science and Technology in America xiv (1995) (highlighting the difficulties faced by judges and juries in recognizing "good science" and "legitimate expertise").

[66] The term "legal moralism", coined by the famous legal moralist Patrick Devlin, is a theory that implies that it is permissible for the State to use its coercitive power to enforce society's collective morality. See Patrick Devlin, The Enforcement of Morals 10 (1965); Kenneth E. Himma, Philosophy of Law. Internet Encyclopedia of Philosophy (2001–2009) available at http://iep.utm.edu/law-phil (last accessed 28 April 2016).

[67] See Steven Banks, Adr and Litigation Involving Social Problems 35 Fordham Urb. L.J. 109, 118 (2008).

[68] See Frantzeska Papadopoulou, TRIPS and Human Rights, in Intellectual Property Rights in a Fair World Trade System 262, 283 (A. Kur & M. Levin eds., 2011).

[69] Universal Declaration of Human Rights, G.A. Res. 217A (III), art. 27, U.N. Doc. A/810 (Dec. 10, 1948). Article 27 of the Universal Declaration of Human Rights prescribes the enjoyment of cultural rights. It specifies that: "Everyone has the right freely to participate in the cultural life of the community, to enjoy the arts and to share in scientific advancement and its benefits. Everyone has the right to the protection of the moral and material interests resulting from any scientific, literary or artistic production of which he is the author".

[70] International Covenant on Economic, Social, and Cultural Rights Art. 15(1) (a-c), Dec. 16, 1966, 933 U.N.T.S. 3 [hereinafter ICESCR]. Covenant provisions have the rank of constitutional law and they have begun to be applied by the State party's courts. Article 15 of ICESCR states that: "1. The States Parties to the present Covenant recognize the right of everyone: (a) To take part in cultural

here is explicitly defined the right to scientific progress and access to its benefits as well as the rights to cultural participation. In particular, the Covenant's provisions emphasize the right of everyone to access "science and culture" with the clear intention to include in these words all fields of human knowledge[71]: this right comprehends and protects the right of everyone "to participate in the advancement and share in the benefits of human knowledge both scientific and cultural".[72] This target is explicitly marked by the expression "the right of access to knowledge" that is, *de facto*, a different way to look at the right of access to information.[73] The concept of a right to science and culture has not generated a great deal of interest from legal scholars.[74] In addition there is still a lack in thorough understanding of what the right would mean in practice.

However, this right has recently received renewed attention from international human rights institutions: three consecutive reports issued by the United Nations Special Rapporteur for cultural diversity stressed several critiques and concerns about the continuous expansion of intellectual property rights taking into consideration the different implications of copyright and patent policy for the human right to science and culture.[75]

---

life; (b) To enjoy the benefits of scientific progress and its applications; (c) To benefit from the protection of the moral and material interests resulting from any scientific, literary or artistic production of which he is the author.

2. The steps to be taken by the States Parties to the present Covenant to achieve the full realization of this right shall include those necessary for the conservation, the development and the diffusion of science and culture.

3. The States Parties to the present Covenant undertake to respect the freedom indispensable for scientific research and creative activity.

4. The States Parties to the present Covenant recognize the benefits to be derived from the encouragement and development of international contacts and co-operation in the scientific and cultural fields."

[71] See Lea Shaver & Caterina Sganga, The Right to Take Part in Cultural Life: On Copyright and Human Rights, 27 Wis. Int'l L.J. 637, 642 (2010);

[72] Id., at 642–643; see also Lea Shaver, The Right to Science and Culture, 2010 Wis. L. Rev. 121, 137 (2010); Aurora Plomer, The Human Rights Paradox: Intellectual Property Rights and Rights of Access to Science, 35 Hum. Rts. Q. 143 (2012).

[73] See Geertrui Van Overwalle, Human rights' limitations in patent law, in Intellectual Property And Human Rights. A Paradox 236, 261 (Willem Grosheide ed., 2010) (discussing how the right of access to information can be reflected in patent law).

[74] See Aurora Plomer, The Right to Access the Benefits of Science and Intellectual Property Rights in Biotech Innovations & Fundamental Rights 45 (R. Bin, et al. eds., 2011).

[75] See United Nations General Assembly, Human Rights Council, Report of the Special Rapporteur in the Field of Cultural Rights: The Right to Enjoy the Benefits of Scientific Progress and its Applications, Farida Shaheed, U.N. Doc. UA/HRC/20/26 (14 May 2012) at 15; United Nations General Assembly, Human Rights Council, Report of the Special Rapporteur in the Field of Cultural Rights: Copyright policy and the right to science and culture, Farida Shaheed, U.N. Doc. A/HRC/28/57 (24 Dec. 2014); United Nations General Assembly, Human Rights Council, Report of the Special Rapporteur in the Field of Cultural Rights: Patent policy and the right to science and culture, Farida Shaheed, U.N. Doc. A/70/279 (4 Aug. 2015).

Also human rights scholars and members of the access to knowledge movement[76] assert that the right to science and culture is in tension with the current and unprecedented extensions of intellectual property rights that unduly restrict the ability of individuals to take part in cultural life and profit from advances in science and technology.[77] On this ground, various tensions and conflicts grow between the belief that knowledge needs to be free and the fact that property rights establish a very substantial control over certain knowledge products. This antagonism is then intensified by technology's effect on knowledge creation.[78] In addition, as already stressed by other authors, in the context of the right to science and culture, "access" can support multiple dimensions.[79]

> It should be understood to include the ability to actively participate and share with others, not merely to play the passive role of consumer. [...] [t]he right 'to take part in culture consists in the ability to consume and to create, individually and with others. Culture exists to be shared and to inhabit a culture is to contribute to it. Participation, as well as consumption, is the essence of the right to science and culture. "Access" therefore should be understood in terms of access to scientific and cultural materials, tools, and information; access to opportunities to create as well as to consume; and to share in the senses of both taking and giving. Looking to the scientific aspect of the right, access must go beyond sharing in the diffuse benefits of scientific learning in its pure form.[80]

Another important aspect to be considered in this discussion is the question of the freedom of scientific research. This fundamental right is in fact expressly recognized, with specific reference, in some constitutions of European Countries.[81] At the same time, in countries where no specific provisions are provided, such freedom ends up having to be protected as a particular aspect of the wider freedom of speech.[82] It is a matter of fact that gene patent holders can abuse of their complete

[76] See generally Gaëlle Krikorian & Amy Kapczynski (eds.), Access to Knowledge in the Age of Intellectual Property (2010).

[77] See Lea Shaver, The Right To Science And Culture, 10 Wis. L. Rev. 121, 126 (2010); Amy Kapczynski, Access to Knowledge: A Conceptual Genealogy, in Access to Knowledge in the Age of Intellectual Property 16, 47 (G. Krikorian & A. Kapczynski eds. 2010). See also Aurora Plomer, The Right to Access the Benefits of Science and Intellectual Property Rights in Biotech Innovations & Fundamental Rights 45 (R. Bin, et al. eds., 2011).

[78] See Gaëlle Krikorian, Access to Knowledge as a Field of Activism, in Access to Knowledge in the Age of Intellectual Property 57, 79 (G. Krikorian & A. Kapczynski eds. 2010).

[79] See Lea Shaver, The Right To Science And Culture, 10 Wis. L. Rev. 121, 171–172 (2010).

[80] Id. See also Lea Shaver & Caterina Sganga, The Right to Take Part in Cultural Life: On Copyright and Human Rights, 27 Wis. Int'l L.J. 637, 646 (2010).

[81] See Amedeo Santosuosso et al., What Constitutional Protection for Freedom of Scientific Research, 33 Journal of Medical Ethics 342 (2007); Roberto Bin, Freedom of Scientific Research in the Field of Genetics, in Biotech Innovations & Fundamental Rights 131 (R. Bin et al., eds. 2011).

[82] See Amedeo Santosuosso et al., What Constitutional Protection for Freedom of Scientific Research, cit.; Roberto Bin, Freedom of Scientific Research in the Field of Genetics, cit. (the author observes that in countries where freedom of scientific research is not identified with specific constitutional norms, protection of science is often placed under the same category as other rights, for example, freedom of expression, due process or equal protection). Id. at 132.

control to charge disproportionate fees for diagnostic testing and to preclude other researchers from utilizing specific genes for research or from pursuing research in the same field: studies have demonstrated this chilling effect on scientific research[83] even showing a sensible decrease of number of publications on patented genetic information.[84]

Yet another point of tension associated with science and technology advances is related to the right to health. Several levels of protection are given to the right to health as we can find specific and consistent constitutional recognition for such fundamental right.[85] From this point of view, it is claimed that gene patents can have a detrimental impact on health care: for example, they are able to prevent more precise, inexpensive and advanced diagnostic tests from being developed.[86] In addition, gene patents can also constrain the freedom of scientists and health researchers to investigate more about gene-to-disease relationships limiting further developments in fields that could benefit and enhance the health of all people.[87] Particularly relevant in this framework is also the Convention for the Protection of Human Rights and Dignity of the Human Being with regard to the Application of Biology and Medicine: the Convention on Human Rights and Biomedicine (also known as

[83] See Mildred K. Cho et al., Effects of Patents and Licenses on the Provision of Clinical Genetic Testing Services, 5(1) J. Molecular Diagnostics 3 (2003) (analyzing the effect of gene patents on the diffusion of 12 genetic tests); Jon F. Merz et al., Diagnostic Testing Fails the Test: The Pitfalls of Patents Are Illustrated by the Case of Haemochromatosis, 415 Nature 577 (2002) (considering the consequence of gene patents on the diffusion of the Haemochromatosis genetic test); Thomas D. Kiley, Patents on Random Complementary DNA Fragments?, 257 Science 915 (1992); Stuart M. MacLeod & Donald J. Willison, Patenting of Genetic Material: Are the Benefits to Society Being Realized?, 167 Can. Med. Ass'n J. 259, 261 (2002); Arti K. Rai & Rebecca S. Eisenberg, Bayh-Dole Reform and the Progress of Biomedicine, 66 Law & Contemp. Probs. 289, 301 (2003) (expressing the concern that genetic patents can hinder developments in diagnostic tests); Karen Seashore Louis et al., Entrepreneurship, Secrecy, and Productivity: A Comparison of Clinical and Non-Clinical Life Sciences Faculty, 26 J. Tech. Transfer 233, 238–239 (2001); David Blumenthal et al., University-Industry Research Relationships in Biotechnology: Implications for the University, 232 Science 1361 (1986); David Blumenthal et al., Withholding Research Results in Academic Life Science: Evidence From a National Survey of Faculty, 277 J. Am. Med. Ass'n 1224, (1997); Eric G. Campbell et al., Data Withholding in Academic Genetics: Evidence From a National Survey, 287 J. Am. Med. Ass'n 473, (2002); Joel Lexchin, The Secret Things Belong Unto the Lord Our God: Secrecy in the Pharmaceutical Arena, 26 Med. & L. 417, 421 (2007) (evaluating problems on sharing of research results in academia).

[84] See Fiona Murray & Scott Stern, Do Formal Intellectual Property Rights Hinder the Free Flow of Scientific Knowledge? An Empirical Test of the Anti-Commons Hypothesis, 63 J. Econ. Behav. & Org. 648 (2007).

[85] See also ICESCR, art. 12.

[86] See Secretary's Advisory Comm. on Genetics, Health, & Soc'y, U.S. Dept of Health & Human Servs., Revised Draft Report on Gene Patents and Licensing Practices and Their Impact on Patient Access to Genetic Tests (2010), http://oba.od.nih.gov/oba/SACGHS/SACGHS%20Patents%20Report%20Approved%202-5-20010.pdf (last accessed 28 April 2016).

[87] Conflicts and dilemmas within the current patent system will be extensively discussed in the following chapters. See infra chp. 4.

Oviedo Convention).[88] The Convention is the only binding international legal instrument to address the issue of bioethics. Its aim – as specified in Article 1 – is to safeguard the dignity and identity of all human beings and guarantee everyone, without discrimination, respect for their integrity and other rights and fundamental freedoms with regard to the application of biology and medicine. In particular, the Convention is directed at protecting the dignity of individuals in connection with biomedical treatments, research, genetics and transplantation of organs or tissues. The Oviedo Convention also prohibits the creation of human embryos for research purposes.

Finally, the most evident and pervasive conflict of rights in the technological era is the one with the right to freedom of expression and access to information. Freedom of expression is constitutionally protected in many liberal and democratic Countries. It is considered one of the cornerstones of the United Nations Declaration of Human Rights (Article 19)[89] and it is recognized as a fundamental right under Article 10 of the European Convention on Human Rights.[90] Also the EU Charter of Fundamental Rights sets out a series of individual rights and freedoms relevant to this discussion.[91] Largely, it strengthens the rights already recognized in the case law of the Court of Justice of the EU, established in the European Convention on Human Rights, as well as all the other rights, freedoms and principles stemming from the constitutional traditions of EU Member States and other international agreements. In particular, it could be in interesting – mostly in the future – to monitor how the newly formulated rights in the European Charter – the right of the individual in the field of medicine (Article 3 EUCFR) and the individual rights to the information (Article 11 EUCFR) – will be applied to solve "potential conflicts of interests in the constitutional discourse" of the contemporary networked society.[92]

As it will be further discussed in the following chapters, the multimedia revolution has profoundly affected habits of thought and expression, thereby involving also the debate concerning access to knowledge and information.[93] The rules

---

[88] See Convention for the Protection of Human Rights and Dignity of the Human Being with Regard to the Application of Biology and Medicine: Convention on Human Rights and Biomedicine, Council of Eur., Apr. 4, 1997, C.E.T.S. 164, available at http://conventions.coe.int/treaty/en/treaties/html/164.htm (last accessed 28 April 2016).

[89] Universal Declaration of Human Rights, G.A. Res. 217A (III), art. 19, U.N. Doc. A/810 (Dec. 10, 1948).

[90] Convention for the Protection of Human Rights and Fundamental Freedoms, opened for signature Nov. 4, 1950, art. 10, 213 U.N.T.S. 221, 234 [hereinafter European Convention on Human Rights]. See also Ronald J. Deibert, Black Code Redux: Censorship, Surveillance, and the Militarization of Cyberspace, in Digital Media and Democracy: Tactics in Hard Time 140 (M. Boler ed., 2008).

[91] Charter of Fundamental Rights of the European Union art. 8, Dec. 18, 2000, 2000 O.J. (C 364) 1.

[92] See Christine Godt, Intellectual Property and European Fundamental Rights, in Constitutionalization of European Private Law: XXII/2 211, 218 (Hans Micklitz ed. 2014).

[93] Amy Kapzcynski, The Access to Knowledge Mobilization and the New Politics of Intellectual Property, 117 Yale L.J. 804 (2008).

governing the world of information and communication have never been – as they are in the current period – the subject of such profound changes. This has inevitably caused tension in the delicate balance that underpins fundamental rights and basic democratic principles. Regulatory policies could not interfere or restrict freedom of expression. However, freedom of expression is not an absolute right, and consequently some limitations and restrictions may apply under certain legitimate circumstances.[94]

1.7 Theory, Methods and Analysis Approaches

The research methods used in this book are those traditionally related to scientific research in the legal field: identification of the sources, in-depth study of the legal scholarship, case-law analysis, general theory studies, and elaboration of original results on exegesis and analysis of legal concepts. Specifically, the methodological approach involves the analysis of the texts produced by government and regulatory institutions as well as by judicial authorities. In particular, the investigation unfolded in the book is performed and analyzed by using the following methodologies: doctrinal research, interdisciplinary legal research and comparative method. The doctrinal research method is applied to the analysis of the regulatory framework adopted in the United States and in Europe. The comparative method is used to illustrate how different jurisdictions have responded to the opportunities and threats posed by scientific and technological innovations and their major implications for individual rights protection. This technique will contribute to the understanding of laws and the coherent explanation of their particular identities. At the same time, it can provide a more consistent picture suggesting original approaches taken from foreign experience and stimulating the circulation of models.[95] This comparative and multi-perspective analysis looks at the past, the present and the future regulatory framework making assessments of the current landscape and structure with three different levels – the north-American, the European and the global. Following this methodological track, the book also considers and compares the regulatory reforms recently adopted or discussed in Europe and in the United States. Finally, in order to achieve an accurate understanding of specific provisions and principles, the book also considers historical material seeking the policy makers' original intentions. This specific approach is essentially used to illustrate the effectiveness of existing regulation. Uncertain or ambiguous legal ruling are then interpreted observing the proper institutional or social context also considering the industry or the technology to which it relates. This process will involve an evaluation of the effectiveness of a particular

[94] See Michel Verpeaux, Freedom of Expression 42 (2010); Vincenzo Zeno Zencovich, Freedom of expression: a critical and comparative analysis 80 (2008)

[95] See Guy Canivet, The Practice of Comparative Law by the Supreme Courts: Brief Reflections on the Dialogue Between the Judges in French and European Experience, 80 Tulane L. Rev. 1377, 1382 (2006).

piece of legislation in achieving specific social goals as well as an examination of the extent to which it is being complied with.

All the case law is used with the mere purpose of identifying trends and highlighting possible commonalities and differences in the regulation of issues raised by biotechnology or communication technologies. The cases selected were only those who have had jurisprudential impact, specifically cases involving issues at the interface of science, technology and individual rights addressing the application or interpretation of controversial and contentious provisions and that have contributed to policy changes at the national level. Preference was given to recent case law and newly enacted legislation. In providing a clear, concise and direct insight to the subject in a book of limited length, necessarily the selection of case law for comment and analysis can appear uneven or occasionally idiosyncratic. In order to overcome this limit, the selection of cases examined follows a deliberate pattern: in particular we have tried to identify those cases that more than others are able to stimulate the discussion and the circulation of similar legal approaches between different legal systems promoting exchanges, dialogues and contaminations between the doctrine, public authorities, and judges. In order to support the "circulation of models" we have also provided a mixture of civil law and common law elements.

Two are the thematic trajectories of the book. The first is devoted to the analysis and comparison of regulatory regimes adopted in the US and EU. Here the focus is on two main themes: the conflict between freedom of expression and regulation of digital network technologies; and the conflict between individual rights and regulation of biotech innovations. From the first perspective, the analysis will concentrate primarily on the most recent attempts to regulate and monitor digital content and Internet based applications. From the second perspective, the objective is on how to balance freedom of research and other fundamental rights and liberties, such as public safety, right to health, intellectual property and human dignity.[96] The two research paths are complementary, as results from the second could be applied to the first and *vice versa*. In particular they permit to underline how the commodification of information is driving common economic trends in both the digital information and genetic information fields.[97] From the legal perspective this is realized through a continuous expansion of intellectual property rights over various forms of information. On this ground, human information and genetic information reveal their contrasting nature as both public and private goods.[98] The balance between these two contrasting factors remains contentious. Consequently, the investigation concentrates on how to determine the appropriate balance and line of separation between private and public interests.

[96] See Christian Starck, Freedom of Scientific Research and its limits in German Constitutional Law, 39 Isr. L. Rev. 110, 120 (2006) (observing how the right to human dignity creates another restriction on the freedom of scientific research).

[97] See Sandra Braman, The Meta-Technologies of Information, in Biotechnology and Communication: The Meta-Technologies of Information 3, 11 (Sandra Braman ed., 2004).

[98] Id., at 13.

1.8 Organization of the Book

The internal organization of the book essentially reflects the diversity and the interdisciplinary nature of the subject matter of this investigation. It is framed by this introductory chapter, which provides an overview of the main theme, and a closing commentary section with concluding remarks. The book is structured in two main thematic sections in order to provide an easy and accessible way of concentrating on the complexity of the legal issues surrounding scientific and technological innovations integrating legal theory, legal doctrine and the analysis of relevant judicial decisions. The first thematic cluster includes two chapters (Chaps. 2 and 3) dealing with rights claims and legal controversies embedded in the rise of digital communication technologies. The second thematic cluster comprises two chapters (Chaps. 4 and 5) focusing on right claims and legal controversies arising from or related to the implementation of biotechnological inventions.

In this first introductory chapter we have tried to introduce the background of the conflict between legal rights and scientific and technological developments. After a brief introduction to the terms and principles important in this analysis, this opening part outlined the key challenges facing individuals and society as a result of scientific and technological advances, as well as the issues involved with making such technologies accessible. This part also examined – in general terms – the role of law in the global regulation of innovative technologies. Finally, in this section, we have also looked at how scientific and technological developments while providing better conditions of life of people, in a number of instances they can also give rise to social problems as well as threaten the human rights and fundamental freedoms of the individual.

The second and the third chapters of the book discuss the specific issues and challenges posed by recent digital content reforms designed to monitor and control the flow of information over the Internet, indirectly narrowing the freedom of expression and communication. The main question addressed in these chapters is to identify which developments have taken place – from a global perspective – with respect to fundamental rights and new communication technologies. In particular, over the course of the third chapter, we will discuss how – in almost all democratic systems – new and old media have not only posed problems of definition, but have often resulted in attempts to contain and control information flow. This condition raises a number of questions and concerns: what measures and actions can be taken to guarantee freedom of expression, media pluralism and access to knowledge in the digital environment? What are the possible solutions to protect digital freedom of expression and what actions can be taken to better protect citizens' access to information and for their participation in digital life? What are the policy directions for allowing the free flow of information, freedom of expression and protection of individual liberties as they relate to access? How to structure a balanced protection for intellectual property allowing – at the same time – for a better respect of individual users' freedom to express themselves, to access and share content, culture, information and to innovate and create? Chapter 3 tries to provide answers to these questions through an analysis of relevant case law, including both national and international rulings.

The fourth and fifth chapters of the book consider some of the major issues and rights in the field of biotech innovations. One of the most troublesome problems in this area is closely related to the patentability of isolated elements of the human body or other natural organisms and animals. This question is tied to a series of corollary questions concerning human dignity and fundamental legal and moral rights of the individual. In particular, the patenting of biotech inventions involving the use of biological material of human or natural origin can undermine the right of access to scientific knowledge or generate indirect implications on the right to health and the right to use natural resources. After an introductory section (Chap. 4) devoted to define and explain the essential principles and concepts of the life sciences with an emphasis on cellular biology, the book moves the discussion within the context of regulation of biotechnology and individual rights. In this regard, we focus particularly on providing answers to questions surrounding genetic invention patents. Gene patents, in fact, can have an adverse effect not only on the free access to research outputs, but they could also introduce additional barriers to scientific information, health care opportunities and biodiversity conservation. Genes represent the common heritage of mankind and should be passed from generation to generation through natural mechanisms. In light of these concerns, the fifth chapter considers recent litigation over biotech patents and expressed sequence tags (ESTs) focusing on ethical and juridical implications related to the development of personalized medicine and bioprospecting activities.

References

Ahearn, Raymond J. 2011. *U.S. – EU trade and economic relations: Key policy issues for the 112th congress*. Washington, DC: Congressional Research Service.

Aigrain, Philippe. 2012. *Sharing: Culture and the economy in the internet age*. Amsterdam: Amsterdam University Press.

Alexy, Robert. 2002. *A theory of constitutional rights*. Oxford/New York: Oxford University Press.

Balkin, Jack M. 2009. The future of free expression in a digital age. *Pepperdine Law Review* 36: 427.

Banks, Steven. 2008. Adr and litigation involving social problems. *Fordham Urban Law Journal* 35: 109.

Beldiman, Dana (ed.). 2013. *Access to information and knowledge: 21st century challenges in intellectual property and knowledge governance*. Cheltenham/Northampton: Edward Elgar Publishing.

Benedek, Wolfgang, and Matthias C. Kettemann. 2013. *Freedom of expression and the internet*. Strasbourg: Council of Europe Publishing.

Benkler, Yochai. 2006. *The wealth of networks: How social production transforms markets and freedom*. New Haven: Yale University Press.

Bernier, Louise. 2010. *Justice in genetics: Intellectual property and human rights from a cosmopolitan liberal perspective*. Cheltenham/Northampton: Edward Elgar Publishing.

Bin, Roberto, et al. (eds.). 2011. *Biotech innovations & fundamental rights*. Milan/New York: Springer.

Bishop, Cheryl Ann. 2012. *Access to information as human right*. El Paso: LFB Scholarly Publishing.

Blumenthal, David, et al. 1986. University-industry research relationships in biotechnology: Implications for the university. *Science* 232: 1361.

Blumenthal, David, et al. 1997. Withholding research results in academic life science: Evidence from a national survey of faculty. *Journal of the American Medical Association* 277: 1224.

Boldrin, Michele, and David K. Levine. 2010. *Against intellectual monopoly*. New York: Cambridge University Press.

Bozeman, Barry, et al. (eds.). 2003. *Knowledge flows and knowledge collectives: Understanding the role of science and technology policies in development*. New York: Rockefeller Foundation.

Braman, Sandra. 2002. Informational meta-technologies and international relations: The case of biotechnologies. In *Information technologies and global politics: The changing scope of power and governance*, ed. James N. Rosenau and J.P. Singh, 91. Albany: State University of New York Press.

Braman, Sandra (ed.). 2004a. *Biotechnology and communication: The meta-technologies of information*. Mahwah: Lawrence Erlbaum Associates.

Braman, Sandra. 2004b. Technology. In *The sage handbook of media studies*, ed. John D.H. Downing et al., 123. Thousand Oaks: Sage.

Braman, Sandra. 2004. The meta-technologies of information. In *Biotechnology and communication: The meta-technologies of information*. Mahwah: Lawrence Erlbaum Associates.

Brown, Ian, and Christopher T. Marsden. 2013. *Regulating code. Good governance and better regulation in the information age*. Cambridge, MA: MIT Press.

Brownsword, Roger. 2008. *Rights, regulation, and the technological revolution*. Oxford/New York: Oxford University Press.

Brownsword, Roger, and Morag Goodwin. 2012. *Law and technologies of the twenty-first century*. Cambridge/New York: Cambridge University Press.

Callon, Michel, Pierre Lascoumes, and Yannick Barthe. 2009. *Acting in an uncertain world: An essay on technical democracy*. Cambridge, MA: MIT Press.

Campbell, Eric G., et al. 2002. Data withholding in academic genetics: Evidence from a national survey. *Journal of the American Medical Association* 287: 473.

Chapman, Audrey R. 2009. Towards an understanding of the right to enjoy the benefits from scientific progress and its applications. *Journal of Human Rights* 8: 1.

Cho, Mildred K., et al. 2003. Effects of patents and licenses on the provision of clinical genetic testing services. *Journal of Molecular Diagnostics* 5(1): 3.

Claude, Richard Pierre. 2002. *Science in the service of human rights*. Philadelphia: University of Pennsylvania Press.

Cornides, Jakob. 2004. Human rights and intellectual property: Conflict or convergence? *Journal of World Intellectual Property* 7: 135.

Cullet, Philippe. 2007. Human rights and intellectual property rights in a TRIPS Era. *Human Rights Quarterly* 29: 403.

Cutcliffe, Stephen H. 2000. *Ideas, machines and values: An introduction to science, technology and social studies*. Lanham: Rowman & Littlefield Publishers.

Davies, Gillian. 2002. *Copyright and the public interest*, 2nd ed. London: Sweet & Maxwell.

De Azevedo Cunha, Mario Viola, et al. 2013. *New technologies and human rights: Challenges to regulation*. Farnham/Burlington: Ashgate.

Deibert, Ronald J. 2008. Black code redux: Censorship, surveillance, and the militarization of cyberspace. In *Digital media and democracy: Tactics in hard time*, ed. M. Boler, 140. Cambridge, MA: MIT Press.

Devlin, Patrick. 1965. *The enforcement of morals*. London/New York: Oxford University Press

Dutton, William H., et al. 2011. *Freedom of connection – freedom of expression: The changing legal and regulatory ecology shaping the internet*. Paris: UNESCO Report.

Dworkin, Ronald. 1978. *Taking rights seriously*. Cambridge: Harvard University Press.

Eisenstein, Elizabeth. 1979. *The printing press as an agent of change: Communications and cultural transformations in early-modern Europe*. Cambridge/New York: Cambridge University Press.

Elkin-Koren, Niva, and Neil W. Netanel (eds.). 2002. *The commodification of information*. The Hague/New York: Kluwer Law.
Feenberg, Andrew. 1999. *Questioning technology*. London/New York: Routledge.
Feldman, Robin. 2009a. Historic perspectives on law & science. *Stanford Technology Law Review* 12: 1.
Feldman, Robin. 2009b. *The role of science in law*. Oxford/New York: Oxford University Press.
Geiger, Christophe. 2004. Fundamental rights, a safeguard for the coherence of intellectual property law? *International Review of Intellectual Property and Competition Law* 35: 268.
Geiger, Christophe. 2006. 'Constitutionalising' intellectual property law? The influence of fundamental rights on intellectual property in the European Union. *International Review of Intellectual Property and Competition Law* 37: 371.
Geiger, Christophe (ed.). 2015. *Research handbook on human rights and intellectual property*. Cheltenham: Edward Elgar Publishing.
Godt, Christine. 2014. Intellectual property and European fundamental rights. In *Constitutionalization of European private law: XXII/2 211*, ed. Hans Micklitz. Oxford: Oxford University Press.
Goggin, L. Malcom. 1986. *Governing science and technology in a democracy*. Knoxville: University of Tennessee Press.
Griffiths, Jonathan, and Uma Suthersanen (eds.). 2008. *Copyright and free speech. Comparative and international analyses*. Oxford/New York: Oxford University Press.
Grosheide, Willem (ed.). 2010. *Intellectual property and human rights. A paradox*. Cheltenham/Northampton: Edward Elgar.
Hardt, Michael, and Antonio Negri. 2004. *Multitude: War and democracy in the age of empire*. New York: Penguin Press.
Haunss, Sebastian. 2013. *Conflicts in the knowledge society. The contentious politics of intellectual property*. Cambridge: Cambridge University Press.
Helberger, Natali. 2005. *Controlling access to content: Regulating conditional access in digital broadcasting*. The Hague: Kluwer Law International.
Helfer, Laurence R. 2003. Human rights and intellectual property: Conflict or coexistence? *Minnesota Intellectual Property Law Review* 5: 47.
Helfer, Laurence R. 2004. Regime shifting: The TRIPS agreement and new dynamics of international intellectual property lawmaking. *Yale Journal of International Law* 29: 29.
Helfer, Laurence R. 2008. The new innovation frontier? Intellectual property and the European court of human rights. *Harvard International Law Journal* 49: 1.
Helfer, Laurence R., and Graeme W. Austin. 2011. *Human rights and intellectual property: Mapping the global interface*. Cambridge/New York: Cambridge University Press.
Heller, Michael A., and Rebecca S. Eisenberg. 1998. Can patents deter innovation? The anticommons in biomedical research. *Science* 280: 698.
Horner, Lisa, et al. 2010. *Information and communication technologies and human rights*. Brussels: European Parliament.
Hugenholtz, P. Bernt. 2001. Copyright and freedom of expression in Europe. In *Expanding the boundaries of intellectual property. Innovation policy for the knowledge society*, ed. Rochelle Cooper Dreyfuss, Diane Leenheer Zimmerman, and Harry First, 343. Oxford/New York: Oxford University Press.
Hveem, Helge, and Lelio Iapadre (eds.). 2011. *The global governance of knowledge creation and diffusion*. New York: Routledge.
Irwin, Alan. 2001. Constructing the scientific citizen: Science and democracy in the biosciences. *Public Understanding of Science* 10: 1.
Jasanoff, Sheila. 1995. *Science at the bar. Law, science and technology in America*. Cambridge, MA: Harvard University Press.
Jasanoff, Sheila. 2004. Science and citizenship: A new synergy. *Science and Public Policy* 31: 90.
Jasanoff, Sheila. 2005. *Designs on nature: Science and democracy in Europe and the United States*. Princeton: Princeton University Press.

Jasanoff, Sheila. 2011a. Constitutional moments in governing science and technology. *Science and Engineering Ethics* 17: 621.
Jasanoff, Sheila (ed.). 2011b. *Reframing rights: Bioconstitutionalism in the genetic age*. Cambridge, MA: MIT Press.
Kapzcynski, Amy. 2008. The access to knowledge mobilization and the new politics of intellectual property. *Yale Law Journal* 117: 804.
Kiley, Thomas D. 1992. Patents on random complementary DNA fragments? *Science* 257: 915.
Kleinman, Daniel Lee (ed.). 2000a. *Science, technology, and democracy*. Albany: State University of New York Press.
Kleinman, Daniel Lee. 2000b. Democratizations of science and technology. In *Science, technology, and democracy*, ed. Daniel Lee Kleinmann, 139. Albany: State University of New York Press.
Krikorian, Gaëlle, and Kapczynski, Amy (eds.). 2010. *Access to knowledge in the age of intellectual property*. New York: Zone Books.
Krimsky, Sheldon. 1982. *Genetic alchemy: The social history of the recombinant DNA controversy*. Cambridge, MA: MIT University Press.
Krimsky, Sheldon, and Peter Shorett (eds.). 2005. *Rights and liberties in the biotech age: Why we need a genetic bill of rights*. Lanham: Rowman & Littlefield Publishers.
Kur, Annette, and Marianne Levin. 2011. *Intellectual property rights in a fair world trade system: Proposals for reform of TRIPS*. Cheltenham/Northampton: Edward Elgar.
Land, Molly. 2013. Toward an international law of the internet. *Harvard International Law Journal* 54: 393.
Laurie, Graeme. 2004. *Genetic privacy. A challenge to medico-legal norms*. Cambridge/New York: Cambridge University Press.
Lawton, Thomas C. 1997. *Technology and the new diplomacy: The creation and control of EC industrial policy for semiconductors*. Aldershot/Brookfield: Avebury.
Lawton Smith, Helen (ed.). 2002. *The regulation of science and technology*. Houndmills/New York: Palgrave Publishers.
Leenes, Ronald E., et al. (eds.). 2008. *Constitutional rights and new technologies. A comparative study*. The Hague: T.M.C. Asser Press.
Lessig, Lawrence. 2004. *Free culture: How big media uses technology and the law to lock down culture and control creativity*. New York: Penguin Press.
Lexchin, Joel. 2007. The secret things belong unto the Lord our God: Secrecy in the pharmaceutical arena. *Medicine and Law* 26: 417.
Lucchi, Nicola. 2006. *Digital media and intellectual property*. Berlin/New York: Springer.
MacLeod, Stuart M., and Donald J. Willison. 2002. Patenting of genetic material: Are the benefits to society being realized? *Canadian Medical Association Journal* 167: 259.
Mahop, Marcelin Tonye. 2010. *Intellectual property, community rights and human rights*. Milton Park/New York: Routledge.
Matthews, Duncan. 2011. *Intellectual property, human rights and development*. Cheltenham/Northampton: Edward Elgar Publishing.
Merz, Jon F., et al. 2002. Diagnostic testing fails the test: The pitfalls of patents are illustrated by the case of haemochromatosis. *Nature* 415: 577.
Murphy, Thérèse (ed.). 2009. *New technologies and human rights*. Oxford/New York: Oxford University Press.
Murray, Fiona, and Scott Stern. 2007. Do formal intellectual property rights hinder the free flow of scientific knowledge? An empirical test of the anti-commons hypothesis. *Journal of Economic Behavior and Organization* 63: 648.
Ó Siochrú, Seán. 2005. *Assessing communication rights: A handbook*. London: World Association for Christian Communication.
Ozolina, Zaneta, et al. 2012. *Ethical and regulatory challenges to science and research policy at the global level, expert group report, directorate-general for research and innovation of the European Commission*. Luxembourg: Publication Office of the European Union.

Papadopoulou, Frantzeska. 2011. TRIPS and human rights. In *Intellectual property rights in a fair world trade system: Proposals for reform of TRIPS*, ed. Kur Annette and Levin Marianne, 262. Cheltenham/Northampton: Edward Elgar Publishing.

Pestre, Dominique. 2008. Challenges for the democratic management of technoscience: Governance, participation and the political today. *Science as Culture* 17: 101.

Plomer, Aurora. 2012a. After Brüstle: EU accession to the ECHR and the future of European patent law. *Queen Mary Journal of Intellectual Property* 2: 110.

Plomer, Aurora. 2012b. The human rights paradox: Intellectual property rights and rights of access to science. *Human Rights Quarterly* 35: 143.

Plomer, Aurora. 2013. The human rights paradox: Intellectual property rights and rights of access to science. *Human Rights Quarterly* 35: 143.

Plomer, Aurora. 2015. *Patents, human rights and access to science*. Cheltenham: Edward Elgar.

Plomer, Aurora, and Paul Torremans (eds.). 2009. *Embryonic stem cell patents. European law and ethics*. Oxford/New York: Oxford University Press.

Rai, Arti K., and Rebecca S. Eisenberg. 2003. Bayh-Dole reform and the progress of biomedicine. *Law Contemporary Problems* 66: 289.

Resnik, David B. 2004. *Owning the genome. A moral analysis of DNA patenting*. Albany: State University of New York Press.

Resta, Giorgio. 2009. Proprietà Intellettuale e Diritti Fondamentali: Una Relazione Ambigua, In *Persona, Derecho y Libertad: Nuevas Perspectivas. Escritos en Homenaje al Profesor Carlos Fernández Sessarego*, ed. Carlos Alberto Calderón Puertas et al., 787. Lima: Motivensa Editora Jurídica.

Resta, Giorgio. 2011a. The case against the privatization of knowledge: Some thoughts on the myriad genetics controversy. In *Biotech innovations & fundamental rights*, ed. Roberto Bin et al., 34. Milan/New York: Springer.

Resta, Giorgio. 2011b. Nuovi Beni Immateriali e Numerus Clausus dei Diritti Esclusivi. In *Diritti Esclusivi e Nuovi Beni Immateriali*, vol. 3, ed. Giorgio Resta, 68. Torino: UTET.

Rimmer, Matthew. 2008. *Intellectual property and biotechnology. Biological inventions*. Cheltenham/Northampton: Edward Elgar.

Rose, Mark. 1993. *Authors and owners: The invention of copyright*. Cambridge: Harvard University Press.

Santosuosso, Amedeo, et al. 2007. What constitutional protection for freedom of scientific research? *Journal of Medical Ethics* 33: 342.

Santosusso, Amedeo. 2011. *Diritto, Scienza e Nuove Tecnologie*. Padova: Cedam.

Seashore Louis, Karen, et al. 2001. Entrepreneurship, secrecy, and productivity: A comparison of clinical and non-clinical life sciences faculty. *Journal of Technology Transfer* 26: 233.

Shaver, Lea. 2010. The right to science and culture. *Wisconsin Law Review* 4: 121.

Shaver, Lea, and Caterina Sganga. 2010. The right to take part in cultural life: On copyright and human rights. *Wisconsin International Law Journal* 27: 637.

Sinjela, Mpazi (ed.). 2007. *Human rights and intellectual property rights: Tensions and convergences*. Leiden/Boston: Martinus Nijhoff Publishers.

Starck, Christian. 2006. Freedom of scientific research and its limits in German constitutional law. *Israel Law Review* 39: 110.

Thomas, John R. 2005. On proprietary rights and personal liberties: Constitutional responses to post-industrial patenting. In *Death of patents*, ed. Peter Drahos, 110. London: Lawtext Publishing Limited.

Torremans, Paul L.C. (ed.). 2008. *Intellectual property and human rights*. Alphen aan den Rijn: Kluwer Law International.

van den Hoven, Jeroen. 2010. The use of normative theories in computer ethics. In *The Cambridge handbook of information and computer ethics*, ed. Luciano Floridi, 59. Cambridge/New York: Cambridge University Press.

Van Overwalle, Geertrui. 2010. Human rights' limitations in patent law. In *Intellectual property and human rights. A paradox*, ed. Willem Grosheide, 236. Cheltenham/Northampton: Edward Elgar Publishing.

Verpeaux, Michel. 2010. *Freedom of expression*. Strasbourg: Council of Europe Publishing.
Vila De Azevedo Cunha, Mario, et al. (eds.). 2013. *New technologies and human rights: challenges to regulation*. Farnham/Burlington: Ashgate Publishing.
Weeramantry, Christopher Gregory (ed.). 1990. *Human rights and scientific and technological development: studies on the affirmative use of science and technology for the furtherance of human rights*.Tokyo: United Nations University Press.
Wiener, Jonathan B. 2004. The regulation of technology, and the technology of regulation. *Technology in Society* 26: 483.
Wright, Susan. 1994. *Molecular politics: Developing American and British regulatory policy for genetic engineering*. Chicago: University of Chicago Press.
Xalabarder, Raquel (ed.). 2008. Copyright and freedom of expression. *Proceedings of the ALAI 2006 study days*, Huygens Editorial. Barcelona 19–20 June 2006.
Zencovich, Zeno. 2008. *Freedom of expression: A critical and comparative analysis*. Abingdon/New York: Routledge-Cavendish.
Zucca, Lorenzo. 2007. *Constitutional dilemmas: Conflicts of fundamental legal rights in Europe and the USA*. Oxford/New York: Oxford University Press.

Chapter 2
Rights Claims in Digital Media

Abstract This chapter deals with some policy issues arising from the interaction between regulation, freedoms, and security interests in the digital communication environment. Advances in digital communications have opened up a new era of unrestricted freedom of expression and speech, but in recent years a wide range of national and transnational regulators have also attempted or are attempting to implement various levels of control, monitoring or filtering the content delivered across the Internet. The chapter explores these topics by means of a discussion of various policy and regulatory questions.

2.1 Communication Technologies, Social Changes and Individual Rights

Technological developments in communication have brought revolutionary opportunities and changes in the landscape regarding how people obtain, process and exchange information. In this framework, one of the contemporary emerging challenges for the legal and regulatory regime is in shaping a modern interpretation of freedom of thought and expression.[1] The rapidly evolving media revolution has generated a number of new regulatory initiatives designed to reduce systemic risks associated with this means of communication, "ranging from risks to children, to privacy, to intellectual property rights, to nationals' security, which might more indirectly, and often unintentionally, enhance or curtail freedom of expression".[2]

Networked digital communications are now considered crucial components of a democratic system because they are a vehicle for moving "information, knowledge, and culture", which are key elements to develop "human freedom and human development".[3]

[1] William H. Dutton Et al., Freedom of Connection, Freedom of Expression: The Changing Legal and Regulatory Ecology Shaping the Internet, 8 (2011). Available at <http://unesdoc.unesco.org/images/0019/001915/191594e.pdf > (last accessed 28 April 2016).

[2] Id.

[3] Yochai Benkler, The Wealth of Networks: How Social Production Transforms Markets & Freedom 1 (2006).

N. Lucchi, *The Impact of Science and Technology on the Rights of the Individual*, Law, Governance and Technology Series 26,
DOI 10.1007/978-3-319-30439-7_2

As so eloquently expressed by Yochai Benkler in *The Wealth of Networks*:

> A series of changes in the technologies, economic organization, and social practices of production in this environment has created new opportunities for how we make and exchange information, knowledge, and culture. These changes have increased the role of nonmarket and nonproprietary production, both by individuals alone and by cooperative efforts in a wide range of loosely or tightly woven collaborations. Together, they hint at the emergence of a new information environment, one in which individuals are free to take a more active role than was possible in the industrial information economy of the twentieth century. This new freedom holds great practical promise: as a dimension of individual freedom; as a platform for better democratic participation; as a medium to foster a more critical and self-reflective culture; and, in an increasingly information-dependent global economy, as a mechanism to achieve improvements in human development everywhere.[4]

Digital media constitute also an important part of the digital citizenship discussion, namely "the ability to participate in society online".[5] The Internet – in particular – can effectively act as an instrument for enabling the membership and active participation of individuals within society[6] furthering social inclusion. It also has the concrete potential to be a place that values personal freedom and individual rights, a place where people can express and share their views with much less chances and risks of being excluded for what they say or do. There is also a growing awareness and evidence on the increasing opportunities opened by the Internet for social movement participation and mobilization.[7] As thoroughly articulated by public policy scholars, Internet use is integral to citizenship in the information age because it has "the potential to benefit society as a whole, and facilitate the membership and participation of individuals within society".[8] In this sense, digital citizenship could now be considered as a prerequisite for an active participation and engagement in society both online and offline. Digital citizens can be defined as

> those who use the Internet every day, because frequent use requires some means of access (usually at home), some technical skill, and the educational competencies to perform tasks such as finding and using information on the Web, and communicating with others on the Internet. Because of the explosion of political information and opportunities on the Web, digital citizenship is an enabling factor for political citizenship, whether practiced online by responding to Listserv solicitations for campaign contributions or offline at the voting booth.[9]

As a consequence of this scenario, citizens are required to have "a regular access to information technology" as well as "the effective use of technology" in order to act their distinctive role.[10] It also follows that to enable communication and use of

---

[4] Id., at 2.

[5] See Karen Mossberger, Caroline J. Tolbert, and Ramona S. McNeal, Digital citizenship: The Internet, society, and participation 1 (2008)

[6] Id.

[7] Eric Turner, The Grillini in Italy: New Horizons for Internet-based mobilization and Participitation, 12 Soc. Mov. Studies 214 (2013).

[8] See Karen Mossberger, Caroline J. Tolbert, and Ramona S. McNeal, Digital citizenship: The Internet, society, and participation 1, cit.

[9] See Karen Mossberger, Toward digital citizenship, in Routledge Handbook of nternet Politics (Andrew Chadwick and Philippe. N. Howard eds.), 173, 174 (2008).

[10] Id., at 174.

information across electronic networks it is necessary to guarantee a regular and effective Internet access.

2.1.1 Communication Technologies and Regulatory Dilemmas

The Internet, as a global medium, has the potential to reach an unlimited number of people instantaneously, with minimum expenses, and with no restrictions in terms of time and geographical limits.[11] Ubiquitous networking and low-cost computing offer an environment where products that were typically distributed as physical goods can now be delivered completely in digital form.[12] This transformation has extensive implications for the cost structure[13] and strategies of content intermediaries.[14] More importantly, the Internet has eroded the role played by traditional media in becoming the most appropriate place for freedom of speech, expression and pluralism. This completely new dimension has also created regulatory concerns regarding the question of access and control over the network services. Although digital media offer more opportunity to be heard – as precisely noted by Robert Picard – the real problem today is not "share of voice", but "share of ear".[15] In particular, current threats to media pluralism are represented by concentration of enterprises and convergence of media: this is especially facilitated by "the Internet service providers, content aggregators, search engines, and video on demand services that pursue their own interests through in-transparent practices and algorithms that skew the access to and distribution of information, even when it is 'personalized' by individuals".[16] This debate about media ownership concentration and its impact on pluralism has a long and rich tradition representing one of the many aspects of the much wider reflection on media freedom and pluralism.

At the same time – but from a different perspective – most Internet-related disputes are now framed – either explicitly or implicitly – with reference to the creation of new exclusive rights and the expansion of a wide range of enforcement mechanisms not directly related to the proper scope of intellectual property rules.

---

[11] See Manuel Castells, The Internet Galaxy: Reflections on the Internet, Business, and Society 2–5 (2001).

[12] See Digital Dilemma, cit., note 3, at 32 (observing that "information in digital form is largely liberated from the medium that carries it"); see also John M. Gallaugher et al., Revenue Streams and Digital Content Providers: An Empirical Investigation, 38 Info. & Mgmt. 473, 476 (2001).

[13] Production of information goods has high fixed costs but low marginal costs, or "is costly to produce but cheap to reproduce." Carl Shapiro & Hal R. Varian, Information Rules: A Strategic Guide to the Network Economy 3 (1999).

[14] See George M. Giaglis et al., The Role of Intermediaries in Electronic Marketplaces: Developing a Contingency Model, 12 Info. Sys. J. 231 (2002).

[15] See Robert G. Picard, The thorny problem of media pluralism, available at http://themediabusiness.blogspot.se/2012/04/thorny-problem-of-media-pluralism.html (last accessed 28 April 2016).

[16] Id.

This tension is due to the emergence of a new "digital dilemma"[17] which arises as a result of controversial information management practices. Here the problem is twofold: on the one hand we face the problem of information overload. On the other hand, we need to determine how to limit access to information. Of central importance in this regard are the rules governing the use and dissemination of information.[18] It is only in recent years that we have seen a growing use of exclusive rights as an indirect instrument to manage and monitor the communication of works encoded in digital form. Observations of this phenomenon may provide evidence concerning how effectively this method of control may introduce a severe erosion of traditional civil liberties and freedoms. As remarked by Robin Gross,

> clashes between fundamental freedom of expression guarantees and intellectual property rights are upsetting the traditional balance struck between creators and the public. The ease of copying and re-distribution of digital information concerns industries dependent on traditional publishing business models. These companies have successfully petitioned for changes in the copyright laws at the national and international levels. But these recent increases in copyright holders' rights have come at the expense of the public's rights to use media and communicate freely.[19]

Much of this conflict between private rights in information and knowledge exchange is essentially based on the fact that both copyright protection and freedom of speech have a constitutional dimension.[20] In particular, copyright has – at the same time – the potential to be a tool for limiting and enhancing freedom of expression. This particular feature has been described as "copyright's paradox".[21] The main concern here is that, in the digital environment, it appears that copyright protection is more effective to limiting rather than expanding freedom of expression. In a truly free society there is no reason for limiting the access to knowledge and information generated in the course of time: on the contrary it is essential to extend the free movement of culture and ideas. The upward drift of intellectual property rules provides a perfect example of this reduction of freedom. The problem with intellectual property is that the products are not material objects but expressions of ideas.[22] In other words "protection for intellectual

[17] Initially, the digital dilemma was faced when intellectual property law – for the first time – confronted with digital technologies. Now the phrase "digital dilemma" is a term used to define a variety of issues that arise in addressing the intellectual property balancing problem in the new world of digital technology. See Comm. on Intellectual Property. Rights in the Emerging Information Infrastructure, The Digital Dilemma: Intellectual Property in the Information Age 199 (2000).

[18] See Robin Gross, Intellectual Property Rights and the Information Commons, in Human Rights in the Global Information Society 107 (Rikke Frank Jorgenson ed., 2006).

[19] Id.

[20] See Christophe Geiger, *The Constitutional Dimension of Intellectual Property*, in Intellectual Property and Human Rights 111 (Paul L.C. Torremans ed., 2008); Enrico Bonadio, File Sharing, Copyright and Freedom of Expression, 33 European Intell. Prop. Rev. 619 (2011) (discussing the relationship between copyright and freedom of speech in the digital context).

[21] See Neil Weinstock Netanel, Copyright's Paradox (2008).

[22] See Susumu Morimura, Justifying Private Property, in Law, Justice and the State 190, 192 (Aleksander Peczenik & Mikael M. Karlsson eds., 1995).

freedom should be of highest priority in an information age" because "freedom of thought and freedom of expression are fundamental human rights that require access to ideas and information to develop fully."[23]

A growing number of scholars are openly acknowledging that a continually expanding umbrella of copyrights could result in loss of traditional civil liberties. The increasing demand for a stronger intellectual property protection press and compress the protection accorded to other kind of rights and interests. Furthermore, the institutionalization of stronger rights protection through the adoption of new anti-circumvention provisions gives government "more power to control the use and flow of information". It is always Robin Gross to comment on this matter observing that:

> The impact of expanding copyrights reaches a spectrum of existing fundamental legal rights: freedom of expression, freedom of the press, freedom of thought, intellectual freedom, and more are all harmed by such a dramatic shift in the traditional balance of rights.
>
> Historically, when society was primarily an agricultural economy, the key ingredient to wealth and development was ownership and use of land. When society moved into an industrial era, the key to wealth and development shifted to ownership and use of capital. Now as we move into an information society, access to knowledge is the key factor for continued development and wealth on a personal and national level.
>
> Just as human bodies require food and medicine for good health, our minds require knowledge to function and develop. Technology promises the unprecedented opportunity to disseminate information and foster collaboration that will dramatically expand human knowledge and social development. But only if we do not allow the technology to be crippled first by an over-reaction of industries rooted in the past.
>
> The free speech guarantee in the United Nations Universal Declaration of Human Rights, although adopted by the UN General Assembly in 1948, speaks directly to the Internet age: Article 19 guarantees that "Everyone has the right to freedom of opinion and expression; this right includes freedom to hold opinions without interference and to seek, receive, and impart information and ideas through any media and regardless of frontiers".

This universal guarantee to freedom of expression is not limited to speech only in analogue media, but rather explicitly, "... in any media and regardless of frontiers".[24] While proponents of limiting freedom of expression guarantees argue that "digital is different" and traditional rights must be sacrificed to protect private property rights, the Universal Declaration of Human Rights has already answered that digital is no different and that our traditional rights are meant to continue with us into a digital environment.[25] All these factors and their combined effect suggest that – as recently affirmed in a resolution of the United Nations Human Rights Council – to promote and facilitate access to networked communication, it is necessary to recognize that the same "rights that people have offline must also be protected

[23] See Robin Gross, Intellectual Property Rights and the Information Commons, cit. 118.

[24] Universal Declaration of Human Rights, art. 19, G.A. Res. 217 (III) A, U.N. Doc. A/RES/217(III) (Dec. 10, 1948).

[25] See Robin Gross, Intellectual Property Rights and the Information Commons, cit. 119.

online, in particular freedom of expression"[26] which include the right to media freedom and the right of access to information.

2.1.2 *Digital Communication Technologies, Protest Movements and Democracy*

Mass communications media, mobile computing and digital technologies (mainly the Internet) are generally recognized as contributing factors in the rise of mass democracy. In particular, the relevance of networked communication as a tool of mass democracy has proven increasingly evident.[27] Social networking and blogging platforms including Facebook, Twitter, YouTube, Linkedin, Wordpress, Instagram and all other forms of digital and social media have completely changed the way people use and share information. In some countries, the Internet-based communication tools serves as the only source of pluralistic and independent information.[28] In addition, these new media formats have also shown to have significant effects on political processes and institutions. Society ability to take advantage of communication opportunities is in fact a determining pillar of democracy. In this respect, the Inter-American Court of Human Rights has correctly observed – long time ago – that "it is the mass media that make the exercise of freedom of expression a reality."[29] Information and communication technologies have therefore rapidly appeared as a key instrument for political activism and civil rights movements.[30] At the same time, the innovative use of digital media has also significantly enhanced "democratic governance by facilitating more direct participation by citizens in the political decision-making arena".[31] In this respect, the information technology revolution can be seen as a vehicle for reinvigoration of democracy – at least in its literal and basic definition.

[26] See Human Rights Council Res. 20, The Promotion, Protection and Enjoyment of Human Rights on the Internet, 20th Sess., June 18-July 6, 2012, 67th Sess., Supp. No. 53, A/HRC/20/L13 P 3 (June 29, 2012).

[27] See Toby Mendel and Eve Salomon, Freedom of Expression and Broadcasting Regulation, 11 (2011); Ronald J. Deibert et al. (eds.) Access Controlled: The Shaping of Power, Rights, and Rule in Cyberspace, xvii (2010). See also Human Rights and The Internet 7 (Steven Hick, Edward F. Halpin, & Eric Hoskins eds., 2000) (arguing that the Internet has proven to be an effective instrument for the promotion and protection of human rights by disseminating and communicating information).

[28] See Mendel and Salomon, Freedom of Expression and Broadcasting Regulation, cit. at 11; Deibert et al. (eds.) Access Controlled: The Shaping of Power, Rights, and Rule in Cyberspace, cit., at xvii.

[29] See Inter-American Court of Human Rights Advisory Opinion OC-5/85 of November 13, 1985, Inter-Am. Ct. HR (Ser. A) No. 5, 1985, para. 34.

[30] See Human Rights and The Internet, cit., at 8.

[31] See David Bell et al., Cyberculture: The Key Concepts 58 (2004).

For example, the events associated with the so called "Arab Spring" – as well as other similar protests around the world – are a clear demonstration of how important new communication and information technologies have become.[32] The surprising outcomes of these social movements are partially attributed to the greater availability of Internet access and to the power of social media technology.[33] Using a mix of blogs and social networking sites, the new medium has revealed its power to support spontaneous democratic mobilization from below – a concrete and participatory form of democracy.[34] These protests were a direct consequence of the rapidly deteriorating living conditions and enhanced perceptions of intolerable levels of corruption and absence of democracy in these countries.[35] Popular demonstrations started in Tunisia and quickly spread to Egypt, Syria, Bahrain, Jordan, Oman, Yemen, Algeria, and Libya.[36] They were driven by well-educated "digital natives" – young people who have grown up with web technology.[37] Most of these physical protests were organized through virtual communications channels, merging together virtual and physical spaces.[38] The result of these online movements was surprising, with hundreds of thousands of people being summoned to action. Most unexpectedly, these new forms of political and social expression occurred simultaneously in many parts of the world. Up until now, only great political and union organizations possessed this level of influence. Events have shown that digital communication tools can yield enormous impacts on public opinion and decision-making.

Social networks like Twitter and Facebook have played key roles in characterizing the dynamics of these pro-democracy protests. The Arab Spring was planned, organized, and executed through viral demonstrations launched through digital and

---

[32] See Eben Moglen, Why Political Liberty Depends on Software Freedom More Than Ever, speech given at the 2011 FOSDEM conference in Brussels, February 5, available at http://www.softwarefreedom.org/events/2011/fosdem/moglen-fosdem-keynote.html (last accessed 28 April 2016).

[33] If it is true that so-called Arab springs were characterized by the use of social networks, it seems equally true that many of the promoters of these protests have previously participated in training courses sponsored by non-profit organizations such as the National Endowment for Democracy or the Open Society Foundation. See Luca Mainoldi, I Padroni di Internet, 1 Limes "Media come Armi" 10 (2012).

[34] See Jack M. Balkin, The Future of Free Expression in a Digital Age, 36 Pepp. L. Rev., 427, 438 (2009).

[35] See Kenneth Roth, Time to Abandon the Autocrats and Embrace Rights, in World Report 2012, 1, 9 (Human Rights Watch, 2012); Gabriel Ben-Dor, Democratization Processes in the Middle East and the Arab World, in The Arab Spring, Democracy and Security: Domestic and International Ramifications 12, 14 (Efraim Inbar ed., 2013).

[36] See Roth, Time to Abandon the Autocrats and Embrace Rights, cit., at 9

[37] See John Palfrey & Urs Gasser, Born Digital: Understanding the First Generation of Digital Natives (2008) (illustrating inter-generational differences in the use of digital technologies).

[38] See Wael Salah Fahmi, Bloggers' street movement and the right to the city. (Re)claiming Cairo's realand virtual "spaces of freedom", 21 Environ. and Urban. 89 (2009). On this point, see also Lorenzo Mosca, From The Streets To The Net? The Political Use Of The Internet By Social Movements, 1 Int. J. of E-Pol., 1.

electronic media.[39] The use and availability of digital and social media is probably considered one of the most significant and effective elements for explaining both the vulnerability of these autocratic regimes and the relative success of social movements.[40] Twitter was used by activists as one of the key methods of communications "to draw the international community into Egyptian events".[41] The capture of Colonel Muammar Gaddafi was immediately widespread on YouTube; the locations of protests by the Spanish "indignados" were posted via Twitter; and the riots and violence in Syria effectively captured on Facebook.[42] The ubiquitous "Arab satellite channels also broadcasted nearly nonstop coverage" of antigovernment demonstrations, helping to undermine the legitimacy of these repressive and authoritarian regimes.[43] Notably, people have used these global interconnected networks and platforms to challenge the sovereignty and legitimacy of their governments.[44] However, an obvious and significant difference exists between using the Internet to protest against a nasty regime and using it to build up a robust and functional democracy. As observed by several commentators, the current state of affairs in the Maghreb region is far more complicated than before (despite the successful uprising), and a new challenge has reared its ugly head in the area.[45] Four years after the beginning of these movements, the status of democracy in these countries seems still far to be entirely completed. The democratic and libertarian revolts against the authoritarian regimes have also brought unintended and unexpected consequences. That does not detract from the fact that information revolution can facilitate the expression of dissent and opportunities for participation. Democracies are inherently unstable because democracy – by its nature – is always in movement.[46] This means that democracy can always be carried forward or forced back, even in societies where it is considered a kind of given.

[39] See Philip N. Howard and Muzammil M. Hussain, Democracy's Fourth Wave?: Digital Media and the Arab Spring 27 (2013); Ben-Dor, Democratization Processes in the Middle East and the Arab World, cit., at 14.

[40] See generally Howard and Hussain, Democracy's Fourth Wave?: Digital Media and the Arab Spring.

[41] Id., at 55

[42] See Peter Beaumont, The Truth About Twitter, Facebook and the Uprisings in the Arab World, The Guardian (Feb. 24, 2011), www.guardian.co.uk/world/2011/feb/25/twitter-facebook-uprisings-arab-libya; Narseo Vallina-Rodriguez, et al., Los Twindignados: The Rise of the Indignados Movement on Twitter, SocialCom/PASSAT, 496 (2012); Jean-Pierre Filiu, The Arab Revolution: Ten Lessons from the Democratic Uprising 53, 54 (2011); Kareem Fahim et al., Violent End to an Era as Qaddafi Dies in Libya, N.Y. Times, Oct. 20, 2011, at A1; Lyombe Eko, New Media, Old Regimes: Case Studies in ComparativeCommunication Law and Policy, 147, 148 (2012).

[43] See Jeffrey Ghannam, In the Middle East, This Is Not a Facebook Revolution, Washington Post, February 18, 2011.

[44] See Howard and Hussain, Democracy's Fourth Wave?: Digital Media and the Arab Spring, cit., at 38.

[45] See After the Arab Spring: Power Shift in the Middle East? (2011).; Ben Wagner, After the Arab Spring: New Paths for Human Rights and The Internet in European Foreign Policy 8–12 (2012).

[46] See Andrew Levine, The General Will: Rousseau, Marx, Communism 79 (1994).

It is, however, evident that these new forms of political and social activism are intrinsically linked to the growing power of technology and are common in Western liberal democracies as well as developing countries.[47] The US "Occupy Wall Street" and the trans-European "Indignados" protesters also provide empirical evidence of the mobilizing and political potential of the Internet.[48] Both movements are concrete examples of the features and capabilities offered by new horizontal communication channels.[49] In this view, the Internet has revivified "the notion of freedom of expression as an individual liberty"[50] no longer mediated by other elements. The Internet has effectively returned more power to individuals with a profound redistribution of control of information flow and a completely new approach to how society operates.[51] It is therefore reasonable to agree that digital networks, along with the physical occupation of the urban spaces, can reasonably provide the platform for a new form of democratic and pluralistic political process.[52]

In this respect, the UN Human Rights Council has stated that this latest wave of demonstrations has also "shown the key role that the Internet can play in mobilizing the population to call for justice, equality, accountability and better respect for human rights. As such, facilitating access to the Internet for all individuals, with as little restriction to online content as possible, should be a priority for all States."[53] Blogs, videos, and social networking sites have become key instruments for political debate and expression of dissenting views – "so much so that they have provoked counter-responses," not just from repressive states, but also in the so-called

---

[47] See e.g., Eric Turner, The Grillini in Italy: New Horizons for Internet-based mobilization and Participitation, 12 Soc. Mov. Studies 214 (2013) (exploring the Grillini and internetworked movements in Italy); Ernesto Castañeda, The Indignados of Spain: A Precedent to Occupy Wall Street, 11 Soc. Mov. Studies 309 (2012) (analyzing the Indignados movement in Barcelona, Spain); Hardt, Michael, and Antonio Negri. 11 October 2011. The fight for "real democracy" at the heart of Occupy Wall Street. Foreign Affairs. Available from http://www.foreignaffairs.com/print/98542?page=show (last accessed 28 April 2016); Jeffrey J. Juris, Reflections on Occupy Everywhere: Social Media, Public Space, and Emerging Logics, 39 Am. Ethnologist 259 (2012) (arguining that in the trans-national Occupy movements social media have significantly contributed to powerful logics of aggregation).

[48] See After the Arab Spring: Power Shift in the Middle East? cit..; Ben Wagner, After the Arab Spring: New Paths for Human Rights and The Internet in European Foreign Policy cit.

[49] Id.

[50] See Vincenzo Zeno Zencovich, Freedom of Expression: A Critical and Comparative Analysis, 100 (2008).

[51] See Andrew Shapiro, The Control Revolution: How The Internet Is Putting Individuals In Charge And Changing The World We Know xiii (1999) (observing how new technology is allowing individuals to take power from large institutions such as government, corporations and the media). See also, Manuel Castells, Networks of Outrage and Hope: Social Movements in the Internet Age 106 (2012) (observing how social movements were not mediated by formal political organization).

[52] See Castells, Networks of Outrage and Hope: Social Movements in the Internet Age, cit. at 106.

[53] United Nations General Assembly, Human Rights Council, Commission on Human Rights, Report by the Special Rapporteur on the Promotion and Protection of the Right to Freedom of Opinion and Expression, Frank La Rue, U.N. Doc. A/HRC/17/27 (16 May 2011), 2, available at http://www.unhchr.ch/Huridocda/Huridoca.nsf/0/16583a84ba1b3ae5802568bd004e80f7/$FILE/G0010259.pdf (last accessed 28 April 2016) [hereinafter: UN. Human Rights Council 2011].

free world.[54] A recent Freedom House study of 47 countries attempted to measure each country's level of Internet and digital media freedom, examining obstacles to access, limits on content, and violations of user rights.[55] According to the study, despite some specific recent improvements in selected countries, restrictions on Internet freedom and access to information continue to grow.[56] In particular, the study shows how Internet content restrictions are partly connected to the increasing success of social media and networking sites often used for political and social activism.[57] More positively, in an important contingent of states among the countries covered by this survey, the Internet remains a relatively more free domain for freedom of expression when compared to the more repressive or hostile environment for traditional media.[58] We cannot, however, ignore the fact the Internet could be also used by totalitarian regimes as an influential tool for engaging in digital surveillance, political repression, as well as for dissemination of terrorist and extremist propaganda.[59] It is in fact undeniable that the Internet can be a great way not only to spread positive messages and build influence through social media, but it can be also a promotional instrument enabling individual supporters to take part in the creation and distribution of hate and extremist propaganda. The recent rise and expansion of the Islamic State of Iraq and Syria (ISIS) represents a particularly interesting example in this regard. Its increasingly sophisticated social media communication and recruitment strategies influenced a diverse group of people from around the world questioning the democratizing possibilities offered by new media. That does not detract from the necessity to separate the technologies from the content and information being distributed or communicated. Technologies are simply the medium for distribution and dissemination of the message to the audience. It is the people behind the medium that makes the difference. It should not be forgotten that a tool is just a tool and it is up to the user to decide how to use it conveying both positive and negative messages to the target audience.

All of these observations suggest that web-based social networks can really allow for the free flow of information between equals in an autonomous social space; a place in which individuals can critically debate different kinds of issues, with possible migration from the virtual environments to the physical. In addition, these new ways of communication can also serve to activate and strengthen other fundamental rights.[60] The dynamics under these information diffusion models seem

[54] See Douwe Korfs and Ian Brown, Social media and human rights, in Human Rights and a Changing Media Landscape, Strasbourg: Council of Europe Publications, 2012, at 175.

[55] Sanja Kelly, Sarah Cook and Mai Truong (eds.) (2011), Freedom on the Net 2012: A global assessment of Internet and digital media, Freedom House, Washington, DC; available at http://www.freedomhouse.org/sites/default/files/FOTN%202012%20FINAL.pdf (last accessed 28 April 2016).

[56] Id.

[57] Id.

[58] Id.

[59] See generally Evgeny Morozov, The Net Delusion: The Dark Side of Internet Freedom (2011).

[60] See UN. Human Rights Council 2011, cit.

likely to reify Habermas' famous theory of the "public sphere."[61] In fact, the central aspect of Habermas' public sphere model was exactly based on the disjunction of this entity from the powers of the state and the market.[62] This public sphere model operates through an expectation of accessibility that allows all citizens to participate without restraint, and public debate is required to be open in both content and format.[63] According to Habermas, a fully operable public sphere is fundamental to the functioning of democratic societies.[64] The elements of the access to the public sphere include physical and social access.[65] The relevant aspect is that even in a networked society, access remains a democratic key element. Citizens can now stand in front of an "online public sphere" based on the same elements and principles but moved from the physical world to the network.[66]

2.1.3 Reshaping the Boundary of Freedom of Expression in the Digital Age

As discussed and illustrated in the previous pages, the Internet is undoubtedly the most widely recognized and utilized digital communication technological tool employed to propagate information. Through its cables individuals have new opportunities to exchange and share knowledge, ideas, release their creativity and participate in social and political life. It is therefore incontrovertible that the Internet and its technology is perceived and proved to be a fundamental instrument to guarantee also an effective freedom of expression.[67] It is no exaggeration to conclude that the Internet has commonly be seen as providing a technological enrichment of individual

---

[61] See Jürgen Habermas, The Structural Transformation of the Public Sphere: An Inquiry Into a Category Of Bourgeois Society 27 (Thomas Burger & Frederick Lawrence trans., 1989). According to Habermas, the public sphere "may be conceived above all as the sphere of private people come together as a public; they soon claimed the public sphere regulated from above against the public authorities themselves, to engage them in a debate over the general rules governing relations in the basically privatized but publicly relevant sphere of commodity exchange and social labor". Id., at 27.

[62] See Jürgen Habermas, The Public Sphere: An Encyclopedia Article, New German Critique 3, 49 (1974) (defining the public sphere as "the realm of our social life in which something approaching public opinion can be formed".)

[63] Id.

[64] See Peter Uwe Hohendahl, Jürgen Habermas: 'The Public Sphere' (1964), New German Critique 3, 45 (1974).

[65] See Stephen Carr et al., Public Space 138 et seq. (1992).

[66] For a modern application of Habermas' theory, see Mark Poster, Cyberdemocracy: The Internet and the Public Sphere, in Reading Digital Culture, 259, 265 (David Trend ed., 2001) (noting that "the age of the public sphere as face to face talk is clearly over; the question of democracy must henceforth take into account new forms of electronically mediated discours".); see also generally Manuel Castells, The Information Age: Economy, society, and culture, Vol. 1: The Rise of the Network Society (1996).

[67] Zeno Zencovich, Freedom of Expression: A Critical and Comparative Analysis cit. at 99.

freedom of expression.[68] Also for this reason, digital rights defenders and digital libertarians "have raised growing concerns over how legal and regulatory trends might be constraining freedom of expression" over the Internet.[69] The Internet challenges and encourages the right to freedom of expression; in particular, it has the potential to strengthen freedom of expression by providing, developing and facilitating new mechanisms for exchanging data and, as a consequence, ensuring a more intense flow of information.[70] At the same time, however, such conditions are used as a justification for content regulation targeted in part at trying to counteract the pervasiveness and anarchic nature of the medium.[71]

It is a matter of fact that, in almost all democratic systems, use of both new and old forms of information media have not only posed problems of boundary definition, but have often resulted in attempts to contain and control information flow.[72] The key point is that computer-mediated communication is beyond the control of the nation-state.[73] The problem of information control has thus become amplified by the phenomenon of new media.[74] It is recognized that the economic problem of information is essentially its protection and disclosure that is a problem of public goods.[75] In order to contain information and maintain control over access, some countries have made legislative attempts to regulate and monitor digital content. For example, specific state legislation has been adopted in the United States, United Kingdom, Canada and Australia. In particular, number of regulations designed to monitor and control the flow of information on the Internet certainly increased since September 11, 2001.[76] As has been observed by some scholars, virtually every industrialized country and many developing countries have passed laws that expand "the capacities of state intelligence and law enforcement agencies to monitor

[68] Ronald Deibert & Rafal Rohozinski, Good for Liberty, Bad for Security? Global Civil Society and the Securitization of the Internet in Access Denied: The Practice And Policy Of Global Internet Filtering 140 (Ronald Deibert et al. eds., 2008).

[69] William H. Dutton Et al., Freedom of Connection, Freedom of Expression: The Changing Legal and Regulatory Ecology Shaping the Internet, cit. at 8.

[70] Zeno Zencovich, Freedom of Expression: A Critical and Comparative Analysis cit. at 101.

[71] See generally Regulating Content: European Regulatory Framework For The Media And Related Creative Sectors (Michael Holoubek et al. eds., 2007); Zeno Zencovich, Freedom of Expression: A Critical and Comparative Analysis cit. at 107.

[72] See Manuel Castells, The Power of Identity 320 (2nd ed., 2010); Carl J. Couch, Mass Communications and State Structures, 27 Soc. Sci. J. 111 (1990).

[73] Id., at 319.

[74] See Dominique Foray, The Economics of Knowledge 5 (2004). Here the term "new media" refers to the broad concept of digital communications media. For a discussion about this definition, see Lev Manovich, The Language of New Media 19 (2001).

[75] Id. at 5–6.

[76] See Ronald Deibert & Rafal Rohozinski, Good for Liberty, Bad for Security? Global Civil Society and the Securitization of the Internet, cit. at 137; Yochai Benkler, The Wealth of Networks, cit. at 31; Timothy Wu & Jack Goldsmith, Who Controls the Internet? Illusions of a Borderless World 65 (2006).

Internet communications".[77] Furthermore such ongoing attempts to regulate the Internet "reflect the natural maturation process that previous media, such as print, radio, and television, all experienced as they evolved out of unrestrained and experimental to tightly controlled and regulated environments".[78] The experience of democratic countries with provisions designed to monitor and control the flow of information on the Internet, reveals that restriction of the freedom of the media may not withstand constitutional scrutiny. Many regulatory instruments implemented in various countries in the last decade with the intent to police the Internet were often criticized for their inability to reconcile technological progress, protection of economic interests, as well as other conflicting interests. Essentially these policy measures "alter the environment within which Internet communications take place".[79] Illustrative examples include: the controversy over the constitutionality of the US Communication Decency Act of 1996 in *Reno v. American Civil Liberties Union*, invalidating certain provisions of a proposed law designed to regulate indecent and obscene speech on the Internet[80]; the US Supreme Court ruling in *Ashcroft v. American Civil Liberties Union*, holding that the enforcement of the Child Online Protection Act should be enjoined because the law likely violated the First Amendment[81]; and the French case of the "Loi Fillon," where the French Constitutional Council censored most of the dispositions of the Fillon amendment concerning regulation of the Internet and the linked power given to the Conseil Supérieur de l'Audiovisuel.[82] Another interesting example is the most recent decision regarding the French HADOPI law designed to reduce file-sharing,[83] which was partially censored by the French Constitutional Council[84] on the grounds of its inconsistency with Article 11 of the 1789 Declaration of the Rights of Man and of the Citizen.[85]

---

[77] Deibert & Rohozinski, Good for Liberty, Bad for Security? Global Civil Society and the Securitization of the Internet, cit. at 138.

[78] Id. at 137.

[79] Access Denied: The Practice and Policy of Global Internet Filtering, 152 (Ronald J. Deibert et al. eds., 2008); Cass Sustein, Republic.com 134 (2001).

[80] 521 U.S. 844 (1997).

[81] 535 U.S. 564, 656 (2002).

[82] See Conseil constitutionnel [CC] [Constitutional Council] decision no. 96–378 DC, Jul. 23, 1996, Journal Officiel de la République Française [J.O.] [Official Gazette of France], Jul. 27, 1996, p. 11400 (Fr.) (censoring most of the dispositions of the Fillon amendment concerning regulation of the Internet and the linked power given to the Conseil Supérieur de l'Audiovisuel [Audiovisual Regulatory Authority]).

[83] Loi 2009–669 du 12 juin 2009 favorisant la diffusion et la protection de la création sur internet, 135 Journal Officiel de la République Française [J.O.] [Official Gazette of France], June 13, 2009, p. 9666.

[84] The Conseil constitutionnel [Constitutional Council] is the French body in charge of reviewing the conformity of statutes with the Constitution. See Introduction to French Law 30 (George A. Berman & Etienne Picard eds., 2008); Francis Hamon & Michel Troper, Droit Constitutionnel 834 (31st ed. 2009).

[85] See See Conseil constitutionnel [CC] [Constitutional Court], decision No. 2009–580 DC, June 22, 2009, relative à la loi favorisant la diffusion et la protection de la création sur internet, June 13,

In the context of these judicial decisions, two basic questions arise: (1) what restrictions and safeguards should be imposed on the fundamental freedom of expression in a democratic society and (2) under which conditions and guarantees are these restrictions and safeguards feasible? Discussing the Internet's communications potential requires an evaluation of the preconditions that facilitate or inhibit the effective use of information resources. One of these preconditions is for sure the right of access to communication resources or – as already defined – the right to communicate.[86]

2.2 A Legal Framework for the Internet

The use of technological tools raises the question of what rules professionals must follow in the communication and dissemination of information. The aim of these rules is to set the boundaries of legality within which the dissemination of ideas and opinions may be established and conducted.[87] The intensity of these questions are increased mostly because technological advances and the Internet have completely changed the way people access, distribute, and share information putting under pressure copyright-protected material. One of the most important changes deriving from these new conditions is that copyright protection has become a serious concern. Traditional regulatory approaches are – in fact – ineffective to fight digital infringements requiring alternative ways of protection. One of the most recent legal measures introduced to address this problem was the so called "graduated response" system. This term refers to an indirect mechanism to target Internet piracy essentially based on a co-operation with the internet access providers that goes beyond the classical "notice and take down" approach, where online content is simply taken down after a complaint.[88] In particular, this enforcement method implies a

2009, Journal Officiel de la République Française [J.O.] [Official Gazette of France] p. 9675, http://www.conseil-constitutionnel.fr/conseil-constitutionnel/root/bank/download/cc-2009580dc.pdf (in French), and available at http://www.conseil-constitutionnel.fr/conseil-constitutionnel/root/bank_mm/anglaconstitutionnel/root/bank_mm/anglais/2009_580dc.pdf (in English) [hereinafter Decision 2009–580].

[86] See generally Desmond Fisher and L. S. Harms (eds), The Right to Communicate: A New Human Right (1983); Christopher Gregory Weeramantry, Access to Information: A New Human Right. The Right to Know, 4 Asian Y.B. Int'l L. 99 (1994).

[87] See generally Carl Shapiro and Hal R. Varian, Information Rules (1999) (describing the rules of the new information economy).

[88] This system is common in the United States (see 17 U.S.C. § 512(c) (3)) and Europe (see EU's Copyright Directive and E-Commerce Directive) and it recognizes that Internet companies do not have any obligation to monitor the activity of every user. In other words, they are not obliged to prevent the misuse of their services proactively, but when informed of specific infringements, they must promptly "take down" the infringing material.

"notification mechanism for alleged online infringers before more stringent measures can be imposed, including" the suspension of the internet service.[89]

The main problem with this new mechanism is that it places a high level of responsibility on intermediaries – such as internet service providers – imposing sanctions directly against their customers even avoiding a court decision. France and the United Kingdom are the first two European countries to have implemented and experienced the graduated response measures. In both cases, there were deep concerns expressed by opponents regarding threats to fundamental rights and liberties like freedom of expression, protection of privacy, due process and the right to a fair trial.

In the following paragraphs we will examine the most controversial digital content reforms adopted across Europe and in the United States as well as their legal implications.

2.3 Controversial Internet Control Rules

In almost all democratic societies, new media, besides incurring definitional problems, have led to attempts to restrict and control online information.[90] This has often led to the adoption of legislative measures criticized for their inability to reconcile technological progress with economic and other interests.

In recent years, there have been several attempts by states to regulate the content on the Internet. One of the most famous, and certainly one of the most debated, was the United States Communication Decency Act of 1996 (CDA).[91] It was the first important effort by the United States Congress to control pornographic content on the Internet. In the landmark 1997 case of Reno v. ACLU,[92] the U.S. Supreme Court held that the CDA violated the freedom of speech provisions of the First Amendment.[93] In an attempt to protect minors from "indecent" and "patently

[89] See Alain Strowel, Internet Piracy as a Wake-up Call for Copyright Law Makers – Is the "Graduated Response" a Good Reply?, 1 World Intell. Prop. Org. J.. 75, 77 (2009).

[90] See Sunstein, Republic.com, cit. at 138.

[91] The Communications Decency Act of 1996, Pub. L. No. 104–104, 110 Stat. 56 (1996) (codified as amended in scattered parts of section 47 of the United States Code). For a complete overview of the case, see Mike Godwin, Cyber Rights: Defending Free Speech in the Digital Age 323 (rev. ed. 2003).

[92] Reno v. Am. Civil Liberties Union, 521 U.S. 844 (1997). The Communications Decency Act of 1996 was designed to regulate indecent and obscene speech on the Internet and to prevent the transmission of similar information to any person under the age of 18. The Supreme Court held that the Communications Decency Act placed "an unacceptably heavy burden on protected speech". Id. at 882. Furthermore the Court remarked that the statute, in protecting children from harmful content, "suppresses a large amount of speech that adults have a constitutional right to receive and to address to one other". Id. at 874.

[93] The essence of the Court's holding was that the restriction of indecent adult speech on the Internet to safeguard minors was a violation of the First Amendment freedom of speech right of adults to receive and view similar content. Id at 885. Justice Stevens summed up the decision by

offensive" materials, the CDA had the effect, *inter alia*, of restricting access to material that was not harmful to adults: "in order to deny minors access to potentially harmful speech, the Communications Decency Act effectively suppresses a large amount of speech that adults have a constitutional right to receive and to address to one another. That burden on adult speech is unacceptable if less restrictive alternatives would be at least as effective in achieving the legitimate purpose that statute was enacted to serve".[94]

The case generated significant international press coverage, as well as heated legal debate over freedom of expression on the Internet and with regards to developing technologies.[95] Many of the findings and conclusions made at that time by the court are still relevant today. Among the essential findings, the Court was able to set out the nature of cyberspace, the techniques of accessing and communicating over digital networks, and alternative means of restricting access to the Internet.[96] In particular, the Court recognized that the Internet "constitutes a vast platform from which to address and hear from a world-wide audience of millions of readers, viewers, researchers, and buyers."[97] In this way, "any person or organization with a computer connected to the Internet can 'publish' information."[98] But the remarkable aspect of this case is that, for the first time, the Supreme Court introduced a sort of legal recognition to have unrestricted access to the Internet through a broad interpretation of the First Amendment.[99] In other words, the Court extended free speech rights to the Internet. The rationale expressed by the Supreme Court confirmed the opinion of the District Court. In particular, Justice Stevens reported one of the district court's conclusions: "As 'the most participatory form of mass speech yet developed'... [the Internet] is 'entitled to the highest protection from governmental intrusion'".[100] Moreover, the Court, through a fact-based approach, came to the conclusion that speech on the Internet, even when indecent, is entitled to the protection of the First Amendment. Finally, the decision made also clear that: "As a matter of constitutional tradition, in the absence of evidence to the contrary, we presume that governmental regulation of the content of speech is more likely to interfere with the free exchange of ideas than to encourage it. The interest in encouraging freedom of expression in a democratic society outweighs any theoretical but unproven benefit

stating: "As a matter of constitutional tradition, in the absence of evidence to the contrary, we presume that the governmental regulation of the content of speech is more likely to interfere with the free exchange of ideas than to encourage it. The interest in encouraging freedom of expression in a democratic society outweighs any theoretical but unproven benefit of censorship." Id. at 885.

[94] Reno v. Am. Civil Liberties Union, 521 U.S. 874 (1997).

[95] See, Mike Godwin, Cyber Rights: Defending Free speech in the Digital Age 323 (2003).

[96] See Stephen C. Jacques, Reno v. ACLU: Insulating the Internet, the First Amendment and the Marketplace of Ideas, 46 Am. U. L. Rev. 1945 (1997).

[97] Reno v. ACLU, 521 U.S. 844, 853 (1997).

[98] Id.

[99] Id.

[100] Reno v. Am. Civil Liberties Union, 521 U.S. 863 (1997).

of censorship".[101] With this ruling, the Supreme Court had also the opportunity to clarify that communications over the Internet deserve the highest level of constitutional protection.[102] In addition, the Court has also acknowledged the democratizing and emancipatory power of the Internet, in that "through the use of [Internet communication tools], any person with a phone line can become a town crier with a voice that resonates farther than it could from any soapbox."[103] Inappropriate, intrusive, or unbalanced regulatory measures could serve to greatly increase the barrier to entry, thus jeopardizing the foundational structure of the Internet and chilling free speech. In other words, the constitutional protection of freedom of expression implies a constitutional protection of the access to information through the Internet.

The US Congress reacted to the Supreme Court's decision in *Reno* by enacting a new legislation, the Child Online Protection Act (COPA). But also this second attempt to regulate Internet content did not completely resolve the constitutional objections already posed by the provision of the CDA.[104] As a matter of fact, the new piece of legislation "essentially incorporated the traditional standards of obscenity law (which in theory deny any protection to speech that is found to be 'obscene')."[105] After three separate rounds of litigation, the Supreme Court held the statute invalid on the ground that the government had not shown COPA to be the least restrictive means of regulating indecent content on the Internet. The legal challenge to the Communication Decency Act seems to be connected with a red thread to the current debate over Internet access and regulation of illegal material. Today, as in the past, the need to find the most appropriate balance between the protection of individual rights and the general interests of the community is a very complex issue. Currently, the most recent digital content reforms pose similar challenges and risks that can be dealt with in similar ways.

2.4 Digital Content Reforms Recently Introduced or Discussed in Europe and in the U.S.

The use of both new and old forms of information media have not only posed problems of boundary definition, but have often resulted in attempts to contain and control information flow.[106] In particular, policy discussions regarding better regulation of the Internet started to gain ground as soon as protection of intellectual property

[101] Id., at 885.

[102] Id.; see also American Library Association, Resolution on the Use of Filtering Software in Libraries (July 2, 1997), available at http://www.ala.org/advocacy/intfreedom/statementspols/ifresolutions/resolutionuse (last accessed 28 April 2016).

[103] Reno v. Am. Civil Liberties Union, 521 U.S. 844, 870 (1997).

[104] See Ronald J. Deibert et al. (eds.) Access Controlled: The Shaping of Power, Rights, and Rule in Cyberspace, cit., at 371.

[105] See Glen O. Robinson and Thomas B. Nachbar, Communications regulation 33 (2008).

[106] See Manuel Castells, The Power of Identity 320 (2d ed., 2010).

rights became a pressing issue due to the rapid growth of digital transmission techniques.[107] Commercial interests act as the prime agents behind the huge development of content over the Internet.[108] Consequently, when intellectual property rights are at stake, more control for online behavior is often requested.[109] Traditionally, the relationship between intellectual property rights and individual rights was mainly seen in terms of mutual balance and harmony, but as a result of a new enforcement agenda, parties are witnessing exponential growth in the number of controversies that lie at the intersection of these two domains.[110]

In order to contain information and preserve control over access, several countries have adopted legislative measures to regulate and monitor digital content. Regulations designed to monitor and control the flow of information on the Internet increased in the name of protecting national security.[111] Under the mantle of security fears and the "War on Terror," a general decline of fundamental rights has occurred.[112] Virtually every industrialized country and many developing countries have passed laws that expand "the capacities of state intelligence and law enforcement agencies to monitor Internet communications."[113] Online media faces a massive increase in regulation at the transnational and national levels.[114] Important digital content reforms have been recently introduced or discussed in Europe and the United States.[115] These legislative instruments have pursued two broad approaches in order to regulate traffic on the Internet: imposing obligations on Internet intermediaries

---

[107] See National Research Council, Committee on Intellectual Property Rights and the Emerging Information Infrastructure, The Digital Dilemma: Intellectual Property in the Information Age (National Academy Press 2000) (reporting the complex challenge to established norms created by the radical growth in information technology).

[108] See Jamal, B., Shahin, The Internet: A Case Study for Global Governance, 5 Swiss Pol. Sci. Rev. 120 (1999).

[109] Id.

[110] See Laurence R. Helfer, The New Innovation Frontier? Intellectual Property and the European Court of Human Rights, in 49 Harv. Int. L. J. 1 (2008); Id., Human Rights and Intellectual Property: Conflict or Coexistence?, in 5 Minn. Int. Prop. Rev. 47 (2003). See also generally Laurence Helfer and Graeme Austin Human Rights and Intellectual Property: Mapping the Global Interface (Cambridge University Press, Cambridge, 2011).

[111] See Ronald J. Deibert, Black Code Redux: Censorship, Surveillance, and the Militarization of Cyberspace, in Digital Media and Democracy: Tactics in Hard Times 137, 137 (Megan Boler ed., 2008); Benkler, The Wealth of Networks, cit. at 32; Jack Goldsmith and Tim Wu, Who Controls the Internet? 65 (2006).

[112] See Hamelink, Human Rights for the Information Society, in Communicating in the Information Society cit., at 154.

[113] See Ronald J. Deibert, Black Code Redux: Censorship, Surveillance, and the Militarization of Cyberspace, in Digital Media and Democracy: Tactics in Hard Times 137, 138 (Megan Boler ed., 2008);

[114] Id.

[115] See e.g. the French Hadopi Law, the Spanish "Sinde law", the UK Digital Economy Act, the U.S. SOPA, PIPA and OPEN and, finally, the international ACTA Treaty.

and imposing restrictions on Internet users.[116] They have also created a social climate and legal environment that hamper information use and broad access to information sources.

Already introduced and enacted legislation, like the "Sinde law" in Spain,[117] the Digital Economy Act in the United Kingdom,[118] and the Haute Autorité pour la diffusion des œuvres et la protection des droits sur internet (HADOPI) law in France,[119] directly threaten the Internet as a free, egalitarian, and democratic way of communicating. The same issues were raised during the discussion of proposed legislation like the international Anti-Counterfeiting Trade Agreement (ACTA),[120] the Stop Online Piracy Act (SOPA),[121] and the Protect Intellectual Property Act (PIPA)[122] considered in the United States. These legislations are often aimed to fight online piracy and copyright infringement, as well as newer forms of cyber-crime and cyber-terrorism. But Internet activists and freedom of expression defenders fear that similar legal instruments can also be used to establish a surveillance regime that allows restrictions on freedom of movement over different types of communication platforms.[123] Such ongoing attempts to regulate the Internet "reflect the natural maturation process that previous media, such as print, radio, and television, all experienced as they evolved out of unrestrained and experimental to tightly controlled and regulated environments."[124] The experience of democratic countries with provisions designed to monitor and control the flow of information on the Internet reveals that

---

[116] See e.g. Center for Democracy and Technology, Shielding the Messengers: Protecting Internet Platforms for Expression and Innovation (2012) available at https://www.cdt.org/files/file/Intermediary-Liability-6p.pdf (last accessed 28 April 2016); Joel R. Reidemberg, States and Internet Enforcement, 1 U. Ottawa L. & Tech. J. 213, 222(2003) (addressing concerns and motivation of different types of enforcement of decisions through internet instruments).

[117] Ley 2/2011, de 4 de marzo, de Economía Sostenible [Law 2/2011, of March 4, 2011, on Sustainable Economy], 55 Boletín Oficial del Estado [J.O.] [Official Gazette of Spain] March 5, 2011, Sec. I. p. 25033.

[118] Digital Economy Act, 2010, 59 Eliz. 2, c. 24, § 124A (U.K.).

[119] Loi 2009-669 du 12 juin 2009 favorisant la diffusion et la protection de la creation sur Internet [Law 2009-669 of June 12, 2009 Favoring the Dissemination and Protection of Creation on the Internet], 135 Journal Officiel de la Republique Francaise [J.O.] [Official Gazette of France], June 13, 2009, p. 9666.

[120] Anti-Counterfeiting Trade Agreement, Dec. 3, 2010, available at http://www.ustr.gov/webfm_send/2 417.

[121] Stop Online Piracy Act (SOPA) (2012), H.R. 3261, 112th Cong.

[122] Preventing Real Online Threats to Economic Creativity and Theft of Intellectual Property Act, (2012) S. 968, 112th Cong.

[123] See Center for Democracy and Technology, Shielding the Messengers: Protecting Internet Platforms for Expression and Innovation (2012) available at https://www.cdt.org/files/file/Intermediary-Liability-6p.pdf (last accessed 28 April 2016).

[124] See Ronald J. Deibert, Black Code Redux: Censorship, Surveillance, and the Militarization of Cyberspace, in Digital Media And Democracy: Tactics In Hard Times 137, 137 (Megan Boler ed., 2008).

restrictions on the freedom of the media may not withstand constitutional scrutiny.[125] The degree to which the different constitutional protections in each nation can interact in this area varies across medium and nature of content. In particular, constitutional scrutiny of media access regulation has traditionally varied significantly by the predefined category of technology (print, radio and television), but constitutional debates surrounding modern digital platforms continue to be perceived in traditional terms.[126] Media freedom is usually guaranteed or limited by media laws, but the advent of the Internet has highlighted how traditional regulation and control policy can go beyond the regulatory mechanisms used for traditional media.[127] The global dimension of the Internet requires a shift from conventional media regulation. The promotion of freedom, access to information, and pluralism of the media (including unrestricted media regulation) are all key aspects for supporting a concrete implementation of freedom of expression, which represents one of the basic elements of all democratic societies.

Regulations on the Internet have often been criticized for their inability to reconcile technological progress with protection of economic interests, as well as other conflicting interests. Essentially, these policy measures “alter the environment within which Internet communications take place.”[128]

References

Acquisti, Alessandro. 2008. *Digital privacy: Theory, technologies, and practices published/created*. New York: Auerbach Publications.

Aigrain, Philippe. 2012. *Sharing: Culture and the economy in the internet age*. Amsterdam: Amsterdam University Press.

Alexy, Robert. 2002. *A theory of constitutional rights*. Oxford: Oxford University Press.

Allan, Trevor R.S. 2003. *Constitutional justice: A liberal theory of the rule of law*. Oxford/New York: Oxford University Press.

Bache, Ian, and Matthew Flinders (eds.). 2004. *Multi-level governance*. Oxford/New York: Oxford University Press.

Balkin, Jack M. 2004. Digital speech and democratic culture: A theory of freedom of expression for the information society. *New York University Law Review* 79: 1.

Balkin, Jack M. 2009. The future of free expression in a digital age. *Pepperdine Law Review* 36: 427.

[125] See e.g. the case of the US 1996 Communications Decency Act which attempted to limit minors' access to Internet pornography, but it was overturned by the Supreme Court's decision in Reno v. ACLU (1997); or the more recent case of the French Hadopi law which was enacted to fight Internet piracy, but it was partly censored by the Conseil Constitutionnel.

[126] See John Blevins, The New Scarcity: A First Amendment Framework for Regulating Access to Digital Media Platforms, 79 Tenn. L. Rev. 353, 366 (f2012)

[127] See EUI Center for Media Pluralism and Media Freedom, European Union competencies in respect of media pluralism and media Freedom, Report 14–15, 27 (2013).

[128] See Ronald J. Deibert et al. (eds.) Access Controlled: The Shaping of Power, Rights, and Rule in Cyberspace, 152 (2010); Cass R. Sunstein, Republic.com, 134 (2001).

Barron, Anne. 2011. 'Graduated Response' à l'Anglaise: Online copyright infringement and the digital economy act 2010. *Journal of Media Law* 3: 305.
Becker, Eberhard, et al. (eds.). 2003. *Digital rights management: Technological, economic, legal and political aspects*. Berlin/New York: Springer.
Benedek, Wolfgang, and Matthias C. Kettemann. 2013. *Freedom of expression and the internet*. Strasbourg: Council of Europe Publishing.
Benhabib, Seyla. 2006. Twilight of sovereignty or the emergence of cosmopolitan norms? Rethinking citizenship in volatile times. *Citizenship Studies* 11: 19.
Benkler, Yochai. 2000a. An unhurried view of private ordering in information transactions. *Vanderbilt Law Review* 53: 2063.
Benkler, Yochai. 2000b. Constitutional bounds of database protection: The role of judicial review in the creation and definition of private rights in information. *Berkeley Technology Law Journal* 15: 535.
Benkler, Yochai. 2006. *The wealth of networks: How social production transforms markets and freedom*. New Haven: Yale University Press.
Bertozzi Jr., Dan, and Lee F. Bergunder. 1990. *Business, government and public policy: Concepts and practices*. New Jersey: Prentice Hall.
Bimber, Bruce. 2003. *Information and American democracy: Technology in the evolution of political power*. Cambridge/New York: Cambridge University Press.
Bohman, James. 2004. Constitution making and democratic innovation: The European union and transnational governance. *European Journal of Political Theory* 3: 315.
Boldrin, Michele, and David K. Levine. 2010. *Against intellectual monopoly*. New York: Cambridge University Press.
Bonadio, Enrico. 2011. File sharing, copyright and freedom of expression. *European Intellectual Property Review* 33: 619.
Borghi, Maurizio, and Stavroula Karapapa. 2013. *Copyright and mass digitization*. Oxford: Oxford University Press.
Boyle, James. 2003. The second enclosure movement and the construction of the public domain. *Law & Contemporary Problems* 66: 33.
Bozeman, Barry, et al. (eds.). 2003. *Knowledge flows and knowledge collectives: Understanding the role of science and technology policies in development*. New York: Rockefeller Foundation.
Braman, Sandra. 2002. Informational meta-technologies and international relations: The case of biotechnologies. In *Information technologies and global politics: The changing scope of power and governance*, eds. James N. Rosenau, and J.P. Singh, 91. Albany: State University of New York Press.
Braman, Sandra (ed.). 2004a. *Biotechnology and communication: The meta-technologies of information*. Mahwah: Lawrence Erlbaum Associates.
Braman, Sandra. 2004b. Technology. In *Handbook of media studies*, eds. John D.H. Downing et al, 123. Thousand Oaks: Sage Publications.
Brown, Ian. 2013. *Research handbook on governance of the internet*. Cheltenham: Edward Elgar Publishing.
Brown, Ian, and Christopher T. Marsden. 2013. *Regulating code. Good governance and better regulation in the information age*. Cambridge, MA: The MIT Press.
Brownsword, Roger. 2008. *Rights, regulation, and the technological revolution*. Oxford/New York: Oxford University Press.
Brownsword, Roger, and Morag Goodwin. 2012. *Law and technologies of the twenty-first century*. Cambridge: Cambridge University Press.
Bucci, Massimiano. 2006. *Scegliere il Mondo che Vogliamo. Cittadini, Politica e Tecnoscienza*. Bologna: Il Mulino.
Callon, Michel, Pierre Lascoumes, and Yannick Barthe. 2009. *Acting in an uncertain world: An essay on technical democracy*. Cambridge/New York: The MIT Press.
Castells, Manuel. 2003. *The internet galaxy: reflections on the internet, business and society*. Oxford/New York: Oxford University Press.

Chandra, Rajshree. 2012. *Knowledge as property. Issues in the moral grounding of intellectual property rights*. New Delhi: Oxford University Press.
Chapman, Audrey R. 2009. Towards an understanding of the right to enjoy the benefits from scientific progress and its applications. *Journal of Human Rights* 8: 1.
Claude, Richard Pierre. 2002. *Science in the service of human rights*. Philadelphia: University of Pennsylvania Press.
Cranston, Maurice. 1973. *What are human rights?* London: Bodley Head.
Cutcliffe, Stephen H. 2000. *Ideas, machines and values: An introduction to science, technology and social studies*. Lanham: Rowman & Littlefield Publishers.
David, Paul A. 2002. The political economy of public science: A contribution to the regulation of science and technology. In *The regulation of science and technology*, ed. Helen Lawton Smith, 33. Houndmills/New York: Palgrave.
David, Paul A. 2003. The economic logic of "Open Science" and the balance between private property rights and the public domain in scientific data and information: A primer. In *The role of scientific and technical data and information in the public domain*, ed. Julie M. Esanu and Paul F. Uhlir, 19. Washington, D.C: National Academies Press.
David, Pail, and Dominique Foray. 1995. Accessing and expanding the science and technology knowledge base. *Science Technology Industry Review* 16: 13.
De Marco, Eugenio, ed. 2008. *Accesso alla Rete e Uguaglianza Digitale*. Milano: Giuffrè Editore.
Devlin, Patrick. 1965. *The enforcement of morals*. London/New York: Oxford University Press.
Dinwoodie, Graeme B., and Mark D. Janis. 2007. *Trademarks and unfair competition: Law and policy*. New York: Aspen Publishers.
Donders, Yvonne. 2011. The right to enjoy the benefits of scientific progress: In search of state obligations in relation to health. *Medicine Health Care & Philosophy* 14: 371.
Drake, William J. 2010. *Internet governance: Creating opportunities for all*. New York: United Nations Department of Economic and Social Affairs.
Dutton, William H., et al. 2011. *Freedom of connection – freedom of expression: The changing legal and regulatory ecology shaping the internet*. Paris: UNESCO Report.
Dworkin, Ronald. 1978. *Taking rights seriously*. Cambridge, MA: Harvard University Press.
Efroni, Zohar. 2010. *Access-right. The future of digital copyright law*. Oxford/New York: Oxford University Press.
Elkin-Koren, Niva, and Neil Netanel (eds.). 2002. *The commodification of information*. The Hague/New York: Kluwer Law.
Feenberg, Andrew. 1999. *Questioning technology*. New York: Routledge.
Feldman, Robin. 2009a. *The role of science in law*. Oxford/New York: Oxford University Press.
Feldman, Robin. 2009b. *Historic perspectives on law & science*. Stanford Technology Law Review.
Fischer-Huebner, Simone, et al. (eds.). 2009. *Trust, privacy, and security in digital business: 11th International Conference, Trustbus 2014, Munich, Germany, September 2–3, 2014. Proceedings*. New York: Springer.
Frank, Jørgensen Rikke (ed.). 2006. *Human rights in the global information society*. Cambridge, MA: MIT Press.
Frischmann, Brett M., et al. (eds.). 2014. *Governing knowledge commons*. Oxford/New York: Oxford University Press.
Gaisser, Sibylle, et al. 2009. The phantom menace of gene patents. *Nature* 458: 407.
Geiger, Christophe. 2006. 'Constitutionalising' intellectual property law? The influence of fundamental rights on intellectual property in the European Union. *International Review of Intellectual Property and Competition Law* 37: 371.
Geiger, Christophe. 2008. The constitutional dimension of intellectual property. In *Intellectual property and human rights*, ed. Paul Torremans, 111. Alphen aan den Rijn: Kluwer Law International.

Geiger, Christophe. 2010. Promoting creativity through copyright limitations: Reflections on the concept of exclusivity in copyright law. *Vanderbilt Journal of entertainment & Technology Law* 12: 515.

Geiger, Christophe (ed.). 2015. *Research handbook on human rights and intellectual property*. Cheltenham: Edward Elgar Publishing.

Gervais, Daniel. 2009. The tangled web of UGC: Making copyright sense of user-generated content. *Vanderbilt Journal of Entertainment and Technology Law* 11: 841.

Gibbons, Thomas (ed.). 2009. *Free speech in the new media*. Farnham/Burlington: Ashgate.

Giblin, Rebecca. 2014. Evaluating graduate response. *Columbia Journal of Law & the Arts* 37: 147.

Giordano, Simona, et al. (eds.). 2012. *Scientific freedom*. London/New York: Bloomsbury Publishing.

Godt, Christine. 2014. Intellectual property and European fundamental rights. In *Constitutionalization of European private law: XXII/2*, ed. Hans Micklitz, 211. Oxford: Oxford University Press.

Goggin, L. Malcom, ed. 1986. Governing science and technology: Reconciling science and technology and democracy. In *Governing science and technology in a democracy*, ed. Malcom Goggin. Knoxville: University of Tennessee Press.

Gorz, Andre. 2003. *L'immateriel: connaissance, valeur et capital*. Paris: Editions Galilée.

Griffiths, Jonathan, and Uma Suthersanen (eds.). 2008. *Copyright and free speech. Comparative and international analyses*. Oxford/New York: Oxford University Press.

Grosheide, Willem (ed.). 2010. *Intellectual property and human rights. A paradox*. Cheltenham/Northampton: Edward Elgar.

Guibault, Lucie. 2002. *Copyright limitations and contracts. An analysis of the contractual overridability of limitations on copyright*. The Hague/Boston: Kluwer Law.

Guibault, Lucie. 2008. Accommodating the needs of iConsumers: Making sure they get their money's worth of digital entertainment. *Journal of Consumer Policy* 31: 409.

Hamelink, Cees. 2003. Human rights for the information society. In *Communicating in the information society*, ed. Girard Bruce and Seán Ó. Siochrú. Geneva: United Nations Research Institute for Social Development.

Hardin, Garret. 1968. The tragedy of the commons. *Science* 162: 1243.

Hardt, Michael, and Antonio Negri. 2004. *Multitude: War and democracy in the age of empire*. New York: Penguin Press.

Haunss, Sebastian. 2013. *Conflicts in the knowledge society. The contentious politics of intellectual property*. Cambridge: Cambridge University Press.

Helberger, Natali. 2005. *Controlling access to content: regulating conditional access in digital broadcasting*. The Hague: Kluwer Law.

Helfer, Laurence R., and Graeme W. Austin. 2011. *Human rights and intellectual property: Mapping the global interface*. Cambridge/New York: Cambridge University Press.

Heller, Michael A. 1998. The tragedy of the anticommons: Property in the transition from Marx to markets. *Harvard Law Review* 111: 621.

Heller, Michael A. 2008. *The gridlock economy: How too much ownership wrecks markets, stops innovation, and costs lives*. New York: Basic Books.

Hess, Charlotte, and Elinor Ostrom (eds.). 2006. *Understanding knowledge as a commons: From theory to practice*. Cambridge, MA: MIT Press.

Hveem, Helge, and Lelio Iapadre (eds.). 2011. *The global governance of knowledge creation and diffusion*. New York: Routledge.

Jasanoff, Sheila. 2004. Science and citizenship: A new synergy. *Science and Public Policy* 31: 90.

Jasanoff, Sheila. 2011a. Constitutional moments in governing science and technology. *Science and Engineering Ethics* 17: 621.

Jasanoff, Sheila (ed.). 2011b. *Reframing rights: Bioconstitutionalism in the genetic age*. Cambridge, MA: The MIT Press.

Kaminski, Margot. 2009. The origins and potential impact of the Anti-Counterfeiting Trade Agreement (ACTA). *Yale Journal of International Law* 34: 247.

Karppinen, Kari. 2013. *Rethinking media pluralism*. New York: Fordham University Press.

Keller, Perry. 2011. *European and international media law. Liberal democracy, trade and the new media*. Oxford/New York: Oxford University Press.

Kleinman, Daniel Lee (ed.). 2000a. *Science, technology, and democracy*. Albany: State University of New York Press.

Kleinman, Daniel Lee. 2000b. Democratizations of science and technology. In *Science, technology, and democracy*, ed. Daniel Lee Kleinmann, 139. Albany: State University of New York Press.

Kur, Annette, and Marianne Levin. 2011. *Intellectual property rights in a fair world trade system: Proposals for reform of TRIPS*. Cheltenham/Northampton: Edward Elgar.

Land, Molly. 2013. Toward an international law of the internet. *Harvard International Law Journal* 54: 393.

Lawton, Thomas C. 1997. *Technology and the new diplomacy: The creation and control of EC industrial policy for semiconductors*. Aldershot/ Brookfield: Avebury.

Lawton Smith, Helen (ed.). 2002. *The regulation of science and technology*. Houndmills/New York: Palgrave Publishers.

Leenes, Ronald E., et al. (eds.). 2008. *Constitutional rights and new technologies. A comparative study*. The Hague: T.M.C. Asser Press.

Lessig, Lawrence. 2004. *Free culture: How big media uses technology and the law to lock down culture and control creativity*. New York: Penguin Press.

Levine, Andrew. 1994. *The general will: Rousseau, Marx, communism*. Cambridge/New York: Cambridge University Press.

Litman, Jessica. 1990. The public domain. *Emory Law Journal* 39: 965.

Malcom, Goggin L. 1986. *Governing science and technology in a democracy*. Knoxville: University of Tennessee.

Mansell, Robin, and Edward Steinmueller. 2013. Copyright infringement online: The case of the digital economy act judicial review in the United Kingdom. *Media & Society* 15: 1312.

Marks, Stephen. 2010. *Out of obscurity: The right to benefit from advances in science and technology and its implications for global health*. In Proceedings of the 3rd conference on law, science, and technology: Health and science: Human rights and legal issues. Taipei: Academia Sinica

Mazziotti, Giuseppe. 2008. *EU digital copyright law and the end-user*. Berlin: Springer.

Mazziotti, Giuseppe. 2013. *Copyright in the EU digital single market*. Brussels: Center for European Policy Studies.

McDiarmid, Andrew, and Matthew Shears. 2013. The importance of internet neutrality to protecting human rights online. In *The value of network neutrality for the internet of tomorrow*, eds. Luca Belli and Primavera de Filippi, 26. Dynamic Coalition on Network Neutrality.

Mendis, Dinusha. 2013. Digital economy act 2010: Fighting a losing battle? Why the ‘Three Strikes’ law is not the answer to copyright law’s latest challenge. *International Review of Law, Computers & Technology* 27: 60.

Montagnani, Maria Lillà. 2009. A new interface between copyright law and technology: How user-generated content will shape the future of online distribution. *Cardozo Arts & Entertainment Law Journal* 26: 719.

Moore, Adam D. 2003. Intellectual property, innovation, and social progress: The case against incentive based arguments. *Hamline Law Review* 26: 601.

Morozov, Evgeny. 2012. *The net delusion: The dark side of internet freedom*. New York: PublicAffairs.

Murphy, Thérèse (ed.). 2009. *New technologies and human rights*. Oxford/New York: Oxford University Press.

Murray, Andrew. 2010. *Information technology law*. Oxford/New York: Oxford University Press.

Murray, Fiona, and Scott Stern. 2007. Do formal intellectual property rights hinder the free flow of scientific knowledge? An empirical test of the anti-commons hypothesis. *Journal of Economic Behavior and Organization* 63: 648.

Netanel, Neil Weinstock. 2008. *Copyright's paradox*. Oxford/New York: Oxford University Press.
OECD. 2007. *At a crossroads: "Personhood" and digital identity in the information society*. Available at http://www.oecd.org/dataoecd/31/6/40204773.doc.
OECD. 2009. *The role of digital identity management in the internet economy*. Available at http://www.oecd.org/dataoecd/55/48/43091476.pdf.
Orofino, Marco. 2008. *Profili Costituzionali delle Comunicazioni Elettroniche nell'Ordinamento Multilivello*. Milano: Giuffrè.
Ostrom, Elinor. 1990. *Governing the commons: The evolution of institutions for collective action*. Cambridge: Cambridge University Press.
Ozolina, Zaneta, et al. 2012. *Ethical and regulatory challenges to science and research policy at the global level, expert group report, directorate-general for research and innovation of the European commission*. Luxembourg: Publication Office of the European Union.
Pauwels, Caroline, et al. (eds.). 2009. *Rethinking European media and communications policy*. Brussels: VUB Press.
Pestre, Dominique. 2008. Challenges for the democratic management of technoscience: Governance, participation and the political today. *Science as Culture* 17: 101.
Plomer, Aurora. 2013. The human rights paradox: Intellectual property rights and rights of access to science. *Human Rights Quarterly* 35: 143.
Rannenberg, Kai, et al. (eds.). 2009. *The future of identity in the information society*. Berlin/New York: Springer.
Reichman, Jerome H., and Paul Uhlir. 2003. A contractually reconstructed research commons for scientific data in a highly protectionist intellectual property environment. *Law and Contemporary Problems* 66: 315.
Reidenberg, Joel R. 1998. Lex informatica: The formulation of information policy rules through technology. *Texas Law Review* 76: 553.
Resta, Giorgio. 2011. Nuovi Beni Immateriali e Numerus Clausus dei Diritti Esclusivi. In *Diritti Esclusivi e Nuovi Beni Immateriali*, vol. 3, ed. Giorgio Resta, 68. Torino: Utet.
Roffe, Pedro, and Maximiliano Santa Cruz. 2007. *Intellectual property rights and sustainable development: A survey of major issues*. Santiago, Chile: United Nations Publication.
Romero Moreno, Felipe. 2013. Unblocking the digital economy act 2010; human rights issues in the UK. *International Review of Law, Computers & Technology* 27: 18.
Samuelson, Pamela. 2003. Mapping the digital public domain: Threats and opportunities. *Law and Contemporary Problems* 66: 147.
Samuelson, Pamela. 2006. Enriching discourse on public domains. *Duke Law Journal* 55: 783.
Santosusso, Amedeo. 2011. *Diritto, Scienza e Nuove Tecnologie*. Padova: Cedam.
Shapiro, Carl, and Hal R. Varian. 1999. *Information rules: A strategic guide to the network economy*. Boston: Harvard Business School Press.
Sinjela, Mpazi (ed.). 2007. *Human rights and intellectual property rights: Tensions and convergences*. Leiden/Boston: Martinus Nijhoff Publishers.
Spinello, Richard A., and Maria Bottis. 2009. *A defense of intellectual property rights*. Cheltenham/Northampton: Edward Elgar.
Stamatoudi, Irini A. (ed.). 2010. *Copyright enforcement and the internet*. Alphen aan den Rijn: Kluwer Law International.
Strowel, Alain. 2009. Internet piracy as a wake-up call for copyright law makers – is the "Graduated Response" a good reply? *World Intellectual Property Organization Journal* 1: 75.
Sunrise Winter, Jenifer. 2012. Is internet access a human right? Linking information and communication technology development with global human rights' efforts. *Global Studies Journal* 5: 35.
Symonides, Janusz (ed.). 2000. *Human rights: Concept and standards*. Aldershot/Burlington: Ashgate.
Torremans, Paul L.C. (ed.). 2008. *Intellectual property and human rights*. Alphen aan den Rijn: Kluwer Law International.

Ullrich, Hans. 2004. Harmony and unity of European intellectual property protection. In *Intellectual property in the new millennium*, ed. David Vaver and Lionel Bently, 20. Cambridge/New York: Cambridge University Press.

van den Hoven, Jeroen. 2010. The use of normative theories in computer ethics. In *The Cambridge handbook of information and computer ethics*, ed. Luciano Floridi, 59. Cambridge/New York: Cambridge University Press.

Varju, Marton. 2014. *European union human rights law: The dynamics of interpretation and context*. Cheltenham: Edward Elgar Publishing.

Verpeaux, Michel. 2010. *Freedom of expression*. Strasbourg: Council of Europe Publishing.

Vila De Azevedo Cunha, Mario, et al. (eds.). 2013. *New technologies and human rights: challenges to regulation*. Farnham/Burlington: Ashgate Publishing.

Walterscheid, Edward C. 1998. *To promote the progress of useful arts: American patent law and administration*, 1787–1836. Littleton: Fred B Rothman & Co.

Weeramantry, Christopher Gregory (ed.). 1990. *Human rights and scientific and technological development*. Tokyo: United Nations University Press.

Yu, Peter. 2012. Intellectual property and human rights in the nonmultilateral era. *Florida Law Review* 64: 1045.

Zencovich, Zeno. 2008. *Freedom of expression: A critical and comparative analysis*. Abingdon/New York: Routledge-Cavendish.

Chapter 3
Legal Controversies in Digital Media

Abstract The chapter – drawing upon comparative materials and case law analysis – investigates the potential risks and vulnerabilities related to communication technologies focusing on legislative reforms in the area of digital communications and their implications for individual rights.

3.1 Copyright Protection and the Access to Network Conundrum: The Case of the French Hadopi Anti-piracy Legislation

With the HADOPI anti-piracy legislation, France became the first European country to introduce a warning system to protect digital copyright from end-user infringement on the Internet.[1] The law provided for the creation of an independent administrative Authority to deal with the protection of copyrighted works in the digital environment.[2] According to provisions of the first version of the law (HADOPI 1),[3] all Internet activity had to be monitored to detect illegal content sharing, and suspected infringers tracked back to their Internet service providers (ISPs).[4] The French law essentially provided for the so called "three strikes procedure", namely a procedure based on the submission of three written warnings before applying a

---

[1] See Int'l Fed'n of the Phonographic Indus., Digital Music Report 2012, 17 (2012) available at www.ifpi.org/content/library/DMR2012.pdf.

[2] This new Authority replaces the "Autorité de régulation des mesures techniques" (ARMT) introduced by the so called "Dadvsi Law," Loi 2006-961 du 1 août 2006 relative au droit d'auteur et aux droits voisins dans la société de l'information, 178 Journal Officiel de la République Française [J.O.] [Official Gazette of France], August 3, 2006, p. 11529. For more on the Dadvsi law, see Jane Winn & Nicolas Jondet, A New Deal for End Users? Lessons From a French Innovation in the. Regulation of Interoperability, 51 Wm. & Mary L. Rev. 547 (2009).

[3] Loi 2009-669 du 12 juin 2009 favorisant la diffusion et la protection de la création sur internet, 135 Journal Officiel de la République Française [J.O.] [Official Gazette of France], June 13, 2009, p. 9666 [hereinafter HADOPI 1].

[4] See Code de la Propriété Intellectuelle [French Intellectual Property Code] art. L. 331-13, al. 1, available at http://www.legifrance.gouv.fr/affichCode.do?cidTexte=LEGITEXT000006069414 (last accessed 28 April 2016).

N. Lucchi, *The Impact of Science and Technology on the Rights of the Individual*, Law, Governance and Technology Series 26,
DOI 10.1007/978-3-319-30439-7_3

formal sanction.[5] The first step involved an email warning sent directly by the ISPs at the request of the HADOPI Authority (Haute Autorite pour la Diffusion des Oeuvres et la Protection des Droits sur Internet) according to a claim received from a certain right-holder.[6] In case of continued illegal activity, the HADOPI Authority could send a second email warning followed by a communication by registered mail.[7] Finally, the Authority, on its own initiative, had the power to impose a range of sanctions including a temporary Internet disconnection. When called to evaluate the constitutionality of this first version of the HADOPI law, the *Conseil constitutionnel* highlighted an "essential human interest" to have access to computer networks.[8] This is largely due to the fact that the Internet is able to play a very important role in the life of people affecting not only the daily routine, but also offering a broad range of important and fundamental services. This decision laid also the basis for a debate about the need for a balancing analysis by a jurisdictional authority before any interruptions of the service are applied. As a consequence of this decision, the French National Assembly and the French Senate passed an amended version of this anti-piracy law (HADOPI 2).[9] In this new version, the imposition of any sanctions – including internet disconnection – is determined only by a judge. Finally, the downsizing of the package of sanctions provided by the HADOPI law was further weakened with the approval of the Decree of 8 July 2013, n. 596 (HADOPI 3) which abolished the judicial measure of blocking access to the Internet, replacing it with a fine under the responsibility of another administrative authority.[10]

[5] Id.

[6] Id.

[7] Id. art. L. 331-25, al. 2.

[8] Laure Marino, Le Droit d'Accès à Internet, Nouveau Droit Fondamental, 20 Recueil Dalloz 2045 (2009).

[9] Loi 2009-1311 du 28 octobre 2009 relative à la protection pénale de la propriété littéraire et artistique sur internet, 251 Journal Officiel de la République Française [J.O.] [Official Gazette of France], Oct. 29, 2009, p. 18290 [hereinafter HADOPI 2]

[10] See Loi 2013-596 du 8 juillet 2013 supprimant la peine contraventionnelle complémentaire de suspension de l'accès à un service de communication au public en ligne et relatif aux modalités de transmission des informations prévue à l'article L331-21 du code de la propriété intellectuelle [Decree No. 2013-596 of 8 July 2013 abolishing the additional misdemeanor punishable by suspension of access to a communication service to the public online and on the procedure for transmission of information under Article L. 331-21 of the code IP], Journal Officiel de la République Française [J.O.] [Official Gazette of France], Jul. 9, 2013, p. 11428, available at www.legifrance.gouv.fr/affichTexte.do?cidTexte=JORFTEXT000027678782.

3.1.1 *Ramifications of the Decision of the Conseil Constitutionnel*

The graduated response mechanism adopted in France was at the center of a long and public controversy involving academics, jurists, policy makers and non-profit associations defending the rights and freedom of citizens on the Internet.[11] The French experience with the HADOPI law was also reported not only as an example to follow, but also as a symptom of a large and evident problem that was poorly formulated and incorrectly interpreted. The decision of the *Conseil Constitutionnel* is the only good thing that remains after the failure of this inadequate legislative initiative. In particular, it can be considered as a landmark decision and its relevance has been underlined also in a recent pronouncement of the European Court of Human Rights.[12]

As recognized by the French legislative process, and according to Article 61(2) of the French constitution,[13] the *Conseil constitutionnel* can exercise *a priori* and

[11] Among earlier commentators, see Florence Chaltiel, La loi Hadopi devant le Conseil constitutionnel, 125 Les petites affiches 7 (2009); Lionel Costes, La loi "Creation et Internet" partiellement censurée par le Conseil constitutionnel, 50 Revue Lamy Droit de l'Immatériel 3 (2009); Jean-Philippe Feldman, Le Conseil constitutionnel, la loi "Hadopi" et la présomption d'innocence, 28 Sem. Jur. Éd. gén. 25 (2009); Allan Gautron, La "réponse graduée" (à nouveau) épinglée par le Conseil constitutionnel. Ou la délicate adéquation des moyens aux fins, 51 Revue Lamy Droit de l'Immatériel 63 (2009); Frank Macrez & Julien Gossa, Surveillance et Sécurisation: Ce que l'Hadopi Rate. À Propos de la «Petite loi» «Création et Internet», 50 Revue Lamy Dr. Immatériel, 79 (2009); Dominique Rousseau, Hado-pirate la Constitution: le Conseil sanctionne!, 51 Revue Lamy Droit de l'Immatériel 103 (2009); Michel Verpeaux, La liberté de communication avant tout. La censure de la loi Hadopi 1 par le Conseil constitutionnel, 39 Sem. Jur. Éd. gén. 45 (2009); Iliana Boubekeur, De la «Loi Hadopi» à la «Loi Hadopi 2». Analyse de la décision du Conseil Constitutionnel 2009-580 DC et de ses Conséquences, 51 Revue Lamy Droit de l'Immatériel 107 (2009) For a detailed discussion of the problematic "iter" of the law and its relevant aspects, see also Emmanuel Derieux and agnes Granchet, Lutte contre le téléchargement illégale (2010). For some critical comments in English, see Sandrine Rambaud, Illegal Internet File Downloads Under Hadopi 1 and 2, 15 Cyberspace L. 10 (2010); Lyombe Eko, American Exceptionalism, The French Exception, Intellectual Property Law, and Peer-to-Peer File Sharing on The Internet, 10 J. Marshall Rev. Intell. Prop. L. 95, 146–47 (2010); Grégory Sroussi, The Hadopi Law and France's Controversial Fight Against Piracy, Technology, Media & Telecommunications News (Linklaters, London, U.K.) Oct. 2009, at 12; Patrick Van Eecke & Maarten Truyens, Recent Events in EU Internet Law, 13 J. Internet L. 21, 21–2 (2009); Laurent Szuskin, Sophie Fourques de Ruyter, Jennifer Doucleff, Beyond Counterfeiting: The Expanding Battle Against Online Piracy, 21 No. 11 Intell. Prop. & Tech. L.J. 1, 3–6 (2009); Alain Strowel, Internet Piracy as a Wake-up Call for Copyright Law Makers – Is the "Graduated Response" a Good Reply?,cit., at. 79–84; Trisha Meyer, Graduated Response in France: The Clash of Copyright and the Internet, 2 J. of. Inf. Policy 107 (2012).

[12] See ECtHR 18 December 2012, Appl. no. 3111/10, Ahmed Yildirim v. Turkey., para. 32. In this pronouncement, the European Court of Human Rights held that a decision of the Turkish authorities to block internet access to platform Google sites in order to prohibit further access to a specific website hosted by Google can be considered a breach of art. 10 of the Convention for the Protection of Human Rights and Fundamental Freedoms.

[13] See 1958 Const. art. 61, § 2 (Fr.).

abstract control over the constitutionality of laws before their entry into force.[14] On the basis of this principle, members of the National Assembly referred the first version HADOPI law (HADOPI 1) to the *Conseil constitionnel* for review on the grounds of a potential violation of constitutional rights.[15] When called to evaluate the constitutionality of the act, the Court denied the argument that the protection of intellectual property rights might justify an inappropriate reduction in the full enjoyment of freedom of expression – which finds one of its fullest realizations in the Internet.[16] Moreover, the HADOPI 1 noticeably lacked compliance with the set of procedural safeguards that usually come into play when sanctions are imposed: e.g., the right to a fair trial, the right to a defense and the presumption of innocence.[17]

Besides criticizing the sanctioning mechanism contained in the statute, the decision of the *Conseil constitutionnel* highlighted a sort of "fundamental right" of access to computer networks.[18] At the same time, it also provided the basis for a debate about the need of a balancing analysis by a jurisdictional authority before any sanctions are applied, a debate whose consequences may seem to exceed the French border.[19]

3.1.2 Fair Trial, Administrative Sanctions and Freedom of Communication

The judges of the French Constitutional Court essentially addressed compliance with the principle of a "fair trial" in the context of special measures implemented for certain crimes committed online. Their decision refers to the need to protect procedural rights that constitute "minimum guarantees" of a fair trial.[20] Here, the concept

---

[14] See Introduction to French Law, cit., at 30–31 (highlighting that the judicial review of legislation is the most important power of the Constitutional Council and that the Council is different in some important respects from other constitutional Courts. The most striking difference is that the Constitutional Council only exercises an a priori and abstract control, and that access to the Council is limited to a very small number of authorities). See also Hamon & Troper, Droit Constitutionnel, cit., at 834–35.

[15] See Note sous décision n 2009-580 DC du 10 juin 2009, in 27 Cah. Cons. const., 101 (2009) available at http://www.conseil-constitutionnel.fr/conseil-constitutionnel/root/bank_mm/pdf/pdf_cahiers/cccc27.pdf [hereinafter Note sous decision n 2009-580] (last accessed 28 April 2016).

[16] See Decision 2009-580, cit.

[17] On the constitutional consecration of these rights, see Louis Favoreu et al., Droit constitutionnel 808, 817 (4th ed. 2001).

[18] See Laure Marino, Le Droit d'Accès à Internet, Nouveau Droit Fondamental, 30 Recueil Dalloz 2045 (2009).

[19] See Peter K. Yu, The Graduated Response, 62 Fla. L. Rev. 1373, 1376–77 (2010) (observing that in addition to France, similar laws and policies have been adopted, considered, or rejected by Australia, Hong Kong, Germany, the Netherlands, New Zealand, South Korea, Sweden, Taiwan, and the United Kingdom).

[20] See Decision 2009-580, cit., ¶¶ 16,17,18,19 and 20.

of a fair trial is framed in a way that corresponds to the procedural safeguards understood to be implicit in the due process clause of the United States Constitution[21] or embodied in the European concept of "*procès equitable*."[22]

The most discussed point of HADOPI 1 concerned the procedural safeguards granted to Internet users infringing copyright law.[23] On this point, the French law seemed to weaken procedural safeguard guarantees in certain urgent cases (providing only a generic "right to a fair proceeding"). The law granted to a specific administrative body the authority to block Internet access.[24] It provided for the appointment of an administrative authority whose work depended on seemingly "clear" violations of law, without the need for evaluation by a judge.[25] On the one hand, the creation of this administrative control authority found its justification in the necessity to safeguard copyright – an area of law directly threatened by the advent of digital technologies. On the other hand, however, the law likely weakened constitutional guarantees designed to preserve constitutional freedoms and liberties, consequently moving the debate from one about the principles of legality to one about the principle of judicial protection from administrative acts.[26]

The *Conseil Constitutionnel's* findings primarily addressed the sanctioning procedures in place for violations of the obligation of surveillance imposed on intermediaries of communication for content transmitted, posted or stored by their users

[21] U.S. Const. amends. V, XIV. The constitutional guarantee of due process of law excludes all levels of government from arbitrarily or unfairly depriving individuals of their fundamental constitutional rights to life, liberty, and property. On due process, see generally, Ronald D. Rotunda & John E. Nowak, Treatise on Constitutional Law: Substance and Procedure §§ 15, 17 (4th ed. 2007); Edward L. Rubin, Due Process and the Administrative State, 72 Cal. L. Rev. 1044 (1984). "Fair trial" and "due process," in addition to being general principles incorporated into national constitutions and international conventions, are now considered global principles applicable under European Community law. For more on the argument of so called "process rights," see Takis Tridimas, The general principles of EU law (2d ed. 2006).

[22] See European Convention on Human Rights, art. (6)(1), Nov. 4, 1950, 213 U.N.T.S. 221, http://www.echr.coe.int/NR/rdonlyres/D5CC24A7-DC13-4318-B457-5C9014916D7A/0/ENG_CONV.pdf (last accessed 28 April 2016).

[23] See Gautron, La "réponse graduée" (à nouveau) épinglée par le Conseil constitutionnel. Ou la délicate adéquation des moyens aux fins, cit. at 66; Boubekeur, De la «Loi Hadopi» à la «Loi Hadopi 2». Analyse de la décision du Conseil Constitutionnel 2009-580 DC et de ses Conséquences, cit., at 110; Rousseau, Hado-pirate la Constitution: le Conseil sanctionne!, cit., at 104.

[24] See HADOPI 1, cit., art. 6. Under Article 5, the administrative authority had direct power to decide and to enforce penalties against Internet users. See id. art. 5.

[25] On this point, it is remarkable to note the similarity between the French regulatory measure and the Italian debate concerning the adoption of special measures against crimes of opinion committed through social networks – a debate which commenced following aggression directed at the Prime Minister. This debate was followed by the much-discussed national transposition of the European Directive on Audiovisual Media Services. The Italian transposing decree, in fact, grants wide powers of control to the Communications Regulatory Authority over some categories of online digital content and in instances of infringement of copyright law. See D. Lgs. 15 marzo 2010, n. 44, in G.U. Mar. 29, 2010 (It), available at http://www.camera.it/parlam/leggi/deleghe/10044dl.htm (last accessed 28 April 2016).

[26] See Decision 2009-580, cit..

using services they provide on the Internet. According to the *Conseil constitutionnel's* reasoning, one of the most contentious aspects of the law concerned the "graded response" mechanism.[27] In order to limit illegal downloading of digital content protected by copyright, the French law (HADOPI 1) provided for a tightening of control measures and the introduction of an innovative enforcement process.[28] In particular, the HADOPI Authority could impose a special sanction consisting in the suspension of the Internet access for a period of time ranging from 2 months to 1 year.[29]

Thus, HADOPI 1 resulted in the emergence of a new form of internet network surveillance monitored by a semi-police authority, which consequently created troublesome issues related to the protection of privacy and civil liberties in electronic communications. At the same time, HADOPI 1 also resulted in the introduction of a new set of sanctioning rules, devised with the intention of targeting net users suspected of illegal activities (according to the quantity and type of downloaded data). In its decision, the *Conseil constitutionnel* first considered the nature of access to information networks, and then examined the mechanism of sanctions introduced by the act, evaluating the law's respect for fundamental rights and liberties, such as the presumption of innocence, the separation of powers, the right to defense, the right to a fair trial, the principle of cross-examination, as well as the necessary balance between copyright law and freedom of expression.[30]

In analyzing the decision of the *Conseil Constitutionnel* the first critical point to address is the role of the HADOPI Authority in administrative and judicial enforcement.[31] In particular, it is interesting to observe the relationship between the HADOPI Authority and its competence to ensure protection of constitutionally mandated fundamental rights and freedoms. In other words, how can constitutionally-protected interests avoid being compromised in situations where the HADOPI Authority exercises its legislatively created powers?[32] Here, the important point to consider is whether the defendant's constitutional rights are fully protected; particularly in certain specific situations where administrative agencies impose sanctions without regard for constitutional principles like equality or procedural fairness.[33] In

[27] Id. ¶¶ 8–12, 17.

[28] See Gautron, La "réponse graduée" (à nouveau) épinglée par le Conseil constitutionnel. Ou la délicate adéquation des moyens aux fins, cit., at 66.

[29] See HADOPI 1, cit., art. 5(3). The article reads as follows: "La suspension de l'accès au service pour une durée de deux mois à un an assortie de l'impossibilité, pour l'abonné, de souscrire pendant la même période un autre contrat portant sur l'accès à un service de communication au public en ligne auprès de tout opérateur." [The suspension of the access to the service for a period from 2 months to 1 year combined with the impossibility, for the subscriber, to sign during the same period another contract concerning the access to a service of on-line communication with any other operator].

[30] See Decision 2009-580, cit., ¶¶ 6–16.

[31] Id. ¶¶ 4, 16.

[32] See Marco Cuniberti, Autorità indipendenti e libertà costituzionali [Independent authorities and constitutional freedoms] 70 (2007).

[33] See Rousseau, Hado-pirate la Constitution: le Conseil sanctionne!, cit. at 104.

this context, the protection and defense of constitutional rights was most likely what motivated the *Conseil constitutionnel* to contain the power of the HADOPI Authority in its decision.[34]

As is evident, the main question foresees the problem of a denial of due process rights at the procedural level and on a more strictly administrative level. Can an administrative body assume the role of a judicial body; imposing sanctions, such as the interruption of Internet access on the basis of technically "clear" copyright infringement, but without compliance with any procedural constraint? On this point, it is necessary to note that the first version of the French law did not specifically provide the possibility of an appeal against the HADOPI decision (*rectius* the decision of the *Commission de protection des droits*).[35] An appeal would be only be possible after the adoption of the sanction.[36] Moreover, on the matter of substantial and procedural guarantees, the law stated that the Internet user – previously notified by e-mail communications – would only be provided with the date and time of the alleged infringement.[37] It is self-evident that a similar procedure does not meet judicial and procedural guarantees of fairness: in particular the guarantee of adversarial equality and complete disclosure on the nature and cause of the charges.[38]

In the French legal system, the mechanism of protection of freedoms often hinges on constitutional limits (i.e. reservation of statutory powers and reservation of jurisdiction), as is true in many other countries.[39] This structure implies that administrative

---

[34] See Gautron, La "réponse graduée" (à nouveau) épinglée par le Conseil constitutionnel. Ou la délicate adéquation des moyens aux fins, cit. at 66; Boubekeur, De la «Loi Hadopi» à la «Loi Hadopi 2». Analyse de la décision du Conseil Constitutionnel 2009-580 DC et de ses Conséquences, cit., at 110; Rousseau, Hado-pirate la Constitution: le Conseil sanctionne!, cit., at 104; Marino, Le Droit d'Accès à Internet, Nouveau Droit Fondamental, cit., at 2045.

[35] The Hadopi is composed of two bodies: a board [College] and a Commission for the Protection of Rights [Commission de Protection des Droits]. The board is the chief administrative body of the Hadopi and consists of nine members. The Commission consists of three magistrates and supervises the "graduated response" mechanism. See HADOPI 1, cit., art. 5(1).

[36] Id. art. 5(3) ("The well-founded recommendations on the basis of this article can not be disputed that in support of an appeal against a decision to sanction imposed pursuant to Article L. 331-27") (translation by the author). On this point, see Boubekeur, De la «Loi Hadopi» à la «Loi Hadopi 2». Analyse de la décision du Conseil Constitutionnel 2009-580 DC et de ses Conséquences, cit., at 111.

[37] "Les recommandations adressées sur le fondement du présent article mentionnent la date et l'heure auxquelles les faits susceptibles de constituer un manquement à l'obligation définie à l'article L. 336–3 ont été constatés." [The recommendations on the basis of this Article shall include the date and time to which the facts susceptible to constitute a breach of the obligation defined in Article L. 336–3 were noticed.] See Hadopi 1, cit., art. 5(3).

[38] See Decision 2009-580, cit., ¶ 9.

[39] For example, in the Italian legal system Article 13 of the Constitution stipulates a legal and jurisdictional reservation: nobody can be arrested, imprisoned or deprived of their personal freedom if this deprivation is not imposed by the law and if there is not a regular trial and a judicial authority's oversight. In particular it provides that restrictions of personal freedom can be applied by the police, but they have to inform the judicial authority within 48 h; if the judicial authority does not validate the measures within the following 48 h, they become ineffective. See Costituzione della Repubblica Italiana [Constitution] Dec. 22, 1947, art. 13 (It). For an English translation, see

actions – in areas not covered by jurisdictional limits – are subject to the constraints of the principle of legality.[40] Therefore, decisions on measures resulting in a severe limitation of fundamental freedoms[41] are traditionally attributed to the judicial authority and removed from administrative authority. In addition, French constitutional jurisprudence has recognized a jurisdictional reservation of the protection of the right of property, of which copyright represents an intangible variant, in the judicial authority.[42]

The wide powers of sanction and control given to the heterogeneous universe of administrative authorities – usually appointed by government, parliament or elective assembly (thus, not totally independent)[43] – make their positions closer to that of judges'.[44] A problem arises when a non-jurisdictional authority is granted the power to inflict a sanction which directly affects a constitutionally guaranteed right or freedom. The issue is further complicated when the Constitution stipulates that the limitation of a certain right is necessary to ensure safeguards and procedures laid down by judicial order. For this reason, the *Conseil constitutionnel* held that the HADOPI Authority could not be delegated the role of protecting intellectual property rights due to its nature as an administrative body.[45]

It is also important to consider the separation of powers principle as a basis for the judicial protection of fundamental rights.[46] According to the principle of separation of powers, each branch of government (legislative, executive and judiciary) can exercise its specific powers within a clearly defined and limited framework "in order to avoid the abuse of power."[47] For this reason, legislation that does not provide for

Constitution of the Italian Republic, Senato della Repubblica, http://www.senato.it/documenti/repository/istituzione/costituzione_inglese.pdf (last accessed 28 April 2016).

[40] See Cuniberti, Autorità indipendenti e libertà costituzionali, cit., at 61.

[41] For example, freedom of expression, freedom of religion, freedom of thought, freedom of belief, freedom of peaceful assembly, and freedom of association.

[42] Conseil constitutionnel [CC] [Constitutional Court] decision No. 89–256 DC, July 25, 1989, J.O. 9501.

[43] On the alleged impartiality or neutrality of the independent authorities see Cuniberti, Autorità indipendenti e libertà costituzionali, cit., at 404; see also F. Andrew Hanssen, Independent Courts and Administrative Agencies: An Empirical Analysis of the States, 16 J.L. Econ. & Org. 534, 534 (2000).

[44] Traditionally, independent administrative authorities have been delegated functions that are partly administrative, partly legislative and partly judicial. See Edwin Blythe Stason & Frank Edward Cooper, The Law of Administrative Tribunals: a Collection of Judicial Decisions, Statutes, Administrative Rules and Orders and Other Materials 17 (3d. ed. 1957) (the authors point out that "[o]ne of the great difficulties of properly classifying a particular function of an administrative agency is that frequently – and, indeed; typically – a single function has three aspects. It is partly legislative, partly judicial and partly administrative."). See also Sabino Cassese, Poteri indipendenti, Stati, relazioni ultrastatali, 121 Foro it. V, 8 (1996).

[45] See Note sous décision n° 2009-580 DC, cit., at 105..

[46] See T.R.S. Allan, Constitutional Justice: A Liberal Theory of the Rule of Law 31 (2003); Marino, Le Droit d'Accès à Internet, Nouveau Droit Fondamental, cit., at 2045-46.

[47] See Charles de Secondat Montesquieu, De L'Esprit Des Lois [Spirit of the Laws] 162–64 (Gonzague Truc ed. 1949) (1748); see generally Danilo Zolo, The Rule of Law: A Critical

judicial review must be carefully considered and evaluated.[48] Arguably, judicial protection of fundamental rights is one of the best indicators of the existence of the rule of law.[49] In this respect, it is important to note that judicial protection of fundamental rights is explicitly provided for in Articles 7 and 8 of the 1948 Universal Declaration of Human Rights[50] and Article 13 of the 1950 European Convention on Human Rights.[51]

In order to arrive at its conclusion, the *Conseil constitionnel* conducted a proportionality review seeking to determine whether the sanctions of the HADOPI law (HADOPI 1) seriously undermine the freedom of expression or other fundamental rights.[52] In this regard, the *Conseil constituionnel* concluded that the powers vested in the HADOPI Authority were too broad, because they "are not limited to a specific category of persons but extend to the entire population."[53] The *Conseil constituionnel* explained that for this reason "the powers of this Committee [HADOPI Authority] may thus lead to restricting the right of any person to exercise his right to express himself and communicate freely, in particular from his own home."[54] Furthermore, the restriction or denial of access to the internet was recognized as a sanction which applied not only to the Internet access subscriber, but also to "those persons whom the latter allow to access the internet."[55] As a result, in light of the freedom guaranteed by Article 11 of the 1789 Declaration of the Rights of Man and of the Citizen (1789 Declaration), Parliament was not at liberty – "irrespective of the guarantees accompanying the imposition of penalties" – to allow the Committee

Reappraisal, in The Rule of Law: History, Theory and Criticism 3 (Pietro Costa & Danilo Zolo eds., 2007) (discussing the principle of the differentiation of power as divided and distributed across different political institutions and branches).

[48] On judicial review and the enhancement of the protection of individual rights, see Wojciech Sadurski, Judicial Review and the Protection of Constitutional Rights, 22 Oxford J. Legal Stud. 275 (2002).

[49] For a series of critical studies on the rule of law, see The Rule of Law: History, Theory and Criticism (Pietro Costa & Danilo Zolo eds., 2007). In particular see Pietro Costa, The Rule of Law: A Historical Introduction, in The Rule of Law: History, Theory and Criticism 73, 73–76 (Pietro Costa & Danilo Zolo eds., 2007), (drawing on an historical analysis of the rule of law); Luigi Ferrajoli, The Past and the Future of the Rule of Law, in The Rule of Law: History, Theory and Criticism 323, 355 (Pietro Costa & Danilo Zolo eds., 2007) (providing a definition of the rule of law). On the rule of law in a comparative perspective, see Rainer Grote, Rule of Law, Rechtsstaat and Etat de Droit, in Constitutionalism, Universalism and Democracy: A Comparative Analysis 269 (Christian Starck ed., 1999).

[50] Universal Declaration of Human Rights, G.A. Res. 217 (III), U.N. Doc. A/RES/217(III) (Dec. 10, 1948).

[51] European Convention for the Protection of Human Rights and Fundamental Freedoms, art. 13, Nov. 4, 1950, 213 U.N.T.S. 222. On this point, see Tecla Mazzarese, Towards a Positivist Reading of Neo-constitutionalism, Jura Gentium, n.10 2008 at 233, 238 available at http://www.juragentium.unifi.it/en/surveys/rights/mazzares.htm#10 (last accessed 28 April 2016).

[52] See Marino, Le Droit d'Accès à Internet, Nouveau Droit Fondamental, cit., at 2046.

[53] Decision 2009-580, cit., ¶ 16.

[54] Id.

[55] Id.

for the Protection of Copyright (an administrative body) to decide who should have access to the Internet.[56]

In principle, delegation of judicial power to authorities other than courts is not *per se* unconstitutional.[57] However, in this case the issue was the scope and kind of sanction that could be imposed by an independent administrative agency. This constitutional problem arose as a result of the creation of an independent *ad hoc* administrative authority – the HADOPI Authority – which was not obligated to follow legally prescribed procedures and was not required to guarantee adequate defense rights in relation to the nature of the fundamental freedom affected by the imposed sanction.[58]

3.1.2.1 Freedom of Communication and Access to Public Online Services

One of the most interesting aspects addressed by the French case is probably the one concerning the right of access to online networks.[59] The *Conseil constitutionnel* based its legal reasoning on Article 11 of the 1789 Declaration. According to Article 11 "[t]he free communication of ideas and opinions is one of the most precious of the rights of man. Every citizen may, accordingly, speak, write, and print with freedom, but shall be responsible for such abuses of this freedom as shall be defined by law."[60] The judges concluded that this right also includes the freedom to access online networks, given the diffusion of such services and their growing importance to the participation in democratic life and consequently to freedom of expression.[61]

---

[56] Id. The relevant part of the paragraph reads as follows: "[i]n these conditions, in view of the freedom guaranteed by Article 11 of the Declaration of 1789, Parliament was not at liberty, irrespective of the guarantees accompanying the imposition of penalties, to vest an administrative authority with such powers." Id.

[57] See Kenneth F. Warren, Administrative Law in the Political System 56–58 (4th ed., 2004); Cuniberti, Autorità indipendenti e libertà costituzionali, cit., at 403; Hamon & Troper, Droit Constitutionnel, cit., at 145; Georges Dupuis et al., Droit Administratif 209 (11th ed. 2009).

[58] See Rousseau, Hado-pirate la Constitution: le Conseil sanctionne!, cit., at 104.

[59] On the debate about internet access as a possible constitutional or fundamental right, see generally U.N. Econ. & Soc. Council [ECOSOC], Comm'n on Human Rights, Report by the Special Rapporteur on the Promotion and Protection of the Right to Freedom of Opinion and ExpressionI, delivered to the Comm'n on Hum. Rts., U.N. Doc. E/CN.4/2000/63 (Jan. 18, 2000), available at http://www.unhchr.ch/Huridocda/Huridoca.nsf/0/16583a84ba1b3ae5802568bd004e80f7/$FILE/G0010259.pdf (last accessed 28 April 2016); see also David Banisar, The Right to Information in the Age of Information, in Human Rights in the Global Information Society 85–86 (Rikke Frank Jorgenson ed., 2006); Pasquale Costanzo, voce Internet (diritto pubblico), in Dig. IV (Disc. Pubbl.), vol. XVIII, Torino, 2000, p. 353.

[60] Declaration des Droits de l'Homme and du Citoyen de 1789 [Declaration of the Rights of Man and the Citizen] art. 11 (1789) available at <http://www.conseil-constitutionnel.fr/textes/d1789.htm> (last accessed 28 April 2016).

[61] See Decision 2009-580, cit., ¶ 12. The relevant paragraph in the court's opinion reads as follows: "In the current state of the means of communication and given the generalized development of public online communication services and the importance of the latter for the participation in democracy and the expression of ideas and opinions, this right implies freedom to access such

This has led the judges to consider the disconnection of an individual from the internet without a formal judicial oversight as a violation of Article 11 of the 1789 Declaration. Although the court found that internet access cannot be considered a fundamental right in itself, the freedom of communication – which enjoys a particular *status* as a protected right – certainly deserves strengthened protection with respect to internet access. In fact, this type of communication – as opposed to other forms of access to information – necessarily relates to each individual.[62] It is interesting to observe that the same reasoning has been subsequently developed by the European Court of Human Rights in a recent pronouncement concerning a court decision to block access to all Google Sites in Turkey, which hosted an Internet site whose owner was facing criminal proceedings for insulting the memory of Atatürk, the founding father of Turkish Republic. As a result of this decision, access to all other sites hosted by the service was blocked. In this case, the European Court of Human Rights observed that:

> The right to Internet access is considered to be inherent in the right to access information and communication protected by national Constitutions, and encompasses the right for each individual to participate in the information society and the obligation for States to guarantee access to the Internet for their citizens. It can therefore be inferred from all the general guarantees protecting freedom of expression that a right to unhindered Internet access should also be recognized.[63]

Finally, it is worth mentioning another important background principle enunciated by the French court. In applying its jurisprudence on the assessment of proportionality, it has also argued that the freedom of communication, as applied to the right of access to network services, assumes a peculiar importance.[64] Consequently, the restrictions imposed by the sanctioning power must be limited. In particular, on this issue the court stated that, "violations of freedom of access to the Internet can be analyzed, under the Constitution, as invasions of the liberty guaranteed by the Article 11 of the Declaration of 1789."[65] Access to such an important tool of communication has become, for millions of citizens, an integral part of their exercise of

services." On this matter, see also Michel Verpeaux, La liberté de communication avant tout. La censure de la loi Hadopi 1 par le Conseil constitutionnel [The freedom of communication above all. The censorship of the law Hadopi 1 by the Constitutional Council], 39 La Semaine Juridique Generale 46, 50 (2009).

[62] Id.

[63] See ECtHR 18 December 2012, Appl. no. 3111/10, Ahmet Yildirim v. Turkey, para. 31.

[64] Conseil constitutionnel [CC] [Constitutional Court] decision No. 2008-562 DC, Feb. 21, 2008, ¶ 22 (Fr.), available at http://www.conseil-constitutionnel.fr/conseil-constitutionnel/root/bank_mm/anglais/a2008562dc.pdf (last accessed 28 April 2016).

[65] Note sous décision n. 2009-580, cit. ("La portée de la decision, sur ce point, consiste à affirmer que, 'en l'état,' les atteintes à la liberté d'accéder à internet s'analysent, au regard de la Constitution, comme des atteintes à la liberté garantie par l'article 11 de la Déclaration de 1789." [The impact of the decision, on this point, consists in asserting that, violations of freedom of access to the internet can be analyzed, under the Constitution, as violations of freedom guaranteed by Article 11 of the 1789 Declaration]).

many other constitutionally protected rights and freedoms.[66] Therefore, inhibiting access to such a source of information would constitute a disproportionate sanction, in the sense that it would also have a strong and direct impact on the exercise of those constitutional rights and freedoms.[67] The Internet, as opposed to other forms of media, allows for the exercise of the freedom of communication not only in a passive way, but also in an active way, because the user can be both a producer and consumer of information.[68]

On the same ground, the European Parliament has recently stated that the right to internet access also constitutes a guarantee of the right to access education. Specifically, on March 26, 2009, the European Parliament declared that granting all citizens internet access is equivalent to ensuring access to education, reasoning that such access should therefore not be denied or used as a sanction by governments or private companies.[69] Also the Council of Europe is working with all its member states to guarantee that the Internet provides a safe and open environment where freedom of expression, democracy, diversity, information and knowledge can grow without unacceptable restrictions. A concrete example is the recent Council of Europe "Guide to human rights for Internet users"[70] designed to enable users to fully exercise their human rights and fundamental freedoms in the online environment.

3.2 Defining the Balance Between Freedom of Expression and Property Rights

As illustrated by the French case, copyright enforcement, restrictions on the use of copyrighted works and sanctions based on copyright law can often result in unnecessary interferences with the right of freedom of expression and information. In

[66] See Benkler, The Wealth of Networks: How Social Production Transforms Markets & Freedom, cit., at 15 (observing how internet democratizes culture).

[67] See Marino, Le Droit d'Accès à Internet, Nouveau Droit Fondamental, cit., at 2045 (remembering that this right is a "liberté de premier rang").

[68] See Henry H. Perritt, Jr., Law and the Information Superhighway § 2.01[B], at 43 (2d ed. 2001); Andrew Murray, Information Technology Law 104 (2010).

[69] European Parliament Recommendation of 26 March 2009 to the Council on Strengthening Security and Fundamental Freedoms on the Internet, ¶ Q (Mar. 26, 2009), available at http://www.europarl.europa.eu/sides/getDoc.do?pubRef=-//EP//TEXT+TA+P6-TA-2009-0194+0+DOC+XML+V0//EN ("whereas e-illiteracy will be the new illiteracy of the Twenty-first Century; whereas ensuring that all citizens have access to the Internet is therefore equivalent to ensuring that all citizens have access to schooling, and whereas such access should not be punitively denied by governments or private companies; whereas such access should not be abused in pursuit of illegal activities; whereas it is important to deal with emerging issues such as network neutrality, interoperability, global reachability of all Internet nodes, and the use of open formats and standards.") (last accessed 28 April 2016).

[70] Guide to human rights for Internet users, contained in an Appendix to Recommendation of the Council of Europe's Council of Ministers CM/Rec(2014)6 of 16 April 2014.

order to avoid further antagonistic conflicts, the right to freedom of expression must be considered "universal also in regard to the medium and technology" used to convey this right.[71] The right to freedom of expression and freedom of the media were not "designed to fit a particular medium, technology or platform".[72] Freedom of expression is therefore technology-neutral applying "to all means of communications, including the Internet".[73] Any restrictions to this right are only reasonable if they are in accordance with international norms and standards[74] and if they are balanced against the public interest.

In this respect, the decision of the French Constitutional Court reaffirms that freedom of expression and communication "are all the more precious since they are one of the cornerstones of a democratic society and one of the guarantees of respect for other rights and freedoms."[75] As a consequence, any restrictions "placed on the exercising of such freedom must necessarily be adapted and proportionate to the purpose it is sought to achieve."[76] In other words, the issue is not directly related to the use of sector specific sanctions, but rather about reconciling freedom of expression with property rights.[77]

The question here is in fact the extent of conflict between two basic fundamental rights: the freedom of expression, of which the internet is undoubtedly a key element, and property rights, of which copyright represents an intangible aspect.[78]

It is also interesting to note that the approach followed by the French Constitutional Court is exactly in line with the latest interpretations of the Court of Justice of the European Union (CJEU) concerning the balance of copyright on the Internet with other rights. In particular, in the landmark Scarlet v SABAM case[79] the Court of Justice – referring to its 2008 judgement in the Promusicae v Telefónica[80] – argued

---

[71] See Yaman Akdeniz, Freedom of Expression on the Internet: A Study of Legal Provisions and Practices Related to Freedom of Expression, the Free Flow of Information and Media Pluralism on the Internet in OSCE Participating States 50, available at http://www.osce.org/fom/80723 (last accessed 28 April 2016).

[72] Id.

[73] Id.

[74] Id.

[75] Decision 2009-580, cit., ¶ 15.

[76] Id. ¶ 15.

[77] See Conseil constitionnel [CC] [Constitutional Court] decision No. 84-181 DC, Oct. 11, 1984, Rec. 84. In that case, the Conseil Constitutionnel decided on a law intended to limit the concentration and to ensure financial transparency and pluralism of media companies. Id.

[78] In this respect, it should be recalled that the fundamental right to property, which includes intellectual property rights such as copyright (see Case C-479/04, Laserdisken ApS v. Kulturministeriet, 2006 E.C.R. I-8089, ¶ 65), and the fundamental right to effective judicial protection constitute general principles of European Community law (see Joined Cases 154 & 155/04, Alliance for Natural Health and Others, 2005 E.C.R. I-6451, ¶ 126, and Case C-432/05, Unibet, 2007 E.C.R. I-2271, ¶ 37). In addition, at EU level the protection of the right to intellectual property is enshrined in art.17(2) of the Charter of Fundamental Rights of the European Union.

[79] Scarlet Extended v SABAM (C-70/10) Nov. 24, 2011, [2012] E.C.D.R. 4.

[80] Productores de Música de España (Promusicae) v. Telefónica de España SAU (C-275/06), Jan. 28, 2008 , [2008] E.C.R. I-271.

that intellectual property rights – expressly protected in Article 17(2) of the Charter of Fundamental Rights of the European Union[81] – "must be balanced against the protection of other fundamental rights"[82] including the right to freedom of expression and information. The CJEU specifically held that in the context of regulatory measures implemented to safeguard copyright holders, "national authorities and courts must strike a fair balance between the protection of copyright and the protection of the fundamental rights of individuals who are affected by such measures".[83] In addition, the CJEU specified that, although the right to intellectual property is specifically enshrined in Article 17(2) of the Charter of Fundamental Rights of the European Union, there is "nothing whatsoever in the wording of that provision or in the Court's case-law to suggest that right is inviolable and must for that reason be absolutely protected".[84] From this it follows that European courts need to find a neutral balance between intellectual property rights and other fundamental rights avoiding any preferential treatment.[85]

All these considerations lead to an acknowledgement of the importance and persuasiveness of the French court's decision: in particular it seems quite evident its capacity to provide a guidance on other court's opinions with respect to the prominence of freedom of expression in the networked environment. As already mentioned, the European Court of Justice took basically the same approach in the *Scarlet Extended* decision.[86] Most recently, the French decision was also widely quoted in *Yildirim v. Turkey*, the first case focused on the issue of Internet access decided by the European Court of Human Rights.[87]

3.3 The UK Digital Economy Act

Passed by the United Kingdom Parliament in 2010, the Digital Economy Act is also intended to discourage and prevent online copyright infringement.[88] Specifically, some of the provisions of the act address media policy issues related to digital media including copyright violations and protection of intellectual property in the digital environment. Other provisions stipulate measures relating to the obligations of the

---

[81] See Charter of Fundamental Rights of the European Union art. 17(2), Dec. 7, 2000, 2000 O.J. (C 364) 1.

[82] Scarlet Extended v SABAM, cit., at §. 44.

[83] Id., at § 45.

[84] Id., at § 43.

[85] See Wolfgang Benedek and Matthias C. Kettemann, Freedom of Expression and the Internet 78 (2013) (discussing the linkage between technological neutrality and freedom of expression).

[86] Scarlet Extended v SABAM, cit.

[87] See ECtHR 18 December 2012, Appl. no. 3111/10, Ahmed Yildirim v. Turkey.

[88] Digital Economy Act, 2010, c. 24, available at http://www.legislation.gov.uk/ukpga/2010/24/pdfs/ukpga_20100024_en.pdf (last accessed 28 April 2016).

British telecommunications regulator (OFCOM), Internet domain names registry, as well as rules for television and radio broadcasts. The UK Digital Economy Act is essentially based on a policy strategy document called Digital Britain[89] which defined the United Kingdom Government's plan for its digital economy.[90] In particular, this new piece of legislation amends the UK Communications Act 2003.[91]

The Digital Economy Act is widely considered one of the most controversial UK pieces of legislation to have passed in recent years, both because of its rather extreme provisions and because of the fast-tracked parliamentary process through which it has been enacted.[92] It was – in fact – approved during the so called 'Wash-up' period, which is the time between the calling of a general election and the prorogation of the role of the Parliament.[93] This practice is seen as controversial due to the issue of the effectiveness of parliamentary scrutiny given to bills passed using this process.[94] The most controversial part of the Digital Economy Act is that which addresses copyright infringement attempting to make Internet Service Providers more accountable for the content they host. One of the key points of this legislation is the introduction of technical measures to discourage copyright infringement such as the "graduate response" system.

3.3.1 Terms and Effect of the British Reform

The British implementation of the "graduated response" regime is based on two separate sets of obligations. In particular, the Act imposes on Internet service providers a list of "initial" and "technical" obligations[95] designed to monitor their subscribers' illegal activities on the Internet.[96] The "initial obligations" are essentially

[89] Dept. for Bus. Innovation & Skills, Digital Britain: Final Report, cm7650 (2009) available at https://www.gov.uk/government/uploads/system/uploads/attachment_data/file/228844/7650.pdf (last accessed 28 April 2016).

[90] See Anne Barron, Graduated response à l'Anglaise: online copyright infringement and the Digital Economy Act 2010, 3 Journal of Media Law (2011) 305–347.

[91] Communications Act, 2003, c. 21, available at http://www.legislation.gov.uk/ukpga/2003/21/pdfs/ukpga_20030021_en.pdf (last accessed 28 April 2016).

[92] See e.g. See Rebecca Giblin, Evaluating Graduated Response, 37 Colum. J.L. & Arts 147, 167 (2014); Dinusha Mendis, Digital Economy Act 2010: fighting a losing battle? Why the 'three strikes' law is not the answer to copyright law's latest challenge, 27 Int. Rev. of L., Comp. & Tech. 60 (2013); Nick Cusack, Is the Digital Economy Act 2010 the Most Effective and Proportionate Way to Reduce Online Piracy?, 32 Eur. Intell. Prop. Rev. 559 (2011); Benjamin Farrand, The Digital Economy Act 2010 – A Cause for Celebration, or A Cause for Concern?, 32 Eur. Intell. Prop. Rev. 536 (2010).

[93] See generally Lambert M. Surhone, Wash-up Period (2011);

[94] Id.

[95] See Digital Economy Act, Sections 3–16.

[96] Anne Barron, Graduated response à l'Anglaise: online copyright infringement and the Digital Economy Act 2010, cit., at 324.

two: the first one[97] includes the notification to subscribers – i.e. to the owners of the Internet account – of reported infringement. In this case, copyright holders are requested to send a "copyright infringement report" describing the alleged infringement and providing the appropriate evidence.[98] The second "initial obligation" consists in the creation of a "copyright infringement list" containing details of subscribers that have received a specified number of warning messages.[99] According to Section 4 of the Digital Economy Act, names must be recorded in a manner that does not enable any subscriber to be identified.[100] In case the goal of deterrence was not reached through the use of the "initial obligations", the Act also includes the application of 'technical measures' to prevent copyright infringement. According to the definition provided by the Act, a technical measure is "a measure that limits the speed or other capacity of the service provided to a subscriber; prevents a subscriber from using the service to gain access to particular material, or limits such use; suspends the service provided to a subscriber; or limits the service provided to a subscriber in another way".[101] Limiting the speed or the use of users' connection means to use information management systems. That automatically implies a close relationship between graduated response and digital information management, in particular when the "graduated response requires a restriction on Internet access as a sanction and where traffic management will be used to apply the restriction".[102] In other words, the "technical obligation" can include a temporary slowdown of internet connections, the restriction or denial of access to certain sites and also disconnection schemes for repeat infringers.

In order to implement the "initial" and the "technical" obligations, sections 5 and 6 of the Act foresee the approval of two pieces of secondary legislation: the first one is the "Initial Obligations Code" that is a prerequisite for the Internet Service Providers to send out warning letters to Internet users[103]; while the second one is a "Costs Order," which would define the distribution of the scheme's costs.[104] The competent authority to supervise the implementation of both documents is the British telecommunications regulator (OFCOM). The full implementation of the Digital Economy Act 2010 has not been completed so far, because Ofcom had not yet entirely implemented the requested secondary legislation. Ofcom issued its draft

---

[97] See Digital Economy Act, Sections 3

[98] Id.

[99] See Digital Economy Act, Sections 4. See also Dinusha Mendis, Digital Economy Act 2010: fighting a losing battle? Why the 'three strikes' law is not the answer to copyright law's latest challenge, cit., at 63.

[100] See Digital Economy Act, 2010, c. 24, § 124B (2)–(3).

[101] See Digital Economy Act, Section 9, 124G Obligations to limit internet access: assessment and preparation, cl. 3.

[102] See Monica Horten, Where Copyright Enforcement and Net Neutrality Collide – How the EU Telecoms Package Supports Two Corporate Political Agendas for the Internet, PIJIP Research Paper no. 17. American University Washington College of Law, Washington, DC (2010) at 14.

[103] See Digital Economy Act, 2010, c. 24,§§124D, 124E.

[104] See Digital Economy Act, 2010, c. 24, § 124 M; See also Rebecca Giblin, Evaluating Graduated Response, cit., at 167.

"Initial Obligations Code" in June 2012,[105] but – as a matter of fact – it did not come into effect.[106] The timetable for implementation has been pushed back several times and now it seems that the act have been shelved by the UK government introducing a new scheme, named "Voluntary Copyright Alert Programme".[107] According to such new self-regulatory mechanism, the British representatives of the creative industries and the internet service providers agreed to a new educational scheme based on alert messages – without any sanctions – sent to subscribers when their accounts are suspected to have been used to infringe copyright.[108]

3.3.2 Judicial Review and Criticism

The introduction of the graduated response mechanism in the United Kingdom has resulted in an intense debate surrounding the implications for society and internet users. As happened in France after the adoption of the HADOPI anti-piracy legislation, also the Digital Economy Act was subject to a judicial review. In particular, it has been challenged in UK Courts by two British Internet Service Providers – British Telecommunications (BT) and TalkTalk Telecom – on the grounds of its unbalanced response to online copyright infringement and its legality.[109] The dispute centered on whether the Act was compatible with the European Union's legal framework seeking clarification on a number of issues including whether some provisions were consistent with the right to privacy, data protection and the right to freedom expression, evaluating also the proportionality of the proposed measures. The Court was also required to consider the question on the costs imposed on

[105] Off. Comm., Notice of Ofcom's Proposal to Make by Order a Code for Regulating the Initial Obligations, OFCOM 3 (June 26, 2012), http://stakeholders.ofcom.org.uk/binaries/consultations/onlinenotice/summary/notice.pdf (last accessed 28 April 2016).

[106] See Rebecca Giblin, Evaluating Graduated Response, cit., at 172.

[107] See UK piracy warning letters delayed until 2015, BBC News – Technology, 6 June 2013, available at http://www.bbc.com/news/technology-22796723 (last accessed 28 April 2016); Tim Ingham, Digital Economy Act Delayed AGAIN, MusicWeek (Feb. 7, 2013), available at http://www.musicweek.com/news/read/digital-economy-act-delayed-again/053507 (last accessed 28 April 2016); Digital Economy Act copyright regime shelved by UK government. Out-Law.com (July 24, 2014). Available at http://www.out-law.com/en/articles/2014/july/digital-economy-act-copyright-regime-shelved-by-uk-government/ (last accessed 28 April 2016).

[108] See New Education Programme Launched to Combat Online Piracy, gov.uk (July 14, 2014). Available at https://www.gov.uk/government/news/new-education-programme-launched-to-combat-online-piracy (last accessed 28 April 2016).

[109] See Robin Mansell and W. Edward Steinmueller, Copyright Infringement Online: The Case of the Digital Economy Act Judicial Review in the United Kingdom, 15 New Media & Soc. 1312 (2013); Monica Horten, The Digital Economy Act in the Dock: A Proportionate Ruling?, 3 JIPITEC 81 (2012), available at http://www.jipitec.eu/issues/jipitec-3-1-2012/3323/horten.pdf (last accessed 28 April 2016).

Internet Service providers for processing of data associated with the implementation of the "Initial Obligations".[110]

The Plaintiffs argued that the Digital Economy Act breached users' rights to the protection of personal data in the light of respect for private life and fundamental rights to the protection of personal data, under the Charter of Fundamental Rights of the European Union[111] as well as the European Directive on Privacy and Electronic Communications.[112] Under the purposes and intentions of these pieces of legislation, the collection and use of users' information must be limited to specified and agreed purpose and must be protected by stringent security safeguards. In addition, Internet service providers should not be considered responsible for material sent and received over their network unless informed about violations of the law.[113] In analyzing the claim, the Court found that information acquired from IP addresses to identify users are sensitive personal data but it was also seen as reasonable for copyright holders to use this information to detect counterfeit and piracy infringements.[114]

In its final ruling, the UK High Court of Justice dismissed the case, finding that proceedings concerning a dispute over the balance of interests in copyright law are a matter of parliament and not of judiciary.[115] In particular, the court held that "Parliament, when considering measures such as the contested provisions, which could be expected to enhance copyright protection, is entitled to proceed on the basis that existing copyright law does strike a fair balance between the interests referred to."[116] The decision was then subsequently upheld by the Court of Appeal in March 2012.[117] The only argument the court considered relevant was about the costs imposed on Internet service providers arguing that the government could not compel an Internet service provider to pay a percentage of the case fees attached to the act.

Here the question at stake remains the issue of how to reconcile the protection of different fundamental rights: the right to property – which includes the rights linked

---

[110] See Robin Mansell and W. Edward Steinmueller, Copyright Infringement Online: The Case of the Digital Economy Act Judicial Review in the United Kingdom, cit., at 1314.

[111] Article 8 of the Charter of the European Union states, "Everyone has the right to the protection of personal data concerning him or her." Charter of Fundamental Rights of the European Union art. 8, Dec. 18, 2000, 2000 O.J. (C 364) 1. The content of this article has been also implemented in the EU Data Protection Directive, see Directive 95/46/EC, of the European Parliament and of the Council of 24 Oct. 1995 on the Protection of Individuals with Regard to the Processing of Personal Data and on the Free Movement of Such Data, 1995 O.J. (L 281) 31.

[112] See Directive 2002/58/EC of the European Parliament and of the Council of 12 July 2002 concerning the processing of personal data and the protection of privacy in the electronic communications sector O.J. 2002 (L 201) 37 (as amended by the Directive 2009/136/EC).

[113] See Monica Horten, The Digital Economy Act in the Dock: A Proportionate Ruling? cit.

[114] See The High Court of Justice Queen's Bench Division Administrative Court, case BT & Talk Talk v The Secretary of State for BIS, cit.

[115] See The High Court of Justice Queen's Bench Division Administrative Court, case BT & Talk Talk v The Secretary of State for BIS, No. CO/7354/2010, [2011] EWHC 1021 (admin).

[116] See id., at § 249.

[117] British Telecommunications Plc, R (on the application of) v. BPI (British Recorded Music Industry) Ltd & Ors [2012] EWCA Civ 232 (March 06, 2012).

to intellectual property – against the protection of other fundamental rights. The Charter of Fundamental Rights of the European Union explicitly states in Article 17 section 2 that "Intellectual property shall be protected".[118] There is also an extended jurisprudence confirming that intellectual property rights fall within the domain of the property guarantee.[119] The European Court of Justice as well as the European Court of Human Rights have frequently underlined the necessity of balancing conflicting fundamental rights taking also into account other rights protected by European law (such as the principle of proportionality). Unfortunately, the European Court of Justice has only recently started to refer to the EU Charter of Fundamental Rights in intellectual property cases.[120] Initial answers to these questions can be found in some recent decisions of the European Court of Justice such as the Case C-275/06.[121] In this circumstance, there were essentially two conflicting directives: the ones concerning privacy on electronic communications (2002/58)[122] and the ones on Copyright (2001/29).[123] In essence, the ruling was on whether – under European law – Internet service providers have any obligation to reveal the identities of their subscribers alleged to have committed copyright infringement.[124] The Court of Justice held that Member States must guarantee "a fair balance between the various fundamental rights" stressing the need to balance both copyright and the rights of consumers through the application of national laws. The Court also recognized that any obligation to disclose confidential or sensitive personal data must be consistent with Articles 7 and 8 of the EU Charter of Fundamental Rights. In particular, paragraph 53 of its judgment ruled that:

---

[118] See Charter of Fundamental Rights of the European Union art. 17(2), Dec. 7, 2000, 2000 O.J. (C 364) 1.

[119] For an extended analysis of the intellectual property case law of the European Court of Human Rights, see Lawrence R. Helfer, The new innovation frontier? Intellectual property and the European Court of Human Rights, 49 Harv Int'l L. J. 52 (2008); Ali Riza Coban, Protection of Property Rights Within The European Convention on Human Rights' (2004).

[120] See Christine Godt, Intellectual Property and European Fundamental Rights, cit., at 211

[121] Case C-275/06, Productores de Música de España (Promusicae) v. Telefónica de España SAU, 2008 E.C.R. I-271, at 55; the ruling was then confirmed by order in Case C-557/07, LSG-Gesellschaft zur Wahrnehmung von Leistungsschutzrechten GmbH v. Tele2 Telecommunication GmbH, 2009 E.C.R. I-1227. For an overview of the case, see Irini A. Stamatoudi, Data Protection, Secrecy of Communications and Copyright: Conflicts and Convergences – The Example of Promusicae v. Telefonica, in Copyright Enforcement and the Internet 199 (Irini A. Stamatoudi ed., 2010).

[122] Directive 2002/58/EC, of the European Parliament and of the Council of 12 July 2002 Concerning the Processing of Personal Data and the Protection of Privacy in the Electronic Communications Sector, 2002 O.J. (L 201) 37.

[123] Directive 2001/29/EC of the European Parliament and of the Council of 22 May 2001 on the harmonisation of certain aspects of copyright and related rights in the information society, 2001 O.J. (L 167) 10.

[124] See Xavier Groussot, Case C–275/06, Productores de Música de España (Promusicae) v. Telefónica de España SAU, Judgment of the Court (Grand Chamber) of 28 January 2008, 45 Common Mkt. L. Rev., 1745 (2008).

> It is clear, however, that Article 15(1) of Directive 2002/58 ends the list of the above exceptions with an express reference to Article 13(1) of Directive 95/46. That provision also authorizes the Member States to adopt legislative measures to restrict the obligation of confidentiality of personal data where that restriction is necessary inter alia for the protection of the rights and freedoms of others. As they do not specify the rights and freedoms concerned, those provisions of Article 15(1) of Directive 2002/58 must be interpreted as expressing the Community legislature's intention not to exclude from their scope the protection of the right to property or situations in which authors seek to obtain that protection in civil proceedings.

The fact remains that compliance with the stated obligations under the Digital Economy Act meant significant financial and resource burdens for service providers or other data owners and raised significant fundamental concerns regarding freedom of access to information and users' privacy.

3.4 Freedom of Expression and Freedom of Connection

Although it has been speculated that access to internet network services might play a fundamental role for individuals to exercise certain constitutional rights such as freedom of expression, it is quite hard to consider it as a fundamental right *per se*. The right to access to the Internet is a tricky subject that can be located at the intersection of the right to take part in cultural life and the right to benefit from scientific progress as expressed by the article 27 of the Universal Declaration of Human Rights[125] and article 15 of the International Covenant on Economic, Social and Cultural Rights.[126] Furthermore, other regional human rights treaties address the issue of freedom of expression.[127] Freedom of expression is constitutionally protected in many liberal and democratic countries. In many countries, the right to free expression is then increased by rights to freedom of information "providing citizens with a legal right to request and access government-held information and imposing duties on states to publish open records".[128] The right to free expression is also considered one of the cornerstones of the United Nations Declaration of Human Rights (Article 19)[129] and is recognized as a fundamental right under Article 10 of the

[125] Universal Declaration of Human Rights, G.A. Res. 217A (III), art. 27, U.N. Doc. A/810 (Dec. 10, 1948).

[126] International Covenant on Economic, Social, and Cultural Rights Art. 15(1)(a–c), Dec. 16, 1966, 933 U.N.T.S. 3 [hereinafter ICESCR].

[127] See See William H. Dutton et al., Freedom of Connection – Freedom of Expression: The Changing Legal and Regulatory Ecology Shaping the Internet 21 (2011) (mentioning the African Charter on Human and People's Rights, the American convention implemented by the Inter-American Court of Human Rights; the Charter of Fundamental Rights of the European Union).

[128] Id., at 10.

[129] Article 19, Universal Declaration of Human Rights, GA Res 217A (III), 10 December 1948, A/810 91.

European Convention on Human Rights[130] and Article 19 of the International Covenant on Civil and Political Rights.[131] The reason that justifies the protection of freedom of expression is to enable the self-expression of the speakers.[132] In any democracy it is essential that people can have access to a wide range of information in order to effectively participate in society.[133] The Internet has now become one of the principal means of exercising the right to freedom of expression and information[134] and certainly falls within the scope of all these provisions. In addition, the right to information is recognized in many regional and international treaties and conventions on human rights. In the majority of the cases it is included within the right to freedom of expression, which also embraces the right to seek, receive and impart information and ideas.

Here the point is to determine how to ensure that new media remain an unrestricted and public forum where the exercise of the freedom of opinion and expression can be achieved without undue limitations. In fact, while the right to freedom of expression is generally recognized by most liberal states and international bodies as a fundamental human right, there are currently few countries that have formally acknowledged the value of the right to freedom of connection.[135] However, the international debate about the right to internet access is progressively growing amongst governments, academics, internet activists, and civil liberties groups.[136]

It is however worth noting that there are already several decisions issued by national and international courts arguing that access to information is a human right.[137] In Europe, 40 of the 47 member states of the Council of Europe have adopted access to information laws,[138] and a total of 25 European constitutions recognize some kind of right of access to official documents or information and a total of 35 include the right of access to information or the "freedom of information".[139] Also the European Court of Human Rights acknowledged that there is a fundamen-

[130] Article 10, Convention for the Protection of Human Rights and Fundamental Freedoms 1950, ETS 5.

[131] Article 19, International Covenant on Civil and Political Rights, 16 December 1966, 999 UNTS 171.

[132] Wojciech Sadurski, Freedom of Speech and Its Limits, 18 (1999).

[133] See Herbert J. Gans, Democracy and the News 1 (2003) ("The country's democracy may belong directly or indirectly to its citizens, but the democratic process can only be truly meaningful if these citizens are informed.").

[134] See e.g. ECtHR 18 December 2012, Appl. no. 3111/10, Ahmed Yildirim v. Turkey.

[135] Id., at 22.

[136] See generally Wolfgang Benedek and Matthias C. Kettemann, Freedom of Expression and the Internet, cit.

[137] See e.g. Päivi Tiilikka, Access to Information as a Human Right in the Case Law of the European Court of Human Rights, 5 The Journal of Media Law 79 (2013).

[138] The first "right to information" law was enacted by Sweden in 1766 as part of a Freedom of the Press Act. See Anders R. Olsson, Access to Official Documents, in Human Rights and a Changing Media Landscape 77, 79 (COE 2011).

[139] A Guide for Journalists on how to Access Government Information (2010), available at http://www.osce.org/fom/67866?download=true (last accessed 28 April 2016).

tal right of access to information held by public bodies protected by Article 10 on Freedom of Expression of the European Convention on Human Rights.[140] On the contrary, the same Court has not yet had the opportunity of deciding whether a denial or a restriction of access to the Internet can be considered as a violation of the Convention. However, a similar complaint – based on the breach of the provisions of Article 10 – had already been submitted and a decision on the case is still pending.[141] At the same time, the European Court of Human Rights has recently had an occasion to specify the criteria for Internet censorship in the case of *Ahmet Yildirim v. Turkey*.[142] Here the plaintiff filed a claim against the decision of the Turkish authorities to block internet access to all the Google platform websites in order to prevent further access to a specific website, hosted by Google, accused to insulting the memory of Atatürk, the founding father of Turkish Republic. In its ruling, the court of Strasbourg decided that Turkey had violated Article 10 of the Convention by imposing an unbalanced restriction to Internet access failing to consider less restrictive alternatives.[143]

On this ground, one the most striking examples of these changing attitudes is probably provided by the mentioned decision of the French Constitutional Council affirming that the freedom to access "public online communication services" can be recognized in the French Republic's Declaration of the Rights of Man and of the Citizen of 1789.[144]

3.4.1 Bordering Communication Rights

Attempts to regulate and tackle the incredible growth of the information and communication platforms need to be based on a set of principles that are important foundations for any democratic institution. International human rights standards can represent such principles and should be used as a guiding framework for future

[140] ECtHR 14 April 2009, Appl. no. 37374/05, Társaság a Szabadságjogokért v. Hungary; ECHR 26 May 2009, no. 31475/05, Kenedi v. Hungary. In particular, the Court found that when the state has a monopoly over information of public interest in its possession, denying access to such information is equivalent to a form of censorship (Id. at ¶ 36).

[141] The case involves a Lithuanian prisoner who was denied the access to Internet in order to enroll at the University satisfying his right to education. As speculated by other scholars, the court's decision could be reasonably based on the argument that "the prison authorities have had a positive obligation to provide an Internet access even if limited". In fact, a prisoner's right to study and participate in society "deserves appreciation" also because it contributes to the rehabilitation and reintegration into the society. See ECtHR, Jankovskis v. Lithuania, Application No 21575/08. For a brief overview of the case, see Paul De Hert and Dariusz Kloza, Internet (access) as a new fundamental right. Inflating the current rights framework? 3, Eur. J. of L. and Tech. (2012).

[142] See ECtHR 18 December 2012, Appl. no. 3111/10, Ahmed Yildirim v. Turkey.

[143] Id. In particular, the Court considered that "whatever its legal basis, such a measure was bound to have an influence on the accessibility of the Internet and, accordingly, engaged the responsibility of the respondent State under Article 10". Id. at ¶ 53.

[144] Conseil constitutionnel (2009) Décision No. 2009-580 DC, du 10 Juin, 2009, cit.

government policies and actions.[145] These fundamental values are usually entrenched in bills of rights, treaties, or constitutions and assisted or safeguarded by specialized institutions.[146] Here the question is whether the establishment of new human rights standards (or the extension of existing) for the communication society is needed or not.[147] In this context, one of the most discussed aspects concern the interactions between current "informational developments" and the human rights provisions relevant to this new dimension. Fundamental rights that are relevant to current "informational developments" can be related to freedom of expression, protection of privacy, security of information infrastructures, and protection of intellectual property rights.[148]

The bidirectional interactions between digital communication technologies and society can have legal, political, economic, and ethical dimensions "for which the international community has established human rights standards."[149] The lack of implementation poses a major problem.[150] This situation has arisen precisely because "no effective mechanisms have been established to deal with all the obstacles that hamper the realization of human rights in the field of informational developments. Moreover, current human rights provisions focus exclusively on information and ignore communication."[151] At the time it emerged, the right of access to communication resources was considered a fundamental human right and, as such, an indispensable precondition for other human rights "because communication is intimately bound up with what it means to be human."[152] In recent literature on whether access to the Internet can be regarded as a fundamental right, it has been stressed that "recognizing access to the Internet could be considered the re-ignition of previous attempts to recognize a general right to communication."[153] Communication is a fundamental social process that enables information to be

[145] See Meryem Marzouki and Rikke Frank Jørgensen, Towards an Information and Communication Society Respectful of Civil and Political Rights, as well as Economic, Social and Cultural Rights of Citizens. Statement by the Human Rights in the Information Society (HRIS) Caucus for the WSIS intersessional meeting July 15–18, 2003, Paris, France, available at http://www.itu.int/dms_pub/itu-s/md/03/wsispc3/c/S03-WSISPC3-C-0115!!MSW-E.doc (last accessed 28 April 2016).

[146] Lorenzo Zucca, Constitutional Dilemmas: Conflicts of Fundamental Legal Rights in Europe and the USA 3 (2007).

[147] The question has been thoroughly discussed in literature, see e.g. Hamelink, Human Rights for the Information Society, cit.; Mike Godwin, Cyber Rights: Defending Free Speech in the Digital Age, 323 (rev. edn. 2003); Rikke Frank Jørgensen (ed.) Human Rights in the Global Information Society (2006).

[148] See Cees J. Hamelink, Communication Rights and the European Information Society, in The European Information Society: A Reality Check 121, 122 (Jan Servaes ed., 2003).

[149] Hamelink, Human Rights for the Information Society, cit. at 121.

[150] Id.

[151] Id.

[152] See Michael Traber, Communication as a Human Need and Human Right, 39 Religion and Soc., 202 (1992).

[153] See Alisdair A. Gillespie, Restricting Access to the Internet by Sex Offenders, 19 Int'l. J.L. & Info. Tech. 165, 167 (2011).

exchanged, founding the pillar and core of any democratic system.[154] The freedom to express opinions and receive and communicate information without interference or pressure by public authorities is an essential element of democracy. A concrete pluralism of information media, a broad access to information sources, and the full inclusion of all individuals in the informational processes achieves these objectives.[155] As soon as such a scenario has taken place, it remains necessary to settle a right to communication not simply related to content , but with a wider focus, including provisions imposing "an obligation on the State to facilitate communication between societies" and protecting "communication from arbitrary restrictions or control."[156]

The development of modern communication technologies has inflamed this discussion again. In particular, in the context of the information society, the right of access to all the means of expression – i.e., the right to communicate – is progressively coming into conflict with the government's desire to enforce security and monitor user behaviors.[157]

Even if communication rights have not been properly codified and do not have a clearly outlined legal status, legal scholars hold the view that all of the rights' essential elements have been settled in international treaties or conventions.[158] Communication rights are also defined as "those rights – codified in international and regional human rights instruments – that pertain to standards of performance with regard to the provision of information and the functioning of communication processes in society."[159] "Communication rights" is therefore a useful term that relates directly to a set of preexisting human rights.[160] The core of communication rights emanates directly from the specific provision of Article 19 of the Universal Declaration of Human Rights,[161] and it has since developed in the context of

---

[154] See Hamelink, Human Rights for the Information Society, cit.

[155] See Cees Hamelink & Julia Hoffmann, The State of The Right to Communicate, 7 Global Media Journal (2008) available at http://lass.purduecal.edu/cca/gmj/fa08/gmj-fa08-hamelink-hoffman.htm (last accessed 28 April 2016).

[156] See Alisdair A. Gillespie, Restricting Access to the Internet by Sex Offenders, cit. at 165.

[157] Seán Ó Siochrú et al., Assessing Communication Rights: A Handbook 13 (2005).

[158] See Hannu Nieminen, Towards Democratic Regulation of European Media and Communication in Media Freedom and Pluralism: Media Policy Challenges in the Enlarged Europe 3, 15 (Beata Klimkiewicz ed., 2010); Cess J. Hamelink & Julia Hoffmann, The state of the right to communicate, 7 Global Media Journal (2008) available at http://lass.purduecal.edu/cca/gmj/fa08/gmj-fa08-hamelink-hoffman.htm (last accessed 28 April 2016); Christopher Gregory Weeramantry, Access to Information: A New Human Right. The Right to Know, 4 Asian Y.B. Int'l L. 99 (1994). See also generally Desmond Fisher and L. S. Harms (eds), The Right to Communicate: A New Human Right (1983).

[159] See Cees Hamelink and Kaarle Nordestreng, Towards Democratic Media Governance, in Media Between Culture and Commerce 225, 234 (Els de Bens ed., 2007).

[160] Seán Ó Siochrú et al., Assessing Communication Rights: A Handbook 20 (2005).

[161] Universal Declaration of Human Rights, G.A. Res. 217A (III), art. 19, U.N. Doc. A/810 (Dec. 10, 1948).

subsequent features of the information environment.[162] Furthermore, the fundamental value of communication has been detailed in formal terms in numerous national and international statutes.[163] When referring to the exercise of the rights to communication or the freedom of expression, it is common to refer to the internationally recognized laws and standards for human rights set out in these official documents.[164] This recognized body of international law represents the means whereby individuals may realize their inherent dignity and personal autonomy. Ratification of an international human rights treaty obliges a state party to implement in its domestic law those rights and to guarantee that domestic legal remedies are available for any asserted breaches.[165] The problems come when society, culture, technology, and science change rapidly, producing many new concepts that make it difficult to keep up with new developments. This condition implies that the understanding of what human rights guarantee should change as well. In other words, information and communication rights relating to freedom of expression – embodied in the aforementioned international treaties – need to be reassessed under the new conditions of global interactive communication tools.[166]

In addition, freedom of expression is a right with a high level of specificity. It can actually be considered a *meta*-right because of its true potential to "[enable] enjoyment of so many other rights," such as political participation, cultural rights, and rights to assembly and association.[167] In this context, the Internet can be conceived as an instrument of ensuring the individual's ability to actively participate in democracy and civil and political life, without discrimination or limitation.

---

[162] See Cees Hamelink and Kaarle Nordestreng, Towards Democratic Media Governance, in Media Between Culture and Commerce 225, 234 (Els de Bens ed., 2007).

[163] See e.g., The European Convention for the Protection of Human Rights and Fundamental Freedoms, Nov. 4, 1950, 213 U.N.T.S. 221; The Charter of Fundamental Rights of the European Union, 2000 O.J. (C 364) 1.; The U.S. Const., Bill of Rights, 1791; The Declaration des Droits de l'Homme and du Citoyen de 1789 [Declaration of the Rights of Man and the Citizen] art. 11 (1789), available at http://www.legifrance.gouv.fr/Droit-francais/Constitution/Declaration-des-Droits-de-l-Homme-et-du-Citoyen-de-1789 (last accessed 28 April 2016). [hereinafter: Déclaration des Droits de l'Homme 1789]; The International Covenant on Civil and Political Rights, opened for signature Dec. 16, 1966, 999 U.N.T.S. 171; Declaration of Fundamental Principles Concerning the Contribution of the Mass Media to Strengthening Peace and International Understanding, to the Promotion of Human Rights, and to Countering Racialism, Apartheid and Incitement to War, UNESCO Doc. 20C/20 Rev. (Nov. 21, 1978).

[164] See supra note 163.

[165] See generally Lawrence Preuss, The Execution of Treaty Obligations Through Internal Law – System of the United States and of Some Other Countries, 45 Proc. Am. Soc. Int. Law 82 (1951).

[166] See Molly Land, Toward an International Law of the Internet, 54 Harv. Int'l L.J. 393, 407 (2013) (observing how the protection of individuals with regard to new media also requires an evolutive interpretation of human rights treaties).

[167] See Michael O'Flaherty, Freedom of Expression: Article 19 of the International Covenant on Civil and Political Rights and the Human Rights Committee's General Comment No. 34, 12 Hum. Rts. L. Rev. 627, 631 (2012) (observing how this nexus is not only limited to civil and political rights but could be extended easily to other rights).

From the above considerations, it is evident that the right to communicate is a multifaceted concept that can encompass a wide variety of rights and liberties and is subject to patterns of evolution like any kind of information media.[168] In fact, the right to communicate not only includes rights to information and expression; it also incorporates the right to inform and be informed, the right to active participation in the communication process using different kinds of media, the right of impartial access to information resources, and the right of cultural and individual privacy of communication.[169] In this respect, the current framework of information rights does not explicitly take into consideration the fact that modern communication technologies are essentially based on interactive processes.[170] For this reason, the right to communicate partly diverges from the traditional concepts of freedom of information.[171] The right to communicate emphasizes the process of communication rather than just the content .[172] Accordingly, communication rights relating to freedom of expression should be reconsidered in the context of global interactive communication technologies. This goal could be realized through the expansion or reinterpretation of existing rights, or through the recognition of a new specific right.[173]

Access to digital content and access to the physical networked infrastructure both seem to be covered by the existing legal umbrella.[174] In other words, "there is no need for concern about recognizing new rights" because international law already safeguards all the means necessary to exercise the right to freedom of expression,

---

[168] In its 2005 book, the campaign on Communication Rights in the Information Society (CRIS), grouped the family of rights that comprise communication rights within four pillars: Communicating in the Public Sphere; Communication Knowledge; Civil Rights in Communication; Cultural Rights in Communication. See Seán Ó Siochrú et al., Assessing Communication Rights: A Handbook 40 et seq. (2005).

[169] See Jim Richstad and Michael H. Anderson, Policy context for news and a 'new order', in Crisis in International News: Policies and Prospects 9, 26–27 (Jim Richstad & Michael H. Anderson eds., 1981). See also William J. McIver et al., The Internet and the right to communicate, 8 First Monday 12, (2003), available at http://firstmonday.org/htbin/cgiwrap/bin/ojs/index.php/fm/article/view/1102/1022 (last accessed 28 April 2016).

[170] Seán Ó Siochrú et al., Assessing Communication Rights: A Handbook 22, 23 (2005); Cees J. Hamelink, Human Rights for the Information Society, in Communicating in the Information Society 121, (Bruce Girard & Seán Ó Siochrú, eds., 2003) (observing how no human rights standard has been adopted to address communication as an interactive process).

[171] See William F. Birdsall, Web 2.0 as a social movement, 4 Webology (2007), available at http://www.webology.ir/2007/v4n2/a40.html (last accessed 28 April 2016).

[172] Id.

[173] See Seán Ó Siochrú et al., Assessing Communication Rights: A Handbook 20 (2005). See also Land, Toward an International Law of the Internet, cit.

[174] See UN. Human Rights Council 2011, cit., 1. (The report argues that the special and transformative nature of the Internet can not only facilitate individuals to exercise their right to freedom of opinion and expression, but also functioning as an activating element for the enjoyment of other human rights). See also See Special Rapporteur on the Promotion and Protection of the Right to Freedom of Opinion and Expression, Promotion and Protection of the Right to Freedom of Opinion and Expression, ¶ 61, U.N. Doc. A/66/290 (Aug. 10, 2011) (affirming that States have already a positive obligation to promote and facilitate the enjoyment of the right to freedom of expression and the means necessary to exercise this right, which includes the Internet).

and such means include the Internet.[175] In this perspective, access must be considered a key element, but access alone is not sufficient to guarantee the "full flowering of free expression".[176] As coherently highlighted in a recent analysis by the Center for Democracy and Technology "to maximize the Internet's potential to advance human rights, the Internet must remain free from centralized controls, open to the fullest range of content and services, and truly global"; in particular it should be necessary to establish rules to preserve Internet neutrality because this "is one way to prevent the imposition, by those in a position to control access, of structural inequalities that would distort this environment".[177]

3.5 Digital Media Pluralism and the Question of Internet Regulation

As extensively discussed, the Internet has become an essential tool for various life-related purposes, and it is an instrument necessary for the proper enjoyment of a series of rights – including the right to access knowledge and information and the right to communicate. This new paradigm also implies that all people should have access to the Internet at affordable conditions, and any restrictions should be strictly limited and proportionate. As a consequence, any regulatory and policy measures that affect the Internet and the content that flows over it should be consistent with basic rights and liberties of human beings. The unique nature of the access to networked services has therefore a direct connection with the concept of pluralism. In particular, the growing importance of digital media is challenging the traditional notion of pluralism. In this context, the question of access is thus paramount in order to guarantee an effective protection of freedom of expression and information. In any democratic society, the ability to participate in society (also online) can only be assured through media freedom and pluralism improved by the availability of an open, independent and impartial media outlet. Media freedom implies lack of constraint from government control[178] and involves editorial independence, the protection of journalists and an open public access to information sources. On the other hand, media pluralism implies the ability of individuals to satisfy their information needs providing public access "to the widest possible range of voices".[179] It also means that citizens must have access to a range of information sources and services

---

[175] See Land, Toward an International Law of the Internet, cit.

[176] See Andrew McDiarmid and Matthew Shears, The Importance of Internet Neutrality to Protecting Human Rights Online, in The Value of Network Neutrality for the Internet of Tomorrow, 26, 26 (Luca Belli and Primavera de Filippi eds., 2013).

[177] Id.

[178] See e.g. Fred S. Siebert et al., Four Theories of the Press: The Authoritarian, Libertarian, Social Responsibility, and Soviet Communist Concepts of What the Press Should Be and Do (1956); Lee Becker, et al., An evaluation of Press Freedom Indicators, 69 Int. Comm. Gazette, 5 (2007).

[179] See Kari Karppinen, Rethinking Media Pluralism 4 (2013).

included in the digital communication infrastructure. Given the importance of media freedom and pluralism as fundamental pillars of democracy in Europe[180] it is important to give attention to any possible violations and explore ways to support individuals who are faced with the challenge of these violations.[181]

Internet content governance is therefore posing provocative and fascinating regulatory issues directly related to the growing possibilities offered by computer-mediated communication. This debate is not simply "technical", but also political, legal and social since it involves sustainable and value-oriented solutions, but also – and more importantly – the awareness of the human rights dimension of Internet regulation.[182] The possible answers to these issues are at the center of the discussion concerning the regulation of digital content and communication technologies. In the current legal environment, the range of obstacles to the full realization of the new opportunities offered by digital media still presents a substantial challenge for a full realization of media pluralism.[183] This shows the need for appropriate policies, legal mechanisms and social practices, which can help to better secure the freedom and wealth of the digital information network. Here the point is to determine how to ensure that digital media remain an unrestricted and public forum where the exercise of the freedom of opinion and expression can be achieved without undue limitations.

In this framework, there is an ongoing debate among scholars, policymakers, and civil rights activists concerning the question of the access to the digital communication infrastructure at affordable conditions and without unwarranted government restrictions. A preliminary question concerns the determination of the meaning of "access," which encompasses different functional meanings: access to network infrastructure, access at the transport layer and access to digital content and applications. Generally speaking, when we talk about "Internet access," we refer to the access to network infrastructure, which essentially includes the other two functional meanings.

In order to position the analysis of the issues in the global context, an overview of the different legal approaches to this question is set out below. Indeed, legislation from other countries has come into effect or is proposed to cover much the same ground. In addition to France, Estonia and Finland have recognized that access to

---

[180] See Charter of Fundamental Rights of the European Union art. 11(2), 2000 O.J. (C 364) 1.

[181] On this, see generally Beata Klimkiewicz, Beata (ed.), Media Policy Challenges in the Enlarged Europe (2010).

[182] On this, see e.g. Molly Land, Protecting Rights Online. 34 Yale J. Int'l L. 1 (2009); Land, Toward an international law of the internet, cit.; Rolf H. Weber, Shaping Internet Governance: Regulatory Challenges 207 (2010); Nicola Lucchi, Internet content governance and human rights. 16 Vand. J. Ent. & Tech. L. 809 (2014); Oreste Pollicino and Graziella Romeo (eds), The Internet and Constitutional Law: The protection of fundamental rights and constitutional adjudication in Europe (2016).

[183] Council of Europe, Commissioner for Human Rights, Media Pluralism and Human Rights (2011), available at https://wcd.coe.int/ViewDoc.jsp?id=1881589(last accessed 28 April 2016).

the Internet is a right of particular importance for their citizens.[184] In Finland, Decree no. 732/2009 of the Ministry of Transport and Communications on the Minimum Rate of a Functional Internet Access as a Universal Service[185] simply sets provision on the minimum rate of a functional Internet access, but does not mention an explicit right of individuals to access the network infrastructure. More precisely, Finland has become the first country in the world to make broadband a legal right for every citizen, considering Internet a part of necessary universal services. That is to say that, according to the Finnish law, Internet is considered as staple commodities, and which every consumer and company must have access to.[186] This also means that Finnish telecommunication companies are required to provide all Finnish citizens with Internet connection that runs at speeds of at least 1 megabit per second. In this way Finland, is considered the world's first country to adopt laws guaranteeing broadband access.

In Estonia, according to Section 33 of the Public Information Act, "every person shall be afforded the opportunity to have free access to public information through the Internet in public libraries, pursuant to the procedure provided for in the Public Libraries Act (RT I 1998, 103, 1696; 2000, 92, 597)".[187] More recently, the Constitutional Court of Costa Rica explicitly declared Internet access to be a fundamental right following a decision of the Sala Constitucional de la Corte Suprema de Justicia de Costa Rica.[188]

On the question of "internet access", it is interesting to also mention the provocative proposal to introduce a new Article 21 *bis* in the Italian Constitution. In the Italian legal system, Article 21 of the Constitution stipulates that anyone has the right to freely express their thoughts in speech, writing, or any other form of com-

---

[184] See Doris Estelle Long, Three strikes and you are off the Internet, Chicago Daily Law Bulletin (Oct. 29, 2010), http://www.jmls.edu/news/Long%20CDLB%2010%2010%2029.pdf (last accessed 28 April 2016).

[185] Republic of Finland, Decree no. 732/2009 of the Ministry of Transport and Communications on the Minimum Rate of a Functional Internet Access as a Universal Service, 14 Oct. 2009. Online. Available at http://www.finlex.fi/en/laki/kaannokset/2009/en20090732.pdf (last accessed 28 April 2016).

[186] Finnish Communications Regulatory Authority, Internet is part of necessary universal services, available at http://www.viestintavirasto.fi/en/index/internet/laajakaista/yleispalvelu.html.

[187] Republic of Estonia, Public Information Act of Estonia, 15 Nov. 2000, as amended 2003. Online. Available at: http://www.legaltext.ee/text/en/X40095K4.htm (last accessed 28 April 2016).

[188] Sala Constitucional de la Corte Suprema de Justicia de Costa Rica (2010) Andres Oviedo Guzman v. Ministerio de Ambiente, Energia y Telecomunicaciones, Sentencia No. 2010-012790, 30 July, 2010, (Costa Rica). The relevant part of the decision reads: "[...] en los últimos veinte años en materia de tecnologías de la información y comunicación (TIC's) ha revolucionado el entorno social del ser humano. Sin temor a equívocos, puede afirmarse que estas tecnologías han impactado el modo en que el ser humano se comunica, facilitando la conexión entre personas e instituciones a nivel mundial y eliminando las barreras de espacio y tiempo. En este momento, el acceso a estas tecnologías se convierte en un instrumento básico para facilitar el ejercicio de derechos fundamentales como la participación democrática (democracia electrónica) y el control ciudadano, la educación, la libertad de expresión y pensamiento, el acceso a la información y los servicios públicos en línea, el derecho a relacionarse con los poderes públicos por medios electrónicos y la transparencia administrativa, entre otros".

munication. The proposal officially presented and proposed by Professor Stefano Rodotà and Wired magazine Italy, sparked a lively debate in Italy between supporters and opponents.[189] In December 2010 a group of members of the Italian Parliament submitted a Constitutional Amendment to introduce this new provision in the Italian constitution.[190] However, the prevailing opinion is that, in this context, there is no need for specific legislation of a constitutional provision designed to explicitly protect the right of access to the Internet. Such a principle, it is argued, can be easily derived from existing standards on freedom of speech or of expression through an interpretation of the same principle in a contemporary way. The practical example is given by the interpretive approach adopted by the French Constitutional Council in the evaluation of the HADOPI law.[191]

Finally, it is also worth mentioning the recent approval of another important piece of legislation in Brazil consisting of a real civil rights framework for the Internet.[192] With the adoption of the "Marco Civil da Internet", the Brazil government introduces specific principles, guarantees, rights and usability guidelines for the internet usage. In particular, the Brazilian law provides the recognition of net neutrality and sets out the duties and responsibilities of internet service providers according to their classification as internet connection providers or internet application providers.[193] It also introduces specific sanctions for violation of rules on the protection of personal data and private communications of Brazilian Internet users.[194] This piece of legislation bears all the marks of a bill of rights and it will obviously require further actions to make declared rights fully enforced. Nevertheless, it appears to be a very interesting and innovative way for creating a safer and more free Internet.[195]

All these recent regulatory initiatives strongly suggest that, in order to preserve the nature of Internet and the right to free speech, it is necessary to arrive at a

---

[189] Internet in Costituzione: Ecco il Disegno di Legge, Wired.it, available at http://mag.wired.it/news/disegno-legge-internet-diritto.html (last accessed 28 April 2016); See also Stefano Rodotà, Un Articolo 21-bis per Internet, Articolo21.info, available at http://www.articolo21.org/2183/notizia/un-articolo21bis-per-internet-.html (last accessed 28 April 2016); Id., Una Costituzione per Internet, 41 Politica del Diritto, 337 (2010).

[190] Senato della Repubblica Italiana, Disegno di Legge Costituzionale, 6 Dec. 2010, n. 2485. Available at: http://www.senato.it/service/PDF/PDFServer/BGT/00519114.pdf (last accessed 28 April 2016).

[191] See Decision 2009-580, cit.

[192] Lei 12.965/2014, de 24 de Abril de 2014, Diario Oficial Da Uniao [D.O.U.] de 4.24.2014 (Braz.), available at http://www.planalto.gov.br/ccivil_03/_ato2011-2014/2014/lei/l12965.htm (last accessed 28 April 2016).

[193] See Evy Marques and Marilia Bortolotto, Brazil's New Legal Framework Strengthens Internet Freedoms, 16 E-Commerce Law &Policy (2014); Monica Salgado, New Data Protection Law in Brazil, 14 Privacy & Data Protection 13 (2014).

[194] Id.

[195] On the topic of the Internet Bill of Rights, see Rikke Frank Jørgensen, An Internet Bill of Rights?, in Research Handbook on Governance of the Internet 353 (Ian Brown ed., 2013); Stefano Rodotà, Perchè Serve un Internet Bill of Rights, 347 Aut Aut, 52 (2010); Marco Bassini and Oreste Pollicino, Verso un internet bill of rights (2015).

democratic balance between the different parties involved in the communication activity. As Jack Balkin interestingly points out:

> The digital age makes increasingly clear that the point of the free speech principle is to promote not merely democracy, but something larger: a democratic culture. What is a democratic culture? It is a culture in which ordinary people can participate, both collectively and individually, in the creation and elaboration of cultural meanings that constitute them as individuals. Participation in culture is important to us as human beings because, in an important sense, we are made out of culture; we draw on culture to be the sort of individuals we are. [...] A democratic culture is not democratic because people get to vote on what culture should be like. It is democratic because people get to participate in the production of culture through mutual communication and mutual influence. Democratic culture invokes a participatory idea of democracy.[196]

It is also relevant to observe that even the United Nations has declared that "access to the Internet" is a right of all individuals not to be subjected to arbitrary restrictions. In particular, a recent report published by the UN Human Rights Council, declares that States should not institute any laws that prevent its citizens from accessing the Internet and other digital means of communication. It also underlines the fundamental nature of the Internet as a powerful communication medium given that "the Internet has become a key means by which individuals can exercise their right to freedom and expression." In addition, the document, prepared by the United Nations Special Rapporteur on the Promotion and Protection of the Right to Freedom of Opinion and Expression, states that

> Given that the Internet has become an indispensable tool for realizing a range of human rights, combating inequality, and accelerating development and human progress, ensuring universal access to the Internet should be a priority for all States. Each State should thus develop a concrete and effective policy, in consultation with individuals from all sections of society, including the private sector and relevant Government ministries, to make the Internet widely available, accessible and affordable to all segments of population.[197]

In this context, the advent of the Internet has placed in front of lawyers the very important question of how to interpret the right to participate in the virtual society,[198] in other words, how to assess, from a legal perspective, the optimal setting of the freedom to use digital communication tools both to provide information and obtain information. It is no longer just a mere exercise of the traditional right to freedom of thought and expression. It is increasingly perceived as a constitutional dilemma and the Courts and legislatures are more often asked to resolve this dispute concerning the evolutionary interpretation of law.

---

[196] See Jack M. Balkin, The Future of Free Expression in a Digital Age, 36 Pepperdine L. Rev. 427, 438 (2009). On the new approaches to freedom of expression in the digital environment, see also the essays in Thomas Gibbons, Thomas (ed.), Free Speech in the New Media (2009).

[197] See United Nations General Assembly, Human Rights Council (2011) Commission on Human Rights, Report by the Special Rapporteur on the Promotion and Protection of the Right to Freedom of Opinion and Expression, Frank La Rue, U.N. Doc. A/HRC/17/27 (16 May 2011). Available at http://www.unhchr.ch/Huridocda/Huridoca.nsf/0/16583a84ba1b3ae5802568 bd004e80f7/$FILE/G0010259.pdf (last accessed 28 April 2016).

[198] See Vittorio Frosini, L'orizzonte Giuridico dell'Internet, 16 Dir. Inf., 271–280 (2000).

3.6 Digital Media Regulations at the Bar

This chapter addressed the complexity of balancing copyright interests and fundamental constitutional rights in the sphere of increasingly pervasive information technologies. This perspective has been employed to read some recent controversies over Internet access control, including the French controversy over the constitutionality of the HADOPI law, the controversy over the constitutionality of the U.S. Communication Decency Act of 1996, and some other debated digital content reforms adopted in other countries. Using these cases as a paradigmatic example, we have reflected on the importance of fundamental rights as an institutional safeguard against the expansionary tendency of market powers. We have also seen the fundamental role played by Courts in shaping and adapting the frontiers of fundamental legal rights in the context of new technologies. In this regard, useful reference can be also made to some very recent decisions of the Court of Justice of the European Union as well as to decisions of the European Court of Human Rights. For example, in the joined Cases C-293/12 and C-594/12,[199] the Court of Justice held that the Directive on Data Retention seriously interferes with the right to respect for private life and the protection of personal data under articles 7, 8 and 11 of the EU Charter of Fundamental Rights. In another recent decision,[200] the Court argued that the fundamental rights recognized in articles 7 and 8 of the Charter of Fundamental Rights of the European Union are binding rules that take precedence over the economic interests of search engines' activities. For the first time, these decisions define precise limits on the action of private and public subjects operating in the digital space. At the same time, the European Court of Human Rights has recently had occasion to address also the question of blocking injunctions against the intermediaries whose websites and networks are used by third parties to commit infringements specifying the criteria for Internet censorship.[201]

All these elements can be considered together as levels of awareness that digital communication need to be adequately protected above the economic interests of few influential Internet players.

It is no coincidence that in democratic countries, tension over new media and its potential principally revolves around the demarcation of a boundary between information control and the free flow of information. Communication technologies are not only an instrument for free expression, but also a way to access culture and enhance education.[202] With this understanding in mind, it is easy to realize that decisions as the one reached by the French *Conseil constitutionnel* are of enormous importance not only on a national, but also on a transnational level. For the first

---

[199] See Joined Cases C-293/12 and C-594/12, Digital Rights Ireland and Seitlinger, ECJ, Preliminary Ruling of April 8, 2014.

[200] Google Spain SL & Google Inc v Agencia Española de Protección de Datos (AEPD) & Mario Costeja González (C-131/12) May 13, 2014, ECJ.

[201] See ECtHR 18 December 2012, Appl. no. 3111/10, Ahmed Yildirim v. Turkey.

[202] See Strowel, Internet Piracy as a Wake-up Call for Copyright Law Makers – Is the "Graduated Response" a Good Reply?, cit., at 82.

time, the constitutional principle of freedom of expression has been formally expanded to include Internet access as part of freedom of speech.[203] The rationale for this expansion is based on the idea that the right of each individual to access Internet network services is an essential ingredient in the freedom of communication and expression and its lack can negatively affect other rights.

In addition, we have also seen that 40 of the 47 member states of the Council of Europe have adopted access to information laws, and a total of 25 European constitutions recognize some kind of right of access to official documents or information, and a total of 35 include a specific right of access to information or the "freedom of information". Also the European Court of Human Rights acknowledged that there is a fundamental right of access to information held by public bodies protected by Article 10 on Freedom of Expression of the European Convention on Human Rights. There is finally a pending case before the European Court of Human Rights questioning if the denial or the restriction of access to the Internet can be considered as a violation of the Convention.[204]

The pervasiveness of digital platforms begs also the question of whether an elaboration of new rights and constitutional liberties is required, or whether existing legal instruments can be adjusted to meet the demands of a new reality.[205] This point opens the topical and recurrent debate about the necessity of a specific Internet bill of rights.[206] The recent approval of the "Marco Civil da Internet" (Internet Bill of

[203] In addition to France, Estonia and Finland have recognized that access to the Internet is a human right of their citzens. See Doris Estelle Long, Three strikes and you are off the Internet, Chicago Daily Law Bulletin, (Oct. 29, 2010), http://www.jmls.edu/news/Long%20CDLB%2010%20 10%2029.pdf (last accessed 28 April 2016). For the Finnish approach, see Decree no. 732/2009 of the Ministry of Transport and Communications on the Minimum Rate of a Functional Internet Access as a Universal Service, Oct. 14, 2009, available at http://www.finlex.fi/en/laki/kaannokset/2009/en20090732.pdf (last accessed 28 April 2016). In Estonia, according to § 33 of the Public Information Act, "[e]very person shall be afforded the opportunity to have free access to public information through the Internet in public libraries, pursuant to the procedure provided for in the Public Libraries Act (RT I 1998, 103, 1696; 2000, 92, 597)." See Public Information Act of Estonia, Nov. 15, 2000, as amended 2003, available at http://www.legaltext.ee/text/en/X40095K4.htm (last accessed 28 April 2016). More recently, the Constitutional Court of Costa Rica also declared internet access a fundamental right. See Andres Oviedo Guzman v. Ministerio de Ambiente, Energia y Telecomunicaciones, Sentencia No. 2010-012790, July 30, 2010, Sala Constitucional de la Corte Suprema de Justicia de Costa Rica [Constitutional Chamber of the Supreme Court] (Costa Rica).

[204] See ECtHR, Jankovskis v. Lithuania, Application No 21575/08, communicated on 27 September 2010.

[205] See Marco Cuniberti, La libertà della comunicazione nello scenario della convergenza, in Nuove tecnologie e libertà della comunicazione 6 (Marco Cuniberti ed., 2008).

[206] On this debate, see e.g. Stefano Rodotà, Perchè Serve un Internet Bill of Rights, 347 Aut Aut, 52 (2010); Francesca Musiani, The Internet Bill of Rights: A Way to Reconcile Natural Freedoms and Regulatory Needs?, 6 Scripted. A Journal of Law, Technology and Society, 504 (2009); Rikke Frank Jørgensen, An Internet Bill of Rights?, cit., at 353; Klint Finley, Inventor of Web is Right: We Need an Internet Bill of Rights, Wired (Mar. 12, 2014), available at http://www.wired.com/wiredenterprise/2014/03/web25/ (last accessed 28 April 2016); Lex Gill et al.,Towards Digital Constitutionalism? Mapping Attempts to Craft an Internet Bill of Rights, Berkman Center Research Publication No. 2015-15 (2015) available at http://ssrn.com/abstract=2687120.

Rights) in Brazil has forcefully brought again this question to the fore.[207] The idea behind an Internet bill of rights arises from the need to respond to the challenges posed by the evolution of communication technologies to legally protect the observance of the principles considered integral part of any democracy and linked to the evolution of digital media.[208] Do we really need a bill of rights for the Internet? Even if it is argued that we probably simply need to guarantee the full application of all the existing globally recognized international agreements and national statutory laws, it should however be said that an Internet bill of rights can be a useful instrument for "translating" into a one single document all the fundamental rights standards relevant to the online environment.[209] Recently there has been a new and increasing enthusiasm towards this idea to list some general and fundamental principles to be implemented by national legislation.[210] For example, a public consultation was launched in Italy on a draft declaration of Internet rights.[211] It consists of a list of articles, each identifying a specific right, such as the right to internet access, the respect for net neutrality and the right to be forgotten.[212] Several European countries were already taking steps in the same direction: the German Bundestag established a parliamentary standing commission on the digital agenda; the French Parliament established a brainstorming committee on law and freedoms in the digital age and the British House of Commons established a commission on digital democracy.[213]

A final consideration can be made about the possibility of implementing new control measures designed to prevent online copyright infringement at the international level. Can a "graduated response" or "three strikes" mechanism be effectively enforced? Are they effective instruments? A number of European countries have sought to implement legislation along the lines adopted in the Digital Economy Act or in the HADOPI Law. It is perhaps fair to say – as lucidly argued by Ian Lloyd – that success "has been limited and it is perhaps time to recognize that the model may be lawful but is flawed". It has been almost 4 years since the first implementation of the graduated response mechanism.[214] Similar legal tools now exist or are being considered in various jurisdictions.[215] Even if right-holders describe these mechanisms as effective, the evidence and case studies seem to indicate that such practices are not only ineffective, but they are also not entirely consistent with individual rights and freedoms.

---

[207] See supra § 3.7.

[208] See Stefano Rodotà, Perchè Serve un Internet Bill of Rights, cit.

[209] Rikke Frank Jørgensen, An Internet Bill of Rights? cit., at 353.

[210] See Lex Gill et al, Towards Digital Constitutionalism? Mapping Attempts to Craft an Internet Bill of Rights, Berkman Center Research Publication No. 2015-15 (2015) available at http://ssrn.com/abstract=2687120 (last accessed 28 April 2016).

[211] See Declaration of Internet Rights, available at http://nexa.polito.it/declaration-internet-rights (last accessed 28 April 2016).

[212] Daniela De Pasquale, Italy circulates proposed draft Declaration of Internet Rights, 16 E-commerce Law & Policy (December 2014).

[213] Id.

[214] See Rebecca Giblin, Evaluating Graduated Response, cit. at 147.

[215] Id.

Different considerations can be made regarding the consistency of the current regulatory framework. It is definitely a matter of fact that to ensure an effective functioning of copyright law under the changed technological conditions, it is necessary to move away from the traditional rigid system of regulation.[216] The creative and digital sector could potentially perform much better by introducing flexibilisation mechanisms especially with regard to the limitations and exceptions provisions.[217] Traditionally, scholarly attention has mainly focused on how to expand the copyright system and how to adapt it to the challenges posed by new technologies.[218] Now, however, it is time to realize the need to shift the attention to the question of how to guarantee an appropriate balance between competing rights and interests.[219] This is much more imperative when the conflict involves the curtailment of fundamental rights and freedoms. Fortunately this new approach is not only being pursued by certain legal scholars, but it is gaining ground even within European institutions and national governments. We definitely need to stop obsessing about copyright. The time has come to discuss the importance to create a new legal framework in which different models can develop organically, flexibly, in ways that support creators and consumers to get the best out of new technology.[220]

The challenge before us is to safeguard pluralism and media freedom by avoiding the risk of sacrificing them on the altar of copyright enforcement.

References

Alexy, Robert. 2002. *A theory of constitutional rights*. Oxford: Oxford University Press.

Allan, Trevor R. S. 2003. *Constitutional justice: A liberal theory of the rule of law*. Oxford/New York: Oxford University Press.

Bache, Ian, and Matthew Flinders (eds.). 2004. *Multi-level governance*. Oxford: Oxford University Press.

Balkin, Jack M. 2004. Digital speech and democratic culture: A theory of freedom of expression for the information society. *New York University Law Review* 79: 1.

Balkin, Jack M. 2009. The future of free expression in a digital age. *Pepperdine Law Review* 36: 427.

---

216 See Christophe Geiger, Flexibilising Copyright – Remedies to the Privatisation of Information by Copyright Law, 39 Int'l Rev. Intell. Prop. & Comp. L. 196 (2008); Id., The Future of Copyright in Europe: Striking a Fair Balance between Protection and Access to Information, 14 Intell. Prop. Q. 1 (2010). Commission of the European Communities, Copyright in the Knowledge Economy, Green Paper, (Brussels, 2008), at 5, available at http://ec.europa.eu/internal_market/copyright/docs/copyright-infso/greenpaper_en.pdf (last accessed 28 April 2016).

217 See Christophe Geiger, Promoting Creativity through Copyright Limitations: Reflections on the Concept of Exclusivity in Copyright Law, 12 Vand. J. Ent. & Tech. L. 515, 519 (2010).

218 Id. at 517.

219 Id.

220 Neelie Kroes, Who Feeds the Artist, speech held at the 2011 Forum d'Avignon, 19 November 2011, Avignon, France available at http://europa.eu/rapid/pressReleasesAction.do?reference=SPEECH/11/777&format=HTML&aged=0&language=EN&guiLanguage=en (last accessed 28 April 2016).

Barron, Anne. 2011. 'Graduated Response' à l'Anglaise: Online copyright infringement and the digital economy act 2010. *Journal of Media Law* 3: 305.

Bassini, Marco, and Pollicino, Oreste. 2015. *Verso un internet bill of rights*. Roma: Aracne.

Becker, Lee, et al. 2007. An evaluation of press freedom indicators. *International Communication Gazette* 69: 5.

Benedek, Wolfgang, and Matthias C. Kettemann. 2013. *Freedom of expression and the internet*. Strasbourg: Council of Europe.

Benkler, Yochai. 2006. *The wealth of networks: How social production transforms markets and freedom*. New Haven: Yale University Press.

Bimber, Bruce. 2003. *Information and American democracy: Technology in the evolution of political power*. Cambridge: Cambridge University Press.

Birdsall, William F. 2007. Web 2.0 as a social movement. *Webology* 4(2). Available at www.webology.ir/2007/v4n2/a40.html.

Bohman, James. 2004. Constitution making and democratic innovation: The European union and transnational governance. *European Journal of Political Theory* 3: 315.

Borghi, Maurizio, and Stavroula Karapapa. 2013. *Copyright and mass digitization*. Oxford: Oxford University Press.

Boubekeur, Iliana. 2009. De la «Loi Hadopi» à la «Loi Hadopi 2». Analyse de la décision du Conseil Constitutionnel 2009-580 DC et de ses Conséquences. *Revue Lamy Droit de l'Immatériel* 51: 107.

Brown, Ian. 2013. *Research handbook on governance of the internet*. Cheltenham: Edward Elgar Publishing.

Brown, Ian, and Christopher T. Marsden. 2013. *Regulating code. Good governance and better regulation in the information age*. Cambridge, MA: The Mit Press.

Bucci, Massimiano. 2006. *Scegliere il Mondo che Vogliamo. Cittadini, Politica e Tecnoscienza*. Bologna: Il Mulino.

Callon, Michel, Pierre Lascoumes, and Yannick Barthe. 2009. *Acting in an uncertain world: An essay on technical democracy*. Cambridge, MA: The MIT Press.

Cassese, Sabino. 1996. Poteri indipendenti, stati, relazioni ultrastatali. *Foro Italiano* 121: 8.

Chaltiel, Florence. 2009. La loi Hadopi devant le Conseil constitutionnel. *Les Petites Affiches* 125: 7.

Çoban, Ali Riza. 2004. *Protection of property rights within the European Convention on Human Rights*. Aldershot/Burlington: Ashgate.

Costes, Lionel. 2009. La loi "Creation et Internet" partiellement censurée par le Conseil constitutionnel. *Revue Lamy Droit de l'Immatériel* 50: 3.

Cuniberti, Marco. 2007. *Autorità indipendenti e libertà costituzionali*. Milano: Giuffrè.

Cuniberti, Marco. 2008. La libertà della comunicazione nello scenario della convergenza. In *Nuove tecnologie e libertà della comunicazione: profili costituzionali e pubblicistici 6*, ed. Marco Cuniberti. Milano: Giuffrè.

Cusack, Nick. 2011. Is the digital economy act 2010 the most effective and propor-tionate way to reduce online piracy? *European Intellectual Property Review* 32: 559.

De Hert, Paul and Kloza, Dariusz. 2012. Internet (access) as a new fundamental right. Inflating the current rights framework? *European Journal of Law and Technology* 3.

Derieux, Emmanuel, and Agnes Granchet. 2010. *Lutte contre le téléchargement illégale*. Paris: Lamy.

Drake, William J. 2010. *Internet governance: Creating opportunities for all*. New York: United Nations Department of Economic and Social Affairs.

Dutton, William H., et al. 2011. *Freedom of connection – Freedom of expression: The changing legal and regulatory ecology shaping the internet*. Paris: UNESCO Report.

Eko, Lyombe. 2010. American exceptionalism, the French exception, intellectual property law, and peer-to-peer file sharing on the internet. *Journal Marshall Review of Intellectual Property Law* 10: 95, 146–47.

Farrand, Benjamin. 2010. The digital economy act 2010 – A cause for celebration, or a cause for concern? *European Intellectual Property Review* 32: 536.

Feldman, Jean-Philippe. 2009. Le Conseil constitutionnel, la loi "Hadopi" et la présomption d'innocence. *La Semaine Juridique Edition Générale* 28: 25.

Finley, Klint. 2014. Inventor of web is right: We need an internet Bill of Rights. *Wired* (Mar. 12, 2014): Available at http://www.wired.com/wiredenterprise/2014/03/web25/.

Fisher, Desmond and L.S. Harms. (ed.). 1983. *The right to communicate: A new human right*. Dublin: Boole Press.

Frischmann, Brett M., et al. (eds.). 2014. *Governing knowledge commons*. Oxford: Oxford University Press.

Frosini, Vittorio. 2000. L'orizzonte Giuridico dell'Internet. *Il Diritto dell'informazione dell' Informatica* 16: 271.

Gans, Herbert J. 2003. *Democracy and the news*. Oxford/New York: Oxford University Press.

Gautron, Allan. 2009. La "réponse graduée" (à nouveau) épinglée par le Conseil constitutionnel. Ou la délicate adéquation des moyens aux fins. *Revue Lamy Droit de l'Immatériel* 51: 63.

Geiger, Christophe. 2006. 'Constitutionalising' intellectual property Law? The influence of fundamental rights on intellectual property in the European union. *International Review of Intellectual Property and Competition Law* 37: 371.

Geiger, Christophe. 2008. Flexibilising copyright – remedies to the privatisation of information by copyright law. *International Review of Intellectual Property and Competition Law* 39: 196.

Geiger, Christophe. 2010. Promoting creativity through copyright limitations: Reflections on the concept of exclusivity in copyright law. *Vanderbilt Journal of Entertainment & Technology Law* 12: 515.

Geiger, Christophe. 2010. The future of copyright in Europe: striking a fair balance between protection and access to information. *Intellectual Property Quarterly* 14: 1.

Geiger, Christophe (ed.). 2014. *Research handbook on human rights and intellectual property*. Cheltenham: Edward Elgar Publishing.

Gibbons, Thomas (ed.). 2009. *Free speech in the new media*. Burlington: Ashgate.

Giblin, Rebecca. 2014. Evaluating graduate response. *Columbia Journal of Law & the Arts* 37: 147.

Gill, Lex et al. 2015. Towards digital constitutionalism? Mapping attempts to craft an internet bill of rights, Berkman Center Research Publication No. 2015-15. Available at http://ssrn.com/abstract=2687120.

Gillespie, Alisdair A. 2011. Restricting access to the internet by sex offenders. *International Journal of Law and Information Technology* 19: 165.

Godt, Christine. 2014. Intellectual property and European fundamental rights. In *Constitutionalization of European private law: XXII/2 211*, ed. Hans Micklitz. Oxford: Oxford University Press.

Godwin, Mike. 2003. *Cyber rights: Defending free speech in the digital age* (rev. edn.). Cambridge, MA: MIT Press.

Goggin, L. Malcom. 1986. *Governing science and technology in a democracy*. Knoxville: University of Tennessee.

Gorz, Andre. 2003. *L'immateriel: connaissance, valeur et capital*. Paris: Editions Galilée.

Griffiths, Jonathan, and Uma Suthersanen (eds.). 2008. *Copyright and free speech. Comparative and international analyses*. Oxford: Oxford University Press.

Grote, Rainer. 1999. Rule of law, rechtsstaat and etat de droit. In *Constitutionalism, universalism and democracy: a comparative analysis: the German contributions to the Fifth World Congress of the International Association of Constitutional Law*, ed. Christian Starck. Baden-Baden: Nomos.

Groussot, Xavier. 2008. Case C–275/06, productores de música de España (Pro-musicae) v. Telefónica de España SAU, judgment of the Court (Grand Chamber) of 28 January 2008. *Common Market Law Review* 45: 1745.

Guibault, Lucie. 2002. *Copyright limitations and contracts. An analysis of the contractual overridability of limitations on copyright*. The Hague: Kluwer Law.

Hamelink, Cees. 2003. Human rights for the information society. In *Communicating in the information society*, ed. Bruce Girard and Seán Ó. Siochrú. Geneva: United Nations Research Institute for Social Development.

Hamelink, Cees. 2003. Communication rights and the European information society. In *The European information society: a reality check 121*, ed. Jan Servaes. Bristol/Portland: Intellect.

Hamelink, Cees and Nordestreng, Kaarle. 2007. Towards democratic media governance. In *Media between culture and commerce 225*, ed. Els de Bens. Bristol/Chicago: Intellect Books.
Hamelink, Cess, and Julia Hoffmann. 2008. The State of The Right to Communicate. *Global Media Journal* 7: 13.
Hanssen, F. Andrew. 2000. Independent courts and administrative agencies: An empirical analysis of the states. *Journal of Law, Economics, and Organization* 16: 534.
Haunss, Sebastian. 2013. *Conflicts in the knowledge society. The contentious politics of intellectual property*. Cambridge: Cambridge University Press.
Helfer, Lawrence R. 2008. The new innovation frontier? Intellectual property and the European Court of Human Rights. *Harvard International Law Journal* 49: 52.
Helfer, Laurence R., and Graeme W. Austin. 2011. *Human rights and intellectual property: Mapping the global interface*. Cambridge: Cambridge University Press.
Horten, Monica. 2010. *Where copyright enforcement and net neutrality collide – How the EU telecoms package supports two corporate political agendas for the internet*. PIJIP Research Paper, Series no. 17. Washington, DC: American University Washington College of Law.
Horten, Monica. 2012. The digital economy Act in the dock: A proportionate ruling? *Journal of Intellectual Property, Information Technology and Electronic Commerce Law* 3: 81. Available at http://www.jipitec.eu/issues/jipitec-3-1-2012/3323/horten.pdf.
Jasanoff, Sheila. 2011. Constitutional moments in governing science and technology. *Science and Engineering Ethics* 17: 621.
Rikke Frank, Jørgensen (ed.). 2006. *Human rights in the global information society*. Cambridge, MA: MIT Press.
Jørgensen, Rikke Frank. 2013. An internet Bill of Rights? In *Research handbook on governance of the internet* 353, ed. Ian Brown. Cheltenham, UK: Edward Elgar.
Karppinen, Kari. 2013. *Rethinking media pluralism*. New York: Fordham University Press.
Keller, Perry. 2011. *European and international media Law. Liberal democracy, trade and the new media*. Oxford: Oxford University Press.
Klimkiewicz, Beata (ed.). 2010. *Media freedom and pluralism: Media policy challenges in the enlarged Europe*. Budapest/New York: Central European University Press.
Land, Molly. 2009. Protecting Rights Online. *Yale Journal of International Law* 34: 1.
Land, Molly. 2013. Toward an international law of the internet. *Harvard International Law Journal* 54: 393.
Leenes, Ronald E., et al. (eds.). 2008. *Constitutional rights and new technologies. A comparative study*. The Hague: T.M.C. Asser Press.
Long, Doris Estelle. 2010. Three strikes and you are off the Internet. *Chicago Daily Law Bulletin* (Oct. 29, 2010). Available at http://www.jmls.edu/news/Long%20CDLB%2010%2010%2029.pdf.
Lucchi, Nicola. 2014. Internet content governance & human rights. *Vanderbilt Journal of Entertainment and Technology Law* 16: 809.
Macrez, Frank, and Gossa. 2009. Julien Surveillance et Sécurisation: Ce que l'Hadopi Rate. À Propos de la «Petite loi» «Création et Internet». *Revue Lamy Dr Immatériel* 50: 79.
Mansell, Robin, and Edward Steinmueller. 2013. Copyright infringement online: The case of the digital economy Act judicial review in the United Kingdom. *Media & Society* 15: 1312.
Marino, Laure. 2009. *Le droit d'accès à Internet, nouveau droit fondamental*. 20 Recueil Dalloz 20:2045.
Marques, Evy, and Marilia Bortolotto. 2014. Brazil's new legal framework strengthens internet freedoms. *E-Commerce Law and Policy* 16(5).
Mazziotti, Giuseppe. 2013. *Copyright in the EU digital single market*. Brussels: Center for European Policy Studies.
McDiarmid, Andrew, and Matthew Shears. 2013. The importance of internet neutrality to protecting human rights online. In *The value of network neutrality for the internet of tomorrow*, ed. Luca Belli and Primavera de Filippi, 26. 1st Report of the Dynamic Coalition on Network Neutrality.

McIver, William J. et al. 2003. The Internet and the right to communicate. *First Monday* 8: 12. Available at http://firstmonday.org/htbin/cgiwrap/bin/ojs/index.php/fm/article/view/1102/1022.

Mendis, Dinusha. 2013. Digital economy act 2010: Fighting a losing battle? Why the 'Three Strikes' law is not the answer to copyright law's latest challenge. *International Review of Law Computers & Technology* 27: 60.

Meyer, Trisha. 2012. Graduated response in France: The clash of copyright and the internet. *Journal of Information Policy* 2: 107.

Montesquieu, Charles de Secondat. 1949. *De l'esprit des lois* (Gonzague Truc ed.). Paris: Editions Garnier.

Murphy, Thérèse (ed.). 2009. *New technologies and human rights*. Oxford: Oxford University Press.

Murray, Andrew. 2010. *Information technology law*. Oxford: Oxford University Press.

Musiani, Francesca. 2009. The Internet Bill of Rights: A way to reconcile natural freedoms and regulatory needs? *Scripted. A Journal of Law, Technology and Society* 6: 504.

Nieminen, Hannu. 2010. Towards Democratic Regulation of European Media and Communication. In *Media freedom and pluralism: media policy challenges in the enlarged Europe* 3, ed. Beata Klimkiewicz. Budapest/New York: Central European University Press.

OECD. 2009. *The Role of Digital Identity Management in the Internet Economy*. (Available at http://www.oecd.org/dataoecd/55/48/43091476.pdf).

OECD. 2007. *At a Crossroads: "Personhood" and Digital Identity in the Information Society*. Available at http://www.oecd.org/dataoecd/31/6/40204773.doc.

O'Flaherty, Michael. 2012. Freedom of Expression: Article 19 of the International Covenant on Civil and Political Rights and the Human Rights Committee's General Comment No. 34. *Human Rights Law Review* 12: 627.

Olsson, Anders R. 2011. Access to official documents. In *Human rights and a changing media landscape* 77. Strasbourg: Council of Europe Publications.

Ó Siochrú, Seán. 2005. *Assessing communication rights: A handbook*. London: World Association for Christian Communication.

Pestre, Dominique. 2008. Challenges for the democratic management of technoscience: Governance, participation and the political today. *Science as Culture* 17: 101.

Pollicino, Oreste, and Graziella Romeo (eds.). 2016. *The Internet and Constitutional Law: The protection of fundamental rights and constitutional adjudication in Europe*. London/New York: Routledge.

Rambaud, Sandrine. 2010. Illegal internet file downloads under hadopi 1 and 2. *Cyberspace Law* 15: 10.

Reidenberg, Joel R. 1998. Lex informatica: The formulation of information policy rules through technology. *Texas Law Review* 76: 553.

Richstad, Jim and Anderson, Michael H. 1981. Policy context for news and a 'new order'. In *Crisis in international news: policies and prospects*, eds. Jim Richstad and Michael H. Anderson 9. New York: Columbia University Press.

Rodotà, Stefano. 2010. Perchè serve un internet Bill of Rights. *Aut Aut* 347: 52.

Romero Moreno, Felipe. 2013. Unblocking the digital economy Act 2010; Human rights issues in the UK. *International Review of Law Computers & Technology* 27: 18.

Rousseau, Dominique. 2009. Hado-pirate la Constitution: le Conseil sanctionne! *Revue Lamy Droit de l'Immatériel* 51: 103.

Rubin, Edward L. 1984. Due Process and the Administrative State. *California Law Review* 72: 1044.

Sadurski, Wojciech. 2002. Judicial review and the protection of constitutional rights. *Oxford Journal of Legal Studies* 22: 275.

Salgado, Monica. 2014. New data protection law in Brazil. *Privacy and Data Protection* 14: 13.

Siebert, Fred S., et al. 1956. *Four theories of the press: the authoritarian, libertarian, social responsibility, and soviet communist concepts of what the press should be and Do*. Urbana: University of Illinois Press.

Sinjela, Mpazi (ed.). 2007. *Human rights and intellectual property rights: Tensions and convergences*. Leiden: Martinus Nijhoff Publishers.

Sroussi, Grégory. 2009. *The Hadopi Law and France's controversial fight against piracy*, Technology, Media & Telecommunications News. London: Linklaters.

Stamatoudi, Irini A. (ed.). 2010. *Copyright enforcement and the internet*. Alphen aan den Rijn: Wolters Kluwer.

Strowel, Alain. 2009. Internet piracy as a wake-up call for copyright Law makers – Is the "Graduated Response" a good reply? *World Intellectual Property Organization Journal* 1: 75.

Sunrise Winter, Jenifer. 2012. Is internet access a human right? Linking information and communication technology development with global human rights' efforts. *Global Studies Journal* 5: 35.

Surhone, Lambert M. 2011. *Wash-up period*. Betascript Publishing.

Symonides, Janusz (ed.). 2000. *Human concept and standards*. Burlington: Ashgate Rights.

Szuskin, Laurent, et al. 2009. Beyond counterfeiting: The expanding battle against online piracy. *Intellectual Property and Technology Law Journal* 21(11): 1.

Tiilikka, Päivi. 2013. Access to information as a human right in the case law of the European Court of Human Rights. *The Journal of Media Law* 5: 79.

Torremans, Paul L.C. (ed.). 2008. *Intellectual property and human rights*. Alphen aan den Rijn: Kluwer Law International.

Traber, Michael. 1992. Communication as a human need and human right. *Religion and Society* 39: 202.

Ullrich, Hans. 2004. Harmony and unity of European intellectual property protection. In *Intellectual property in the new millennium*, vol. 20, ed. David Vaver and Lionel Bently. New York: Cambridge University Press.

Van Eecke, Patrick, and Maarten Truyens. 2009. Recent events in EU internet law. *Journal of Internet Law* 13: 21.

Varju, Marton. 2014. *European union human rights law: The dynamics of interpretation and context*. Cheltenham: Edward Elgar Publishing.

Verpeaux, Michel. 2009. La liberté de communication avant tout. La censure de la loi Hadopi 1 par le Conseil constitutionnel. *La Semaine Juridique Édition Générale* 39: 45.

Verpeaux, Michel. 2010. *Freedom of expression*. Strasbourg: Council of Europe Publishing.

Vila De Azevedo Cunha, Mario, et al. (eds.). 2013. *New technologies and human rights*. Farnham: Ashgate Publishing.

Walterscheid, Edward C. 1998. *To promote the progress of useful arts: American patent law and administration 1787–1836*. Littleton: Fred B Rothman & Co.

Warren, Kenneth F. 2004. *Administrative law in the political system* (4th ed.). Boulder: Westview Press.

Weber, Rolf H. 2010. *Shaping internet governance: Regulatory challenges*, 2010. Berlin: Springer.

Weeramantry, Christopher Gregory (ed.). 1990. *Human rights and scientific and technological development*. Tokyo: United Nations University Press.

Weeramantry, Christopher Gregory. 1994. Access to information: A new human right. The right to know. *Asian Yearbook of International Law* 4: 99.

Yu, Peter K. 2010. The graduated response. *Florida Law Review* 62: 1373.

Yu, Peter. 2012. Intellectual property and human rights in the nonmultilateral era. *Florida Law Review* 64: 1045.

Zolo, Danilo. 2007. The rule of law: A critical reappraisal. In *The rule of law: History, theory and criticism*. eds. Pietro Costa and Danilo Zolo. Dordrecht: Springer.

Zucca, Lorenzo. 2007. *Constitutional dilemmas: Conflicts of fundamental legal rights in Europe and the USA*. Oxford/New York: Oxford University Press.

Chapter 4
Rights Claims in the Biosciences

Abstract The chapter explores the rapidly growing field of biotechnologies, namely those technologies involved in the collection, processing, distribution, and use of biological information. In particular, it examines the debate around the progressive commodification of genetic resources and connected genetic information realized by means of intellectual property rights and other forms of management of essential public knowledge assets. The chapter includes the necessary background for understanding how biotechnology and genetic engineering works.

The extremely fast technological progress in the field of biosciences has brought about new legislative and judicial attempts to restructure the global regulatory regime especially with regard to intellectual property rights, trying to balance the interests of both rights-holders and consumers. As argued by some social science scholars, the biotech industry has shown a remarkable expansion since the early 1960s.[1] It now constitutes a significant source of innovation in the life sciences as well as a major actor of the global knowledge economy.[2] But the great success of the biotechnology industry was not achieved spontaneously. On the contrary, it was the result of several influencing and favorable government policies toward the sector in combination with a liberalized regime for the governance of biomedical research.[3] The problem is that these favorable conditions are now in the process of turning unfavorable. In addition, as it has already been authoritatively observed by Sheila Jasanoff in *Reframing Rights*, the increased availability of genetic testing and gene therapy can also have serious implications for genetic information privacy and discrimination "through the creation of a genetically stigmatized class with reduced

[1] See Steven Vallas, Daniel Lee Kleinman, and Diana Biscotti, Political Structures and the Making of U.S. Biotechnology, in State of Innovation: The U.S. Government's Role in Technology Development 57 (Fred Block and Matthew Keller eds.) (2011).

[2] Id.

[3] Id.

N. Lucchi, *The Impact of Science and Technology on the Rights of the Individual*, Law, Governance and Technology Series 26,
DOI 10.1007/978-3-319-30439-7_4

access to employment, health care, insurance, and other social goods".[4] It was also noticed that debates and "concerns about the need to regulate the disruptive potential of biological manipulation were apparent almost from the moment when genetic engineering became feasible in the 1970s."[5] The emergence of all these concerns has also shed light on the problem of how to regulate the use, access, distribution and appropriation of individual genetic information as well as the information content of DNA.

The purpose of this part of the book is to scrutinize the debate over the private appropriation of natural and genetic resources increasingly considered as simple elements of the market framework. Discussion focuses on the dispute around the progressive commodification of genetic resources and connected genetic information realized by means of intellectual property rights and other forms of management of knowledge. The chapter considers a select number of cases that demonstrate the effectiveness of human rights arguments to inform and interpret intellectual property rights in a manner that would enhance individual and collective rights without undermining innovation. These cases – in addition to having a national impact – can also create persuasive legal precedent that courts in other countries can look to when evaluating similar questions.

Considering this scenario, the relevant question being asked is how to balance property rights and other fundamental liberties such as freedom of scientific research, human dignity, right to health and public safety.[6] In particular, tensions between patent law and fundamental legal rights more often concern rights such as the right to health or the right to food.[7] However, also freedom of expression concerns are increasingly coming under the scrutiny of courts, regulators and scholars in several different disciplines.[8] Biotechnology is a frontline area of research and its developments can imply several potential risks for the environment, human health and other legitimate uses of shared, public natural resources. In addition, one of the possible detrimental consequences of strong and broad intellectual property rights in these areas might also be to create undue limitations on the freedom of expression.[9]

---

[4] See Sheila Jasanoff, Rewriting Life, Reframing Rights, in Reframing Rights: Bioconstitutionalism and the Genetic Age 1, 9 (Sheila Jasanoff ed., 2011) (citing Lee M. Silver, Remaking Eden: How Genetic Engineering and Cloning Will Transform The American Family 283–84 (1998)).

[5] Id., at 6.

[6] See Amedeo Santosuosso et al., What Constitutional Protection for Freedom of Scientific Research, 33 Journal of Medical Ethics 342, 343 (2007).

[7] Laurence R. Helfer and Graeme W. Austin, Human Rights and Intellectual Property: Mapping the Global Interface, 312 (2011). On the point, see also Jamie Crook, Balancing Intellectual Property Protection with the Human right to Health, 23 Berkeley J. Int'l L. 524 (2005); Geertrui van Overwalle, Patents in Agricultural Biotechnology and the Right to Food (UN Report 2009).

[8] See generally Intellectual Property and Human Rights, En. ed., (Paul L.C. Torremans ed. 2008); Intellectual Property and Human Rights. A Paradox (Willem Grosheide ed., 2010); Biotech Innovations & Fundamental Rights (R. Bin, et al. eds., 2011).

[9] Helfer and Austin, Human Rights and Intellectual Property: Mapping the Global Interface, cit. at 314.

4.1 Introduction

Biotechnology is not a single technology, but a wide suite of techniques for managing genetic information resulting from a number of different disciplines.[10] Using biotechnology, genetic information can be easily manipulated, modified and controlled almost to the point of excluding others from making research or new contributions in the same area of investigation. In this context, one of the most challenging questions we need to address at the outset is whether scientific innovations and their patent protection can really undermine civil liberties and human rights. The argument used by the American Civil Liberties Union (ACLU) in the course of a recent controversy over human gene patents,[11] is that "gene patenting is a civil liberties issue because gene patents undermine the free exchange of information and scientific freedom, bodily integrity" and the health of individuals.[12] In other words, the patent system, by granting exclusive rights to gene patent holders,

> in essence gives those patent holders complete control over those genes and the information contained with them. This interferes with a person's right to know about his or her own genetic makeup and scientists' rights to study the human genome and develop new genetic tests. Granting a monopoly on fundamental pieces of knowledge infringes on First Amendment rights, which protect the freedom of scientific inquiry and the free exchange of knowledge and ideas.[13]

The debate over the impact of patents on fundamental rights and freedoms of individuals was brought to the fore by a recent and landmark U.S. lawsuit. Here a group of plaintiffs, headed by the American Civil Liberties Union, challenged the patentability of gene sequences linked to human health emphasizing potential tensions, not only with the human right to health, but also between patents and freedom of speech.[14]

The responsibility of any free and democratic society is to find a balance between the conflicting arguments of the parties involved in this delicate debate, in order to determine which legal approach is more likely to strike a satisfactory compromise. In this context, the purpose of the following pages will be to identify ways to reconcile economic interests with the indispensable freedom of scientific research and an efficient growth of various innovative products and solutions in the field of healthcare and biodiversity conservation.

---

[10] Sandra Braman, Biotechnology and Communication: The Meta-Technologies of Information X (2004).

[11] Assoc. for Molecular Pathology v US Patent and Trademark Office, 702F Supp 2d 181 (SDNY 2010).

[12] See American Civil Liberties Union, Legal Challenge to Human Gene Patents 1, 5 (May 27, 2009), available at http://www.aclu.org/pdfs/freespeech/brca_qanda.pdf (last accessed 28 April 2016).

[13] Id.

[14] See Association for Molecular Pathology v. US Patent and Trademark Office, 702F Supp 2d 181 (S.D.N.Y 2010). Additional information on the case and on plaintiffs' arguments are available at http://www.aclu.org/free-speech/brca-genes-and-patents (last accessed 28 April 2016).

4.2 Biosciences and the New Frontiers of Rights

Biotechnology is a recognized research area that has increasingly advanced into new technologies and modern practices raising several legal, ethical and regulatory issues. Broadly speaking, biotechnology comprises "any technique that uses living organisms or substances from those organisms to make or modify a product, to improve plants or animals, or to develop microorganisms for specific uses".[15] The term "biotechnology" was first coined in 1919 by the Hungarian scientist Károly Ereky. According to his definition, the term meant "all lines of work by which products are produced from raw materials by the aid of living things."[16] Modern biotechnology can be better defined according to the OECD definition as "the application of science and technology to living organisms as well as parts, products and models thereof, to alter living or nonliving materials for the production of knowledge, goods and services."[17]

Nowadays, biotechnology – especially genetics and genomics – has also had substantial influence on the development of new pharmaceuticals and the methods used to study, predict and treat human disease.[18] At the same time, this revolution has also resulted in a new set of challenges for lawyers. In particular, the revolutionary speed of biotech innovations has had a significant impact on the protection of collective and individual rights. Fundamental rights provide a framework within which the justifications of limitations and restrictions to biotechnology innovations and research results have to be assessed. The legal regulation of scientific research and scientific investigations impact more and more directly on the freedom of research and therapies as well as on the broad diffusion of knowledge commons. As was observed by Hess and Ostrom – modern biology has been, de facto, turned into an "information science".[19] Closely related is also the much debated question of the technological manipulation of life and the boundary of scientific knowledge with regard to the topical question of genetic invention patents and their effects on access to scientific information and health care opportunities. Today, interests antagonistic to freedom of scientific research and access to scientific knowledge are emerging distinctly, requiring a careful balance between public and private domain. As

[15] Office of Technology Assessment, U.S. Congress, Biotechnology in a Global Economy, app. f, at 268 (1991).

[16] Karl Ereky, Biotechnologie der Fleisch-, Fett-, und Milcherzeugung im landwirtschaftlichen Grossbetriebe: für naturwissenschaftlich gebildete Landwirte verfasst (1919); see also Bernard R. Glick & Jack J. Pasternak, Molecular Biotechnology: Principles and Applications of Recombinant DNA 5–7 (3d ed. 2003).

[17] Organization for Economic Co-operation and Development, Scientific, Industrial and Health Applications of Biotechnology, Statistical Definition of Biotechnology (2001).

[18] See e.g. John Travis, Frontiers in Biotechnology: Biotech Gets a Grip on Cell Adhesion, 260 Science 906 (1993); See David B. Resnik, Owning the Genome: A Moral Analysis of DNA Patenting 7 (2004).

[19] See Charlotte Hess and Elinor Ostrom, A Framework for Analysing the Microbiological Commons, 58 International Social Science Journal 335, 336 (2006).

pointed out by other scholars, "the uniquely open-ended nature of biomedical science requires a reassessment of how patenting affects biotech research and innovation."[20] A few questions may arise in this regard: how do technology and science affect law, and vice versa? Do new biotech innovations affect constitutional rights? How does the protection of genetic inventions change the conditions of access to knowledge? What are the public interests considered to be so deserving of protection that they effectively counter-limit rights already embedded with the architecture of many constitutional systems? Within this framework, we will try to put forward a critical analysis of the problems concerning the protection of individual rights in the field of biotechnologies. Drawing on expertise from different disciplines, the investigation comprises the analysis of some recent court cases and their potential impact on regulatory change. Looking at different aspects of the legal and scientific issues involved in the regulation of biological resources, we also investigate the impact that modern DNA-related technology can have on the production and dissemination of knowledge. In particular the focus of attention will be on the question of access of genetic information, the protection of natural collective resources, the freedom of scientific research in genetics and the role of biotech patents. Finally we will try to highlight challenges, opportunities and contradictions regarding the revolutionary technological developments in the life sciences and their consequences for the protection of individual and collective rights.

4.2.1 *Access to Scientific Knowledge and DNA-Based Inventions*

During the last few years we have witnessed incredible progress and achievements of DNA related technologies. This kind of research has undoubtedly had a fundamental role in many scientific and medical advances. However, biotech research is extremely costly and requires many years to develop and implement effective products or diagnostic tools.[21] Often governments must provide grants for research and offer intellectual legal protection to original creative inventions in order to safeguard the investment in research and development of biotech industries.[22] In particular, the patent system is the instrument properly configured to allow innovators to recoup their investment in research and development.[23] For this reason, it is also

[20] See David E. Adelman, A Fallacy of the Commons in Biotech Patent Policy, 20 Berkeley Tech. L.J. 985, 956(2005).

[21] See David B. Resnik, Owning the Genome: A Moral Analysis of DNA Patenting 67 (2004).

[22] Id., at 81. See also Arti K. Rai, Knowledge Commons: The Case of Biopharmaceutical Industry, 12 First Monday, Jun. 4, 2007, http://firstmonday.org/issue12_6/rai/index.html (last accessed 28 April 2016).

[23] U.S. Dep't of Justice & Fed. Trade Comm'n, The Evolving IP Marketplace: Aligning Patent Notice and Remedies With Competition 1 (2011) [hereinafter 2011 Marketplace Report], available at http://www.ftc.gov/os/2011/03/110307patentreport.pdf (last accessed 28 April 2016). See

considered to play a critical role in the growth of the biotechnology industry and in promoting innovation across biotech industries.[24]

However, along with some benefits, there are also adverse effects associated to some forms of DNA-based inventions. For example, people begin to wonder whether it might be acceptable to patent part of the human body. Similar questions and concerns are common not only among the general public but also among scientist and legal scholars.[25] These debates are highly intense and contentious, and focus much more on ideological, ethical and economic arguments than on factual considerations. Now here the whole question is whether a gene can be considered simply a chemical compound or rather an information-carrying structure which, even if manipulated or isolated, maintains the quality or state of being produced by nature. On this argument, there are essentially two schools of thoughts.[26] There are those who believe that DNA or genetic material is simply a combination of various chemicals.[27] Adopting this chemical approach, patent protection on genes can be allowed.[28]

Dominique Guellec and Bruno van Pottelsberghe de la Potterie, The Economics of the European Patent System: IP Policy for Innovation and Competition 123 (2007) (noting that patents constitute the main asset for biotech industries).

[24] Id. See also Rebecca Eisemberg, Patenting the Human Genome, 39 Emory L.J. 721, 736 (1990). In this article, the author argues that "A rule that limits the first inventor to process patent protection may consequently provide a considerably weaker incentive to invest in developing the first means of making an obviously desirable product than a rule that offers product patent protection. Whether the process patent alone would provide an adequate incentive to induce the necessary inventive effort is ultimately an empirical question with an answer that varies from one invention to the next. Yet the first inventor to develop a means of making an obviously desirable but previously unobtainable product has made an invention that the public may well consider worth the price of a patent monopoly on the product itself. Rather than risk losing valuable inventions by offering too little patent protection in the form of what may eventually become an unenforceable process patent, it may be preferable to offer the higher bounty of a product patent at the outset". Id., at 736.

[25] See e.g. Mark J. Hanson, Patenting Genes and Life: Improper Commodification?, in Who Owns Life? 161, 168–173 (David Magnus et al. eds., 2002); John M. Conley & Roberte Makowski, Back to the Future: Rethinking the Product of Nature Doctrine as a Barrier to Biotechnology Patents (Part II), 85 J. Pat. & Trademark Off. Soc'y 371, 393 (2003) (offering a critical analysis of the so called "isolation and purification doctrine"); David B. Resnik, Owning the Genome: A Moral Analysis of DNA Patenting 73–83 (2004) (illustrating various arguments against patents on DNA-related inventions); Matthew Albright, Profits Pending: How Life Patents Represent the Biggest Swindle of the 21st Century 140–43 (2004) (criticizing gene on patents and on living organisms); David Koepsell, Who Owns You?: The Corporate Gold-Rush To Patent Your Genes 156 (2009) (arguing that gene patents should be forbidden).

[26] Resnik, Owning the Genome: A Moral Analysis of DNA Patenting, cit. at 73–74; Dominique Guellec & Bruno van Pottelsberghe de la Potterie, The Economics of the European Patent System: IP Policy for Innovation and Competition 122 (2007) (observing how opponents to the patentability of genetic stuff claim that living material is a discovery, not an invention, as it exists in nature before being identified by researchers).

[27] See Kathrin Garforth, Life as Chemistry or Life as Biology? An Ethic of Patents on Genetically Modified Organisms", in Patenting Lives: Life Patents, Culture and Development 27,46 (Johanna Gibson ed., 2008).

[28] Id., at 42. The authors notes that: "The legal fiction that assumes away the complexity of life to allow the patenting of organisms also suggests that these organisms are fungible with the other types of things patented under the statute". Id., at 35.

As we will discuss later, this is exactly the current approach adopted by the American, European and Japanese patent authorities.[29] The patentability of genetic information[30] was gradually recognized by a number of decisions of courts including the US Supreme Court in 1980[31] and the board of appeal of the European Patent Office[32] in the 1990s.[33] On the other hand, there are those whose view of the DNA and genetic information is strictly connected to the judicially created doctrine of "product of nature".[34] According to this theory, anything made or intervened by human hand is patentable, but things that exist in nature as it is, are not patentable.[35] However, opponents to DNA patents argue that all DNA is a non-patentable product of nature with no difference between transformation and isolation in the wild or in the lab.[36] Moreover, opponents of gene patents also argue that this praxis can violate the freedom of speech, expression and communication – common to all Western liberal democracies – because patents have the potential to restrict the individual's freedom of expression.[37] Looking over both arguments, it is evident that genes are different from other things that are patented,

> because they are not inventions, and other researchers cannot invent alternative genes. Even if patent-holders publish information about the genes they have identified, there is nothing to invent around – the genetic material contained in the gene is the information. Because this information is the foundation for future diagnostic tests and potential treatments, tying

---

[29] See Melanie J. Howlett & Andrew F. Christie, An Analysis of the Approach of the European, Japanese and United States Patent Offices to Patenting Partial DNA Sequences (ESTs), 34 Int'l Rev. Indus. Prop. & Copyright L. 581 (2003); Jasmine C. Chambers, Patent Eligibility of Biotechnological Inventions in the United States, Europe, and Japan: How Much Patent Policy is Public Policy?, 34 Geo. Wash. Int'l L. Rev. 223 (2002); Leslie G. Restaino et al., Patenting DNA-Related Inventions in the European Union, United States and Japan: A Trilateral Approach or a Study in Contrast?, 2003 UCLA J.L. & Tech. 2 (2003). See also Anne Reese & Brian Opeskin, Current Issues in Gene Patenting, in Disputes and Dilemmas in Health Law 277, 280 (Ian Freckelton & Kerry Petersen eds.) (2006).

[30] Here the term includes: genetic materials and gene fragments, such as expressed sequence tags (ESTs) and single nucleotide polymorphisms (SNPs).

[31] Diamond v Chakrabarty 447 US 303 (1980).

[32] Decision T 19/90-3.3.2, 1990 O.J. Eur. Pat. Off. 476.

[33] See Dominique Guellec & Bruno van Pottelsberghe de la Potterie, The Economics of the European Patent System: IP Policy for Innovation and Competition 123 (2007).

[34] Gottschalk v. Benson, 409 U.S. 63, 67 (1972). But see contra Dan L. Burk, Edifying Thoughts of a Patent Watcher: The Nature of DNA, 60 UCLA Law Rev. Discourse 92 (2013) (arguing that – even if the informational content of the molecules is effectively the same – in reality molecules exist in different dimensions and therefore the configurations of the molecules in a human cell as opposed to in the laboratory can be certainly quite different). Id. at 101.

[35] For a discussion on this topic, see John M. Conley, Gene Patents and the Product of Nature Doctrine, 84 Chi.-Kent L. Rev. 109, 113 (2009); John M. Conley & Roberte Makowski, Back to the Future: Rethinking the Product of Nature Doctrine as a Barrier to Biotechnology Patents, 85 J. Pat. & Trademark Off. Soc'y 301, 303–04 (2003);

[36] See Resnik, Owning the Genome: A Moral Analysis of DNA Patenting, cit. at 74; see also generally Vandana Shiva, Biopiracy: The Plunder of Nature and Knowledge (1997).

[37] Complaint at 19, 22–25, Ass'n for Molecular Pathology v. U.S. Patent & Trademark Office, 702F. Supp. 2d 181 (S.D.N.Y. 2010) (No. 09 Civ. 4515).

it up as intellectual property can inhibit, rather than stimulate, advances in biomedical research.[38]

In the following pages we readdresses this controversial debate in the light of evidence provided by recent court cases investigating how law could better regulate research activity, with a particular consideration to human based research and the dissemination of linked knowledge.

4.3 Nucleic Acids, Genetic Codes and Stem Cells: Uses and Potential Market Value

Before closely examining the problems concerning the protection of individual rights in the field of biosciences, it is necessary to briefly describe some of the basic elements and concepts of molecular biology, biochemistry, genetics and cell biology. The purpose is to provide, in a simplified and schematic format, all the fundamental scientific information needed to understand the complex working of the living system, the functional utilization of the DNA, the proper nature of its activities as well as other key terms.

The genetic code is the set of all the information that regulate metabolism and the composition and the structure of the cell.[39] Cells are the basic unit of all living organisms.[40] They are the smallest elements of plants and animals that are able of carrying on all the necessary life processes.[41] Every single cell "is a complex collection of molecules with many different activities all integrated to form a functioning, self-assembling, self-regulating, and self-reproducing biological unit."[42] DNA (*Deoxyribonucleic acid*) is the molecule that is the repository of genetic information in all organisms.[43] The information coded by DNA determines the structure and function of the all cell. RNA (Ribonucleic acid) is a molecule – chemically similar to DNA – which contains instructions for making proteins (see Fig. 4.1).[44] DNA and RNA are – in fact – nucleic acids present in the cells of any organism. These two nucleic acids – DNA and RNA – have different tasks. The DNA is the molecule that

---

[38] See American Civil Liberties Union, Legal Challenge to Human Gene Patents 8 (May 27, 2009), available at http://www.aclu.org/pdfs/freespeech/brca _qanda.pdf (last accessed 28 April 2016).

[39] See D. L. Hartl, Genetics: Analysis Of Genes And Genomes, 8th ed., Burlington, Jones & Bartlett Learning, 2012, 23; B. Alberts et al., Molecular Biology of the Cell, 5th ed., New York, Garland Publishing, 2008, 2.; W. Klug, M. Cummings et al., Essentials of Genetics, 12th ed., Upper Saddle River, 2012, 5.

[40] See Office of Technology Assessment, U.S. Congress, Ownership of Human Tissues and Cells, New Developments in Biotechnology 31 (1987).

[41] Id.

[42] Id.

[43] Id. at 157.

[44] See B. Alberts et al., Molecular Biology of the Cell, cit., 333 seq.

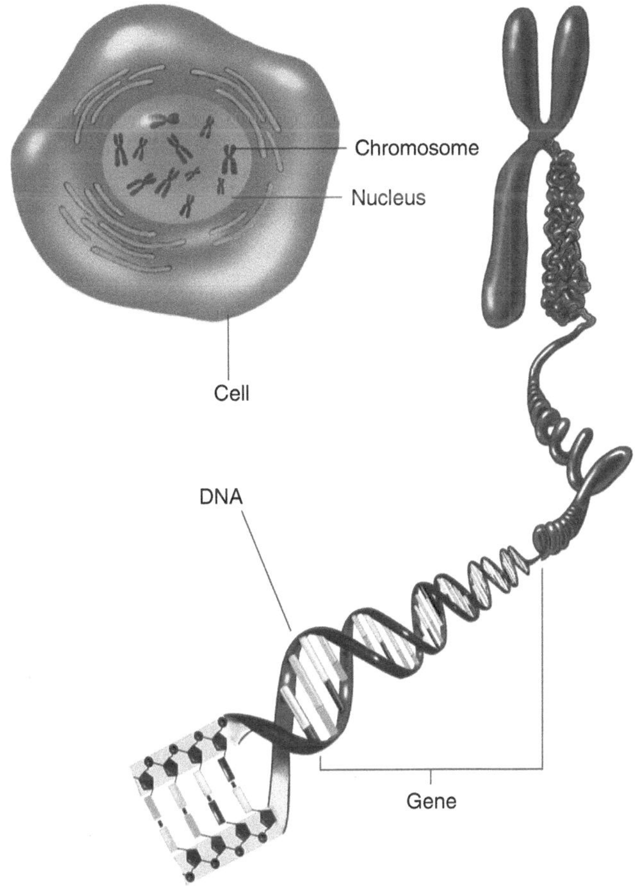

Fig. 4.1 The long, stringy DNA that makes up genes is spooled within chromosomes inside the nucleus of a cell (Images Credit: National Institute of General Medical Sciences. http://images.nigms.nih.gov/index.cfm?event=viewDetail&imageID=2540)

contains the genetic material and which then functions as information carrier.[45] At the same time, the RNA is a molecule involved in the transfer of information from DNA to protein.[46] The DNA is then composed of genes, which are – essentially – traits or fragments of DNA containing the genetic information necessary to build a specific protein. The genes are organized in chromosomes and it is through the chromosomes that the genetic information is transmitted. A gene is then normally segmented in stretches of DNA that encode protein fragments.[47] It is estimated that the chromosomes present in human cells contain about 30,000 genes: this set of

[45] See W. Klug, M. Cummings, Essential of Genetics, cit., 4.

[46] See Bruce Alberts et al., Molecular Biology of the Cell, cit., 333 seq.

[47] Id.

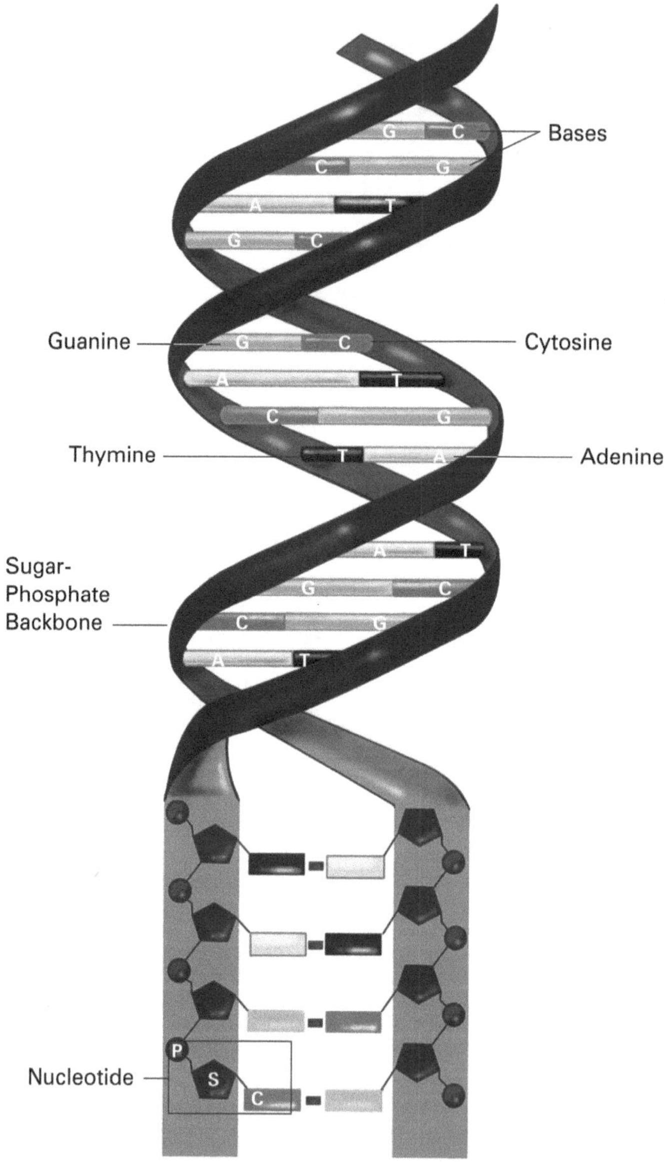

Fig. 4.2 DNA consists of two long, twisted chains made up of nucleotides. Each nucleotide contains one base, one phosphate molecule, and the sugar molecule deoxyribose. The bases in DNA nucleotides are adenine, thymine, cytosine, and guanine (Images Credit: National Institute of General Medical Sciences. http://images.nigms.nih.gov/index.cfm?event=viewDetail&imageID=2542)

genes is known as the human genome.[48] These genes contain the biological information needed to synthesize some proteins.[49] Each gene contains a specific information encoded in a precise sequence composed of four nucleotide bases (adenine, thymine, cytosine and guanine) which combine in pairs to communicate with the cell and instruct its development (see Fig. 4.2).[50]

The combination of these molecules contains the information for synthesizing all the 20 amino acids of which proteins are composed.[51] The classic textbook by Bruce Alberts et al., *Molecular Biology of the Cell*, defines the term "genome" as "the totality of genetic information belonging to a cell or an organism; in particular the DNA that carries this information". Alberts also explains that the genome of a cell

> contains in its DNA sequence the information to make many thousands of different protein and RNA molecules. A cell typically expresses only a fraction of its genes, and the different types of cells in multicellular organisms arise because different sets of genes are expressed. Moreover cells can change the pattern of genes they express in response to changes in their environment, such as signals from other cells.[52]

The Human Genome Project has mapped and sequenced all these genes.[53] This project was a milestone in the field of DNA sequencing, opening the way for the genomic revolution and allowing a direct and ready access to DNA sequence information. The idea of determining the complete nucleotide sequence of the human genome cropped up in the United States inspired by some influential members of the scientific community, high academic scientists-administrators and officials in federal agencies.[54] The Human Genome Project has been considered by some observers as a very open project firmly "entrenched in a highly convergent innovation network" in which "a scientific, technical and market pole are strongly aligned and coordinated",[55] but also a process which involved "assembling a heterogeneous collection of people and objects, without regard for the walls of laboratories."[56] In fact, the original goal of the project was not to sequence and patent as many genes as possible just for profit, but rather to provide a free public database for scientists worldwide working on the study of human genetic variation.

---

[48] See W. Klug, M. Cummings, Essential of Genetics, cit., 4.

[49] See D. L. Hartl, Genetics: Analysis Of Genes And Genomes, cit., 22.

[50] See W. Klug, M. Cummings, Essential of Genetics, cit., 5.; B. Alberts et al., Molecular Biology of the Cell, cit., 4.

[51] See B. Alberts et al., Molecular Biology of the Cell, cit., 5.

[52] See Id. at 415.

[53] See W. Klug, M. Cummings, Essential of Genetics, cit., 7–8. See also Vittorio Ancarani, The Politics of the Human Genome Project. Do Institutions Matter? 6 (2008).

[54] See Vittorio Ancarani, The Politics of the Human Genome Project. Do Institutions Matter? 6 (2008).

[55] See Dirk Stemerding, How to Deal with the Implications of Human Genome Research? On the Bounds of a Politics of Regulation", in Ethics of Human Genome Analysis. European Perspectives 217, 224 (Hille Haker, Richard Hearn and Klaus Steigleder eds.) (1993).

[56] See Brian Balmer, Managing Mapping in the Human Genome Project," 26 Soc. Stu. Sci. 531, 532 (1996).

Today, the use of automated techniques has made it possible to determine the complete DNA sequences of the genome of different organisms.[57] Taken together, "these techniques for analyzing and manipulating DNA" have made it easy to "identify, isolate, and sequence genes from any organism of interest. Related technologies allow scientists to produce the protein products of these genes in the large quantities needed for detailed analyses of their structure and function, as well as for medical purposes."[58] The current scientific and commercial scenario is that "with numerous genome sequences available, the exploration of gene function often begins with a DNA sequence." From the commercial perspective, the challenge is therefore to translate sequence into function.[59] Assigning biochemical and cellular functions to the thousands of uncharacterized gene products discovered by genome sequencing means to able to predict gene functions and identify genes associated with specific disease.[60]

These conditions explain why one of the most significant aspects of the human genome sequence information is the illustration "of how DNA sequence variation leads to differences among individuals (phenotypic variation) and guidance on how to apply that information for the betterment of humankind."[61] In fact, the results of this project allowed the definition of genetic testing and have also created the opportunity to develop various gene therapies. Through a simple blood sample or a tissue sample, it is now possible to determine the specific aspects of the genetic status of an individual who – in combination with the mapping of the human genome – can allow physicians to determine the presence of defective genes that predispose to a given disease.[62] These findings have opened the door to so-called personalized or precision medicine. This term refers to the personalization of medical care based on the individual characteristics of each patient and the related genes.[63] Similar analytical techniques assess the genetic predisposition to diseases and are essentially based on the connection between genetic heritage and susceptibility to a particular organ

[57] See Bruce Alberts et al., Molecular Biology of the Cell 551 (5d ed. 2005).

[58] Id, at 553.

[59] Id.

[60] See Gregory A. Petsko, Dagmar Ringe, Protein Structure and Function 129 (2004).

[61] See National Research Council Committee on Intellectual Property Rights in Genomic and Protein Research and Innovation, Reaping the Benefits of Genomic and Proteomic Research: Intellectual Property Rights, Innovation, and Public Health 37 (Stephen A. Merrill & Anne-Marie Mazza eds., 2005).

[62] See Richard A. Spinello, Privacy, Property Rights and Gene Ownership in Bioinformatics Law 77, 78 (Jorge L. Contreras and A. James Cuticchia eds., 2013).

[63] See Committee on a Framework for Development a New Taxonomy of Disease; National Research Council, Toward Precision Medicine: Building a Knowledge Network for Biomedical Research and a New Taxonomy of Disease, Washington DC, The National Academies Press, 2011, 125. For a more detailed study on the normative implications in the area of personalized medicine see also Shubba Ghosh, Identity, Invention and the Culture of Personalized Medicine Patenting (2012).

system dysfunction.[64] From a practical point of view, personalized medicine applies new methods of molecular analysis to improve the patient's condition. According to some optimistic approaches, personalized medicine would promise a series of medical breakthroughs that can increase the quality of clinical care. In this context, it lays the foundations for a new paradigm of health care; in particular, it is considered a priority for both the biotechnology and the pharmaceuticals industry (both involved in the development of new diagnostic and therapeutic instruments).[65]

Another important notion concerns the definition and the status of the human embryo, in particular for patent purposes. A proper answer to the question of how to define human life can play a key role in the field of stem cell research and regenerative medicine. This concept has proven to be extremely difficult to define. The legal and moral status of the human embryo is also a feature that can differ between countries, and many legal systems do not provide any definitions. For example, the Court of Justice of the European Union explained the concept of human embryo in 2011, in regard to the meaning of Article 6(2)(c) of the Biotech Directive, which prohibits the patents on uses of human embryos for industrial or commercial purposes.[66] In that decision, the Court ruled that processes and products involving human embryonic stem cells are not patentable in Europe.[67]

Finally, the last key concept that needs to be introduced is that of stem cells. A stem cell is an unspecialized cell "that has a unique capacity to renew itself and to give rise to specialized cell types"[68] Although most cells of our body – such as heart cells or skin cells – are generally devoted to serving a precise function, "a stem cell is uncommitted and remains uncommitted, until it receives a signal to develop into a specialized cell."[69] Their marked capacity to promote and stimulate proliferation,

---

[64] For an overview on the recent Developments and Critical Issues in this field, see the two reports issued by the United States Department of Health and Human Services: Dep't Of Health & Human Servs., Personalized Health Care: Opportunities, Pathways, Resources (2007), available at URL www.hhs.gov/myhealthcare/news/phc-report.pdf and Dep't Of Health & Human Servs., Personalized Health Care Pioneers, Partnerships, Progress (2008), alla URL www.hhs.gov/myhealthcare/news/phc_2008__report.pdf. See also, H. F. Willard, G. S. Ginsburg (eds), Essentials of Genomic and Personalized Medicine, Burlington, Academic Press, 2009, 2 ss; Shubba Ghosh, Identity, Invention, and the Culture of Personalized Medicine Patenting, cit., at 39 et seq.

[65] See J. S. Geetter, Another Man's Treasure: The Promise and Pitfalls of Leveraging Existing Biomedical Assets for Future Use, 4 J. Health & Life Sci. L., 2011, 1.

[66] See also Implementing Regulations to the Convention on the Grant of European Patents, Dec. 13, 2001, Rule Rule 23d(c) (now Rule 28c) that states: "Under Article 53(a), European patents shall not be granted in respect of biotechnological inventions which, in particular, concern uses of human embryos for industrial or commercial purposes.". See Gerard Porter et al., The Patentability of Human Embryonic Stem Cells in Europe, 24 Nature Biotechnology 653, 653 (2006).

[67] Oliver Brüstle v Greenpeace eV (C-34/10) [2012] 1 C.M.L.R. 41.

[68] Nat'l Insts. of Health, U.S. Dep't of Health &. Human Servs., Stem Cells: Scientific Progress and Future Research Directions 1 (2001), available at http://stemcells.nih.gov/staticresources/info/scireport/PDFs/fullrptstem.pdf (last accessed 28 April 2016).

[69] Nat'l Insts. of Health, U.S. Dep't of Health &. Human Servs., Stem Cell Basics, 3-4 (2009), available at http://stemcells.nih.gov/staticresources/info/basics/SCprimer2009.pdf (last accessed 28 April 2016).

together with their aptitude to become specialized makes stem cells unique.[70] There are several categories of unspecialized cells: totipotent stem cells are capable of developing into a complete organism[71]; pluripotent stem cells are capable of differentiating into any specialized cell type in the body, but are incapable of forming the complete organism; and multipotent stem cells that are capable of differentiating into more than one type of specialized cell.[72] Embryonic stem cells – as indicated by their name – are originated from embryos. Most embryonic stem cells are obtained from embryos that develop from eggs that have been fertilized in vitro and then are made available for research purposes with informed consent of the donors.[73]

From a more practical point of view, stem cells are able to regenerate tissues and organs acting as building blocks for all tissues in the body serving as a sort of internal repair system. Therefore, stem cell research can offer the possibility of developing new methods to regenerate or replace tissues or cells damaged by injuries or diseases and to treat serious chronic diseases by cell-based therapies such as diabetes, Alzheimer's disease, Parkinson's disease and other neurodegenerative diseases. Stem cells are also used in specific medical applications to provide a basic understanding of disease development and contribute to the discovery of safer and more effective drugs.[74] Accordingly, scientists are trying to use stem cells to recreate the damaged, destroyed or dead cells in different diseases. Despite the potential and numerous benefits, these various processes for duplicating biological organisms are considered a promising but controversial area of biomedical research.[75]

The economic value behind of all these scientific discoveries and the development of new health technologies is normally carried through the instrument of patents. Patents directed to personalized or regenerative medicine are therefore essential tools for promoting the development and commercialization of new treatments or predictive tests in the field of medical diagnostics. The advancement of pharmacogenomics and gene therapy has extremely high costs of research and production. Therefore, these areas of research claim a more extensive legal protection involving both a vertical and horizontal expansion of property rights.[76] As a result

---

[70] Nat'l Insts. of Health, U.S. Dep't of Health &. Human Servs., Stem Cells: Scientific Progress and Future Research Directions 1 (2001), available at http://stemcells.nih.gov/staticresources/info/scireport/PDFs/fullrptstem.pdf (last accessed 28 April 2016).

[71] Kevin A. D'Amour & Fred H Gage, Genetic and Functional Differences Between Multipotent Neural and Pluripotent Embryonic Stem Cells, 100 Proc. Nat'l. Acad. Sci. U.S. 11866 (2003).

[72] Id.

[73] Nat'l Insts. of Health, U.S. Dep't of Health &. Human Servs., Stem Cell Basics, cit., at 5.

[74] Commission of the European Communities Commission Staff Working Paper: Report on Human Embryonic Stem Cell Research (Brussels, 2003); See also Gabriela Gebrin Cezar, Can human embryonic stem cells contribute to the discovery of safer and more effective drugs? 11 Curr Opin Chem Biol. 405 (2007).

[75] James A. Thomson et al., Embryonic Stem Cell Lines Derived from Human Blastocysts, 282 Science 1145, 1145 (1998).

[76] See Giorgio Resta, La privatizzazione della conoscenza e la promessa dei beni comuni: riflessioni sul caso "Myriad Genetics", in Riv. crit. dir. priv., 2011, 281, 282.; G. Colangelo, Mercato e cooperazione tecnologica. I contratti di patent pooling, Milano, Giuffrè, 2008, 27.

of this slow but constant process, intangible assets that – because of their specific nature – were once essentially counted in the category of the commons or of the public domain, are now magnetically attracted into the orbit of exclusivity.[77]

4.4 Challenges and Opportunities in the Biosciences

The issue of scientific and biotechnological innovations presents – from different points of view – a substantial challenge for the law. As we have seen, genetic information can have significant margins of "utility" and, conversely, sensitive profiles of danger. This is a very delicate ground where it is not only involved the freedom of scientific research but also its practical applications.[78] It entails factual consequences, which could potentially result in violation of rights and the necessity of striking a balance between opposing interests.

To whom belongs the right to settle the boundary lines between these two interacting domains? There is no doubt that the function to fix the line between legal and illegal is up to the law, providing the appropriate safeguards and precautions. On the other end there are no certain answers to questions raising moral issues because the principles governing what is ethical and what is unethical are not always clear. It is a question of putting the right approach in the field and the necessary legal instruments to regulate the actual use of genetic data, avoiding misuses: abnormal and arbitrary uses or procedures adversely affecting the rights of others.

Even just thinking about the aforementioned scenarios, it is clear that the question of biotech innovations presents a deep and unexpected analogy with the more intimate nature of the law and, in particular, with certain profiles of constitutional law.

We are required not to think genetic data only as an important subject of legal regulation. The similarities between the nature of genetic data and the legal realm are far more profound and pervasive: accordingly, we believe it is desirable to emphasize and highlight these red threads.

On reflection, genetic data is a "sign" in the semiological sense of the word[79]: not surprisingly the expression "read the genetic code" is frequently used in the common language, thereby emphasizing the necessity to give it a "meaning" (also predictive) starting from a biological point of view.[80] As a "sign", the genetic data

[77] See Giorgio Resta, La privatizzazione della conoscenza e la promessa dei beni comuni: riflessioni sul caso "Myriad Genetics", cit., 282.

[78] See e.g. Jonathan King and Doreen Stabinsky, Life Patents Undermine the Exchange of Technology and Scientific Ideas, in Rights and Liberties in the Biotech Age 49 (Sheldon Krimsky & Peter Shorett eds., 2005).

[79] See Paolo Veronesi, Introduction, in Biotech Innovations & Fundamental Rights 3 (Roberto Bin et al.) (2012).

[80] See Id. See also generally Sandra Braman, Biotechnology and Communication: The Meta-Technologies of Information (2004).

belongs to the same large semiological category as the law.[81] Also the law has to be interpreted by signs. At the same time, lawyers, judges, and legislators are thus always requested to interpret and properly explain different categories of signs.[82] As argued and persuasively documented by other scholars "the law actually and specifically enacted or adopted for the government of an organized society can not, by definition, avoid the comparison with concrete and specific cases."[83] So it could happen that legal acts "may have entirely different significance from those originally identified or abstractly conceived."[84] The categorization of the event and factors determining it, are always critical steps in the identification and interpretation of law.[85] They are also the instruments used to close the circle of interpretation that is involved in the understanding of the text as a whole and the interpretation of its parts:

> The correct "pre-understanding of the case" allows the interpreter to determine the applicable law which is to better identify and attribute a precise meaning to the abstract legal rules governing the matter at hand. Thus, the law distilled from this process, applied to the fact that causes the problem, gives to the fact a more defined physiognomy and a more precise legal meaning. This is the typical way of the "hermeneutic circle".[86]

Now something very similar occurs in genetics. More precisely, the reading of the genetic data rarely can pre-determine with certainty diseases that will affect a person's health.[87]

In order to bring this view into harmony with the nature of the problem addressed by genetic-based inventions, it is of course necessary to take also in account that the notion of a gene is an artificial concept.[88] As already mentioned by other authors:

> Cells contain strands of DNA. Genes are simply locations on that strand. In other words, the idea of a gene is a way of conceptualizing a continuous string as if it were broken up into pieces. It is a very helpful way for scientist to talk about and explore genetic phenomena. Nevertheless, the legal system is assigning rights to those pieces. If we lose sight of the assumptions and the artificiality involved, we lose the ability to ask coherently whether the scientific line fits the legal issues properly as those issues unfold in the cases.[89]

---

[81] See Paolo Veronesi, Introduction, cit. at 3.

[82] Id.

[83] Id.

[84] Id. (observing that it happens because of their interaction with the "environment" within which they are operating).

[85] Id.

[86] Id., at 4.

[87] See e.g. E. Richard Gold & Julia Carbone, Myriad Genetics: In the Eye of the Policy Storm, 12 Genetics Med. S39 (2010) (discussing the global impact of the BRCA1 and BRCA2 patents on personalized medicine). See also Matthew Herder, Patents & the Progress of Personalized Medicine: Biomarkers Research as a Lens, 18 Annals Health L. 187 (2009).

[88] Robin Feldman, The Role of Science in Law 10 (2009).

[89] Id.

The legal issues in this complex and delicate ground cannot be effectively addressed and resolved without taking a scientific line and inserting it into the legal doctrine.[90]

Policy makers, scholars and researchers have raised a number of other serious concerns in relation to biotech patents and their claim. Biotech patents (including genes, cell lines and living processes) may be more problematic than patents in other fields.[91] Especially in genetics, property rights can have the adverse effect of restricting access to research, scientific information and health care opportunities.[92] Some scholars have also speculated that biotechnology patents can hamper biomedical research because of their "anticommons" effect,[93] not encouraging innovation but rather hindering the spread of new ideas.[94] In opposition to these arguments we can observe that some empirical studies exclude a negative impact of patents in genomics.[95] As a matter of fact, there is no positive and unequivocal indication that gene patents block innovation, inhibit research and put us all at risk. But there is no clear evidence to the contrary. The empirical studies on this issue produced diverging and contradictory results, making a firm and reasonable conclusion on the matter highly controversial at this time.

Apart from complex ethical, economical and juridical implications arising from these types of patents, it is clear there are many unanswered questions and controversies regarding the access to health-related technology, environment protection and biodiversity conservation, barriers in the access to scientific research and to knowledge. The vast process of privatization of living organisms and genetic

---

[90] Id. at 13.

[91] See Aurora Plomer et al., Challenges to Human Embryonic Stem Cell Patents, 2 Cell Stem Cell 13, 13–15 (2008).

[92] For relevant scholarship on these issues, see, among others, Christopher Geiger, 'Constitutionalising' Intellectual Property Law? The Influence of Fundamental Rights on Intellectual Property in the European Union, 37 Int'l Rev. Intell. Prop. & Competition L., 2006, 371; Lawrence R. Helfer, Human Rights and Intellectual Property: Conflict or Coexistence?, in 5 Minn. Int. Prop. Rev. 47 (2003); Paul L.C. Torremans (ed.), Intellectual Property and Human Rights (2008); Holger P. Hestermeyer, Human Rights and the WTO: The Case of Patents and Access to Medicines (2007); W. Grosheide (ed.), Intellectual Property and Human Rights. A Paradox, cit.; Louise Bernier, Justice in Genetics: Intellectual Property and Human Rights from a Cosmopolitan Liberal Perspective cit.; L. Helfer, G. Austin, Human Rights and Intellectual Property: Mapping the Global Interface, cit.; Peter Yu, Intellectual Property and Human Rights in the Nonmultilateral Era, 64 Fla. L. Rev., 1045 (2012).

[93] For further discussion on the anticommons problem, see Michael A. Heller & Rebecca S. Eisenberg, Can Patents Deter Innovation? The Anticommons in Biomedical Research, 280 Science 698 (1998); Michael A. Heller, The Tragedy of the Anticommons: Property in the Transition from Marx to Markets, 111 Harv. L. Rev. 621 (1998); Fiona Murray and Scott Stern, Do Formal Intellectual Property Rights Hinder the Free Flow of Scientific Knowledge? An Empirical Test of the Anti-Commons Hypothesis, 63 J. Econ. Behav. & Org., 648 (2007).

[94] For more on this, see the provocative work of Michele Boldrin and David K. Levine, Against Intellectual Monopoly 68 et seq. (2010).

[95] See e.g. Joseph Straus et al., Genetic Inventions and Patent Law, An Empirical Survey of Selected German R&D Institutions, Munich, 2004; D. E. Adelman, A Fallacy of the Commons in Biotech Patent Policy, 20 Berkeley Tech L.J., 985, 985–86 (2005).

materials isolated from natural sources seems to point towards a complete reversal of values, opening the frontier to some form of "commodification of life". Both scientists, legal scholars and the public must be involved in moving these conversations forward in order to properly balance the competing interests.

4.5 Property Rights and the Commodification of Knowledge

Since the value of a genetic resource is basically governed by its informational content, property rights that address information as an intangible good can have a significant impact on the use, control and distribution of genetic resources. The role of exclusive rights in biotechnology innovation is extremely complex. Normally, we consider patents as useful instruments to promote innovation, progress and scientific discoveries, "but that is because most patents are granted for human inventions".[96] Even if patents protect inventions, they fundamentally help also innovation, in that way they promise a possible return on investment to inventors and companies spending resources in developing new products for the civil society. Here the point at issue is whether genes can or cannot be considered a human invention because they are "features of the natural world".[97] In light of this situation, it is necessary to recognize and discuss the possible ramifications of private control over human or natural genetic resources. One potential consequence of this type of patents is a trend toward increasing private appropriation of human genetic resources and natural compounds. As eloquently and in plain words expressed by the novelist and public intellectual Michael Crichton in an open editorial for the New York Times,

> Humans share mostly the same genes. The same genes are found in other animals as well. Our genetic makeup represents the common heritage of all life on earth. You can't patent snow, eagles or gravity, and you shouldn't be able to patent genes, either. Yet by now one-fifth of the genes in your body are privately owned. The results have been disastrous. Ordinarily, we imagine patents promote innovation, but that's because most patents are granted for human inventions. Genes aren't human inventions; they are features of the natural world. As a result these patents can be used to block innovation, and hurt patient care.[98]

According to a 2005 study published in the journal *Science*, more than 4000 genes – 20 % of the almost 24,000 human genes – have been patented in the United States, primarily by private firms and universities.[99] For example, some diseases and human pathogens are privately owned, including haemophilus influenza and Hepatitis C. It implies that – in countries where a specific research exemption in not

---

[96] See Michael Crichton, Op-Ed., Patenting Life, N.Y. Times, Feb. 13, 2007, at A23, available at http://www.nytimes.com/2007/02/13/opinion/13crichton.html (last accessed 28 April 2016).

[97] Id.

[98] Id.

[99] See Kyle Jensen & Fiona Murray, Intellectual Property Landscape of the Human Genome, 310 Science 239, 239 (2005).

incorporated in the legislation – scientists interested to conduct research on a patented invention are obliged to contract with the right-holder to do the work. So, because of patent concerns, research interests can be limited or addressed towards less expensive options.[100]

In parallel with these considerations, it is important to appreciate, that genes have become – at the same time – a new area of research just because of their potential to cure genetic diseases, and to test new treatments and medicines. This is a very peculiar situation, since contrasting rights and interests are involved and they need to be weighted and balanced. Considering this wider framework and to better understand the role of regulatory practices within this sector, it is first necessary to discuss what the principles and legal provisions that deal with the private property regimes of genetic materials.

4.6 Biotech Innovations and Fundamental Rights

Policy makers, scholars and researchers have raised a number of serious concerns in relation to DNA-based inventions. As the scientific and technological manipulation of life constantly increases, individual rights and fundamental liberties are seriously menaced and undermined. The continuous expansion of intellectual property rights probably represents one of the most interesting contemporary challenges to limitations of access to knowledge and information.[101] In this regard, the subject matter of gene patents reveals interesting insights.

Biotech patents (including gene sequences, cell lines and living processes) may be more problematic than patents in other fields.[102] Especially in genetics, patents can have the adverse effect of restricting access to research, scientific information[103] and health care opportunities.[104] Some scholars have also speculated that

[100] See Michael Crichton, Patenting Life, cit. (observing how the owner of the genome for Hepatitis C is paid millions by researchers to study this disease). See also Michele Boldrin and David K. Levine, Against Intellectual Monopoly cit at. 245 (noting that also the results of clinical trials are not made available to the public).

[101] For a comparative overview, see Ronald Leenes et al. (eds.), Constitutional Rights and New Technologies: A Comparative Study (TMC Asser Press 2008).

[102] See Aurora Plomer et al., Challenges to Human Embryonic Stem Cell Patents, 2 Cell Stem Cell 13, 13–15 (2008).

[103] See, e.g., Geertrui van Overwalle, Of Thickets, Blocks and Gaps. Designing Tools to Resolve Obstacles in the Gene Patents Landscape, in Gene Patents and Collaborative Licensing Models 383 (Geertrui van Overwalle ed., 2009); Anders Nordgren, Responsible Genetics: The Moral Responsibility of Geneticists for the Consequences of Human Genetics Research 114 (Kluwer Acad. Publishers 2001); but see contra David E. Adelman & Kathryn L. DeAngelis, Patent Metrics: The Mismeasure of Innovation in the Biotech Patent Debate, 85 Tex. L. Rev. 1677, 1681 n. 11 (2007) (pointing out that the effect of the growth in biotech patenting on innovation is more limited than believed).

[104] See e.g. World Health Organization, Genetics, Genomics and the Patenting of DNA: Review of Potential Implications for Health in Developing Countries 20 (2005), available at http://www.who.

biotechnology patents can hamper biomedical research because of their "anticommons" effect.[105] However, apart from complex ethical, economic and juridical implications arising from these particular types of patents, it is clear there are many challenging aspects to be discussed. Current practices related to genes and genetic research technologies also raise questions concerning the global governance of access to knowledge and the achievement of a new balance between universal public interest and property rights in many fields of innovation and creation.[106] In this respect, we just face the classical and paradigmatic dilemma of the conflict of rights.[107] In fact, in the patenting of living organisms and genetic materials there is a tension between equally important principles. On the one hand, it must take into account the protection of property rights, information assets and knowledge creation. On the other, it is necessary to consider the law and policy relating to the regulation of information and public value: biological materials are also recognized as knowledge or information that should be openly shared for scientific investigation.[108] This conflict makes possible an unexpected reversal of values, opening the frontier to some form of "commodification of life".[109] In this scenario, the patenting of DNA-based inventions presents a series of legal and ethical dilemmas. Particularly troublesome questions arise with regard to biotech innovations and scientific developments. Traditionally, the goal of scientific research is knowledge and the barrier-free and wide dissemination of it. In other words, the purpose is to spread scientific knowledge to the public, contributing to the future development of society. These principles and values particularly come into play in the gene patenting debate. Genes are often seen as products of nature and as such they should be treated as the

int/genomics/FullReport.pdf (last accessed 28 April 2016).

[105] On the anticommons problem, see Michael A. Heller & Rebecca S. Eisenberg, Can Patents Deter Innovation? The Anticommons in Biomedical Research, 280 Science 698 (1998) (arguing that the recent trends in patenting will deter innovation by creating "anti-commons" problems); Michael A. Heller, The Tragedy of the Anticommons: Property in the Transition from Marx to Markets, 111 Harv. L. Rev. 621 (1998); Fiona Murray & Scott Stern, Do Formal Intellectual Property Rights Hinder the Free Flow of Scientific Knowledge? An Empirical Test of the Anti-Commons Hypothesis, 63 J. Econ. Behav. & Org. 648 (2007). In opposition to these arguments we can observe that some empirical studies exclude a negative impact of patents in genomics. On this point, see generally Joseph Straus et al., Genetic Inventions and Patent Law, An Empirical Survey of Selected German R&D Institutions, Munich, 2004.

[106] This concern constitutes a typical example of what has been defined as the "democratic management of technoscience and techno-scientific products". See Dominique Pestre, Challenges for the Democratic Management of Technoscience: Governance, Participation and the Political Today, 17 Science as Culture 101 (2008).

[107] For an interesting discussion in this topic, see Lorenzo Zucca, Constitutional Dilemmas: Conflicts of Fundamental Legal Rights in Europe and the USA, 3–12 (OUP 2007).

[108] See Matthew Albright, Life Patents and Democratic Values, in Rights and Liberties in the Biotech Age: Why We Need a Genetic Bill of Rights 29, 35 (Sheldon Krimsky & Peter Shorett, eds., 2005).

[109] See Sheila Jasanoff, A social Contract for the Life Sciences: The US Case, in Trattato di biodiritto, diretto da S. Rodotà e P. Zatti, vol. I, 103 Ambito e fonti del biodiritto, (Stefano Rodotà & Mariachiara Tallacchini eds.) Giuffrè, Milano, 2010, 115.

common heritage of mankind.[110] Gene identification and collection of biotech data are generally the result of a multi-step effort involving several research groups. Even if a patent usually belongs to the inventor, "public and private institutes and laboratories as well as funders may be involved, who all have divergent expectations of using and sharing the results".[111] According to different scholars, genetic testing, genome sequencing and scientific research can be restricted or limited due to concerns about gene patents.[112] All human inventions are based on past experiences or previous information acquired. They also increase in value the more they are shared and spread. The point of the question here is that scientific information can be progressively more controlled and regulated. This reduction of freedom is partly caused by an improper use of intellectual property protection. Intellectual property rights are key strategic tools in the emerging era of knowledge-based societies. Patents in biotech and gene-related inventions provide an insightful perspective on the regulatory challenges posed by DNA as property and as information. In this context, several questions arise with regard to science, scientific knowledge and their compliance with fundamental rights and public health principles. Who owns human genes? Are gene patents bad for research? Can patents granted over genetic materials limit access to scientific knowledge? Are there detrimental effects for public health? We will also try to investigate in which sense the granting of a patent can potentially implicate freedom of expression concerns. Specifically, the crucial question centers on the patenting of human genetic material. What legal and ethical concerns motivate this challenge to patenting? How could the biotech industry understand to these concerns? The answers to these complex questions are of key importance for the global governance of knowledge.

---

[110] See Melissa L. Sturges, Who Should Hold Property Rights to the Human Genome? An Application of the Common Heritage of Humankind, 13 Am. U. Int'l L. Rev. 219, 246 (1997).

[111] See Sirpa Soini et al., Patenting and Licensing in Genetic Testing: Ethical, Legal and Social Issues, 16 Eur. J. Hum. Gen. S10, S33 (2008).

[112] For a general discussion of the issues, see, among others, Michael Heller & Rebecca Eisenberg, Can Patents Deter Innovation? The Anticommons in Biomedical Research, 280 Science 698 (1998); Lori B. Andrews, The Gene Patent Dilemma: Balancing Commercial Incentives with Health Needs, 2 Hous. J. Health L. & Pol'y 65, 101 (2002); Timothy Caulfield et al., Genetic Technologies, Health Care Policy and the Patent Bargain, 63 Clinical Genetics 15 (2002); Kyle Jensen & Fiona Murray, Intellectual Property Landscape of the Human Genome, 310 Science 239, 239–40 (2005); Lori B. Andrews & Jordan Paradise, Gene Patents: The Need for Bioethics Scrutiny and Legal Change, 5 Yale J. Health Pol'Y L. & Ethics 403, 405–11 (2005); Chris Holman, The Impact of Human Gene Patents on Innovation and Access: A survey of Human Gene Patent Litigation, 76 UMKC L. Rev. 295, 300 (2007); Michele Westhoff, Gene Patents: Ethical Dilemmas and Possible Solutions, 20 Health L. 1, 10 (2008). See also generally S. Krimsky and P. Shorett (eds.), Rights and. Liberties in the Biotech Age: Why We Need a Genetic Bill of Rights (Lanham, MD: Rowman & Littlefield, 2005).

4.6.1 The Protection of Genetic-Based Inventions

The role of property rights in biotechnology innovation is extremely complex. In order to answer the aforementioned questions, it is necessary here to first discuss briefly the principles and legal provisions that deal with the patentability of biotech innovations. In this respect, the set of aims of biotech innovations and human genetic research should also be considered. Specifically, the objectives of human genetic research should be "to enhance understanding of how genes and environmental factors operate and interact to influence the health of individuals and populations and in so doing, to generate knowledge with the potential to improve individual and community health".[113] Genetic research should be able to translate research discoveries "into the development and provision of new forms of healthcare involving, among other things, medical genetic testing, pharmacogenetics, gene therapy, and the use of therapeutic proteins or stem cells.[114]

In terms of law, it is also necessary to map correctly the transatlantic differences that make gene patents much harder to uphold in Europe than in the United States.[115] Both the United States (US) and the European Union (EU) are undoubtedly the world's two leading actors in the fields of science innovations, technology advances and creativity. Despite their extensive differences, they share a common body of fundamental legal principles and values on which the constitutional democratic system of government depends. However, the American legal approach to many scientific and technological issues significantly differ from the European one, producing reciprocal obstacles to trade as well as legal concerns impacting the transatlantic economy. At the same time the evolution of European science and technology governance is heavily influenced by American practices and policies.

4.6.1.1 Patents on Genetic Material: Conditions and Requirements

The current approach of the Trilateral Patent Offices [i.e. the European Patent Office (EPO), the Japan Patent Office (JPO) and the United States Patent and Trademark Office (USPTO)] with respect to biotech patents on biological subject matter is to grant patents only for isolated and purified gene sequences with a demonstrated specific utility.[116] The distinction between a non-patentable "product of nature" and

[113] See Australian Law Reform Commission, Genes and Ingenuity: Gene Patenting and Human Health, Report No 99 (2004) 38, available at http://www.austlii.edu.au/au/other/alrc/publications/reports/99 (last accessed 28 April 2016).

[114] Id.

[115] See Andy Coghlan, Europe revokes controversial gene patent, New Scientist, 19th May 2004.

[116] See Melanie J. Howlett & Andrew F. Christie, An Analysis of the Approach of the European, Japanese and United States Patent Offices to Patenting Partial DNA Sequences (ESTs), 34 Int'l Rev. Indus. Prop. & Copyright L. 581 (2003); Leslie G. Restaino et al., Patenting DNA-Related Inventions in the European Union, United States and Japan: A Trilateral Approach or a Study in Contrast?, 2003 UCLA J.L. & Tech. 2 (2003). See also Anne Reese & Brian Opeskin, Current

a patentable "non-naturally occurring composition of matter" was settled for the first time by the United States Supreme Court in Diamond v. Chakrabarty.[117] This ruling in combination with the decision in Moore v. Regent of University of California paved the way for the patenting of genetic material.[118] Subsequently, in 1998, the USPTO, EPO and JPO issued a joint policy statement asserting that "purified natural products are not regarded as products of nature or discoveries because they do not in fact exist in nature in an isolated form. Rather, they are regarded for patent purposes as biologically active substances or chemical compounds and eligible for patenting on the same basis as other chemical compounds".[119]

In other terms, a purified natural substance is considered patentable if the "purification" results in a compound with such distinct characteristics that it becomes a new product commercially or therapeutically valuable. Formally, through the process of purification and isolation of genetic materials it is possible to achieve the separation of different compounds from a biological cell. However, various criticisms have been made on this point. In particular, it has been observed that even if genetic materials are isolated and purified, the main properties of such substances – which are the 'useful' and exploitable information – "are naturally occurring, not created by the person who isolates and purifies the material".[120] Furthermore, isolated and purified genetic sequences are "structurally similar or identical to the form that exists in nature".[121] The direct result of this interpretation is that patents for biotechnological innovations are consequently limited only by the ability of the individuals drafting the claim.[122]

In recent years, one of the most troublesome aspects for gene patents has been their novelty and, consequently, their status as patentable subject matter.[123] But still

---

Issues in Gene Patenting, in Disputes and Dilemmas in Health Law 277, 280 (Ian Freckelton & Kerry Petersen eds.) (2006).

[117] Diamond v. Chakrabarty, 447 U.S. 303 (1980). In this landmark decision the United States Supreme Court held that a live and human-engineered microorganism is patentable subject matter under Section 1010 of the United States Patent Act. The rule for which the decision is commonly known is that patents can be issued on "anything under the sun that is made by man". For a detailed review of the case, see Rebecca S. Eisemberg, The Story of Diamond v. Chakrabarty: Technological Change and the Subject Matter Boundaries of the Patent System, in Intellectual Property Stories 327 (Jane C. Ginzburg & Rochelle Cooper Dreyfuss eds. Foundation Press 2006).

[118] Moore v. Regents of the University of California, 793 P.2d 479 (Cal. S. Ct) (1990).

[119] 1988 Joint Statement of USPTO, EPO and JPO; see Comparative Study of Patent Practices in the Field of Biotechnology Related Mainly to Microbiological Inventions, 7 Biotechnology L. Rep. 159, 163 (1988); see footnote 9, Nuffield Council of Bioethics Discussion Paper, The Ethics of Patenting DNA (2002) 26, 3.14.

[120] See Australian Law Reform Commission, Genes and Ingenuity: Gene Patenting and Human Health, Report 99. Sydney: Australian Commonwealth (2004) at 126. Available at http://www.austlii.edu.au/au/other/alrc/publications/reports/99/ (last accessed 28 April 2016).

[121] Id.

[122] See Douglas Robinson & Nina Medlock, Diamond v. Chakrabarty: A Retrospective on 25 Years of Biotech Patents, 17 Intell. Prop. & Tech. J. 12, 14 (2005).

[123] See e.g. John J. Doll, The Patenting of DNA, 280 Science 689 (1998); Daniel J. Kevles & Ari Berkowitz, The Gene Patenting Controversy: A Convergence of Law, Economic Interests, and

a further question comes up: "as DNA has existed well before the gene discoverer arrived, how can these molecules be novel?" The answer, as it has been suggested, "is that the actual molecule produced and claimed by the gene discoverer is new in a strict sense of the word".[124] More precisely, "gene sequences exist naturally as part of a much bigger molecule" and "there is no doubt that this much bigger molecule would be unpatentable".[125] But the gene discoverer's thesis is that "purified and isolated gene sequences are distinct from the overall DNA molecule".[126] This view is supported by one of the first U.S. patent infringement litigations involving a gene patent. In Amgen, Inc. v. Chugai Pharm. Co. Ltd., the district court held that the patent in suit was valid because the invention "is not as plaintiff argues the DNA sequence encoding human erythropoietin since that is a nonpatentable natural phenomenon 'free to all men and reserved exclusively to none'. [...] Rather, the invention as claimed in claim two of the patent is the "purified and isolated" DNA sequence encoding erythropoietin."[127]

Currently, both in the EU and the US, to be eligible for patent protection, an innovation must meet three basic requirements[128]: (i) novelty; (ii) inventive step (non-obviousness in the US); and (iii) industrial application (utility in the US). The design of the patenting system for human genes requires not only an understanding of the key issues related to the requirement of inventiveness, but also a careful balancing of conflicting exclusive rights. As pointed out by the U.S. Supreme Court Justice Stephen Breyer in the case of Laboratory Corp. v. Metabolite Industries, too much patent protection can impede rather than promote the objective of patent protection.[129]

The dilemma of patent proliferation in biotech is made more difficult by a confused regulatory framework. The ethical and legal issues surrounding the patenting

---

Ethics, 67 Brook. L. Rev. 233 (2001). For a recent overview of the gene patenting controversies, see also Lisa Larrimore Ouellette, Access to Bio-Knowledge: From Gene Patents to Biomedical Materials, 2010 Stan. Tech. L. Rev. N1, http://stlr.stanford.edu/pdf/ouellette-access-to-bio-knowledge.pdf (last accessed 28 April 2016).

[124] See Oskar Liivak, Maintaining Competition in Copying: Narrowing the Scope of Gene Patents, 41 U.C. Davis L. Rev. 177, fn 53 (2007).

[125] Id.

[126] Id.

[127] See Amgen, Inc. v. Chugai Pharm. Co., 13 U.S.P.Q.2d (BNA) 1737, 1759 (D. Mass. 1989).

[128] See Oliver Mills, Biotechnological Inventions. Moral Restraints and Patent Law, 2nd ed., 4 (Ashgate 2010); Lionel Bently & Brad Sherman, Intellectual Property Law, 3rd ed., 391 (OUP 2009).

[129] In his famous dissent, Justice Breyer stated that "too much patent protection can impede rather than promote the progress of science and the useful arts" that is the U.S. constitutional objective of copyright and patent protection. See Lab. Corp. of America Holdings v. Metabolite Labs., Inc., 548 U.S. 124, 126, 79 U.S.P.Q.2d (BNA) 1065, 1066 (2006) (per curiam) (Breyer, J., dissenting) (quoting U.S. Const. art. I, § 8, cl. 8). This dissent, joined by Justices Stevens and Souter, seems to suggest that at least three of the Supreme Court Justices are becoming increasingly concerned about the quality and quantity of the patents being issued by the United States Patent and Trademark Office. See Terry Wrigh, Patent Trends in the U.S. Supreme Court, http://brandlaw.org/2010/01/patent-trends-in-the-u-s-supreme-court/ (last accessed 28 April 2016).

of genetic sequences are currently the subject of an intense international debate, particularly in the technologically advanced United States and European Union.[130] Based on a principle of non-discrimination with regard to technology, article 27 of TRIPs agrees that biological material should be patentable.[131] Human genes can be patented if they meet the requirements of novelty, inventive step and industrial applicability.[132] In other words, genes can be patented if the inventor meets the general requirements of a patent.[133] States may exclude patents on human genes on their territory, but – up to now – very few countries have used this possibility. On the other hand, the European Directive on the Legal Protection of Biotechnological Inventions, specifies that "elements isolated from the human body or otherwise produced by means of a technical process, including the sequence or partial sequence of a gene" may constitute a patentable invention.[134] In particular, the Directive recognizes that biological material which is isolated from its natural environment or produced by means of a technical process is considered to be an invention even if this material previously occurred in nature.[135] In addition, the European Patent Convention (EPC) prohibits the granting of patents for "methods of treatment of the human or animal body by surgery or therapy and diagnostic methods practiced on the human body".[136] On this basis, the European Patent Office concluded that "all methods practiced on the human or animal body which relate to the diagnosis or which are of value for the purposes of diagnosis" are prohibited from being

[130] Donna M. Gitter, International Conflicts Over Patenting Human DNA Sequences in the United States and the European Union: An Argument for Compulsory Licensing and a Fair-Use Exemption, 76 N.Y.U. L. Rev. 1623, 1624 (2001).

[131] See Agreement on Trade-Related Aspects of Intellectual Property Rights, Apr. 15, 1994, art. 27, Marrakesh Agreement Establishing the World Trade Organization, Annex 1C, 33 I.L.M. 1125 (1994) [hereinafter TRIPS]. On this point, see also Johanna Gibson, Patent Publics, Patent Cultures, in Patenting Lives: Life Patents, Culture and Development 1,3 (Johanna Gibson ed., Ashgate 2008).

[132] According to Art. 27 of the TRIPS Agreement, "patents shall be available for any inventions, whether products or processes, in all fields of technology, provided that they are new, involve an inventive step and are capable of industrial application". See also Bently & Sherman, Intellectual Property Law, cit., at 393–394.

[133] Lori B. Andrews & Jordan Paradise, Essay, Gene Patents: The Need for Bioethics Scrutiny and Legal Change, 5 Yale J. Of Health Pol'y, L. & Ethics 403, 404 (2005).

[134] Council Directive 98/44/EC, art. 5(2), 1998 O.J. (L 213) 13 (EC).

[135] Id., at art. 3(2).

[136] Convention on the Grant of European Patents, art. 53(c), Oct. 5, 1973, 13 I.L.M. 270 [hereinafter EPC]. The EPC provides a uniform method and standard for examining a European patent application, but reserves to members of the European Union the task of interpreting and enforcing a patent: "under the EPC, the EPO grants European patents for one or more of the contracting parties to the EPC. However, a European patent is not a uniform patent. Rather it consists of a bundle of parallel national patents granted as a result of a centralized grant by the EPO". On this, see August Reinisch, Decisions of the European Patent Organization Before National Courts, in Challenging Acts of International Organizations Before National Courts 137, 138 (A. Reinisch ed., 2010).

patented.[137] However, Biotech inventions are considered patentable under both the EPC and the Biotechnology Directive.[138] In particular, the European Patent Convention explicitly acknowledges the patentability of biotechnological inventions in Rule 26(1) EPC.[139] In addition, Rule 27(a) EPC provides supplementary specifications about patentable subject-matter in biosciences stipulating that "biotechnological inventions shall also be patentable if they concern biological material which is isolated from its natural environment or produced by means of a technical process even if it previously occurred in nature".[140]

As private research in biotech becomes increasingly protected by patents, concerns appear to arise from the nature and extent of protection granted to patent holders. Patents, in fact, may play multiple roles in the knowledge-based economy. In the current regulatory framework, patent holders have broad freedom in the use of their patent rights.[141] In fact, patent holders are free to choose how to exercise their exclusive rights.[142] Consequently, they are free to set royalties, to grant or refuse licensing requests, or they may choose the licensees and the licensing terms freely, as long as the arrangement complies with relevant regulations, such as competition or antitrust law.[143] Unfortunately, this system, even though designed to encourage private research, could also bring negative results. When patents are licensed too restrictively or when patents are used excessively to protect information "this could hamper research and development, clinical access, and availability of high-quality tests for patients".[144] These factors suggest that patents may have a chilling effect on research and innovation resulting in a significant obstacle on other researchers' ability to conduct further investigations.[145] In addition, licensing practices have the

[137] See decision T 964/99 (OJ EPO 2002, 4), starting from the interpretation set out in decision T 385/86, decision T 964/99.

[138] See Richard A. Spinello & Maria Bottis, A Defense Of Intellectual Property Rights 64 (2009).

[139] Rule 26(1) of 5 October 1973 as adopted by decision of the Administrative Council of the European Patent Organisation of December 7, 2006 and as last amended by decision of the Administrative Council of the European Patent Organisation of October 26, 2010 [hereinafter Implementing Regulations]. The Rules cited are to the earlier version. On the point, see Giovanni Macchia, Patentability Requirements of Biotech Inventions at the European Patent Office: Ethical Issues, in Biotech Innovations & Fundamental Rights 37 (R. Bin et al. eds, 2011).

[140] Implementing Regulations, Rule 27(a).

[141] See, e.g. Bement v. Nat'l Harrow Co., 186 U.S. 70, 90–92 (1902) ("The general rule is absolute freedom in the use or sale of rights under the patent laws of the United States").

[142] A patent simply grants the patentee the right to exclude others from making, using or selling the claimed invention for a limited period of time in return for the disclosure if technical information. See Bently & Sherman, Intellectual Property Law, cit., at 335.

[143] See Bently & Sherman, Intellectual Property Law, cit. at 570. In the U.S., an intellectual property rights holder has no obligation to either use or license its property rights. On the point, see Herbert Hovenkamp, Mark D. Janis & Mark A. Lemely, Unilateral Refusals to License in the US, 2 J. Competition L. & Econ. 1, 13 (2006).

[144] Geertrui Van Overwalle, Turning Patent Swords into Shares, 330 Science 1630 (2010).

[145] See David B. Resnik, Owning the Genome: A Moral Analysis of DNA Patenting 141 (SUNY Press 2004).

consequence of restricting access to genetic information and to data required for research purposes.[146]

4.7 Genetic Information and Knowledge Commons

The analysis of knowledge as a commons "has its roots in the broad, interdisciplinary study of shared natural resources, such as water resources, forests, fisheries, and wildlife".[147] The exploitation of these collective resources must be regulated to prevent the overuse, depletion or extinction. This phenomenon is known as "the tragedy of the commons" – a key metaphor coined by Garret Hardin – where individuals overuse resources because they are completely detached from the real cost.[148] The "tragedy of the commons" is also an allegory used to exemplify the potential struggle between the benefits of producers and consumers and the common or public good. However, contrary to the Hardin's thesis, common resources can be sustainable and successfully managed by the people who use them rather than by private companies.[149] In particular it is argued that there may be situations where the Hardin's model can be applied, "but many groups can effectively manage and sustain common resources if they have suitable conditions, such as appropriate rules, good conflict-resolution mechanisms, and well-defined group boundaries".[150] Commons may in fact be vital resources for communities and nations as long as those subjects involved in their exploitation are able to define and share rules for their sustainability. So the tragedy can be avoided.

In the Anglo-American legal tradition the concept of commons is linked to goods that are owned by a community and of which the same community can freely dispose. In this sense, the notion of commons identifies all the tangible and intangible resources that constitute a collective heritage of a specific community. Starting from these considerations, we intend to illustrate the progressive development of new forms of enclosure in the realm of the "intangible commons of the mind," through several waves of expansion of intellectual property rights in the area of genetic materials and intangibles goods in general.[151] Such proliferation of new enclosures

---

[146] See generally Amedeo Santosuosso et al., What Constitutional Protection for Freedom of Scientific Research?, 33 Journal of Medical Ethics 342 (2007).

[147] See Charlotte Hess and Elinor Ostrom (eds.) Understanding Knowledge as a Commons: From Theory to Practice 4(2006).

[148] See Garret Hardin, The Tragedy of the Commons, 162 Science 1243 (1968); Elinor Ostrom, Governing the Commons: The Evolution of Institutions for Collective Action 2 (1990).

[149] See Charlotte Hess and Elinor Ostrom (eds.) Understanding Knowledge as a Commons: From Theory to Practice cit., at 11.

[150] Id.

[151] See Paul David and Dominique Foray, Accessing and Expanding the Science and Technology Knowledge Base, 16 Science Technology Industry Review 13 (1995); Arti Kaur Rai, Regulating Scientific Research: Intellectual Property Rights and the Norms of Science, 94 Nw. U. L. Rev. 77 (1999); Yochai Benkler, An Unhurried View of Private Ordering in Information Transactions, 53

is proportional to reduction of genetic materials in the public realm and can lead to a consequent decrease of the public domain and also of new innovation.[152] Scientific knowledge is supposed to be open and free. It also should benefit the general public and with a twofold purpose: on the one hand it should be available to the scientific community; on the other hand, it should be used for further research. All these elements are consistent with the thesis according to which the knowledge is replacing physical inputs as factors of production.[153]

4.7.1 The Structure of Ownership in the Life Sciences

Pharmaceutical companies generally adopt a traditional business model based on "closed innovation" and on a system that is completely covered by intellectual property rights. All ideas are generated internally and remain inside until a new product reaches the market. In this regard, it is also necessary to consider biotech patent policy in the context of so-called "cumulative innovation".[154] Almost any human invention is, in fact, based on previous inventions: this means that innovation is cumulative because innovations are based on previous innovations. The term "cumulative innovation" is used to describe a situation in which a second inventor uses a previous invention covered by a valid patent in order to develop a new invention.[155] In other words, the second innovation would not be possible without the prior development of the first innovation. The subsequent innovator is obliged to negotiate a license from the first innovator to use and market the new invention. The cumulative nature of innovation necessarily raises serious issues about the architecture of access to scientific information.[156] In an article published 10 years ago by professor Jerome Reichman, he prophetically observed "How to enable entrepreneurs to appropriate the fruits of their investments in cumulative and sequential innova-

Vand. L. Rev. 2063 (2000); James Boyle, The Second Enclosure Movement and the Construction of the Public Domain, 66 Law & Contemp Probs, 33 (2003); Pamela Samuelson, Enriching Discourse on Public Domains, 55 Duke L. J. 783 (2006).

[152] Jessica Litman, The Public Domain, 39 Emory L. J. 965 (1990); Michael Heller, Michael & Rebecca Eisenberg, Can Patents Deter Innovation? The Anticommons in Biomedical Research, 280 Science 698, 699 (1998); Arti K. Rai and Rebecca S. Eisenberg, Bayh-Dole Reform and the Progress of Biomedicine, 66 L. Contemp. Probs. 289, 291 (2003); Pamela Samuelson, Mapping the Digital Public Domain: Threats and Opportunities, 66 Law and Contemporary Problems 147, 155 (2003).

[153] Several studies have found similar results, describing the relationship between economic development and resource consumption. See e.g. Cutler J. Cleveland & Matthias Ruth, Indicators of Dematerialization and the Materials Intensity of Use, 2 J. Indus. Ecology 15, 25–26 (1998).

[154] See Clarisa Long, Patents and Cumulative Innovation, 2 Wash. U. J.L. & Pol'y 229, 230–31 (2000).

[155] See also Dan L. Burk & Mark A. Lemley, The Patent Crisis and How the Courts Can Solve It 73–75 (University of Chicago Press 2009) (discussing cumulative innovation in patent law).

[156] See Lawrence Lessig, The Architecture of Access to Scientific Knowledge, Lecture at Cern, Geneve, Switzerland, 18 April 2001, available at http://www.youtube.com/watch?v=2me7hptVGzI (last accessed 28 April 2016).

tion without impeding follow-on innovation and without creating barriers to entry has become one of the great unsolved puzzles that the law and economics of intellectual property rights need to address as the new millennium gets under way".[157] Innovation is therefore performed step by step. But when one step is already patented, new developments could be blocked or barred. The patent holder, in fact, might demand royalties, which would increase research costs, thus discouraging companies to invest in that field of research. In the literature on "cumulative innovation" two additional elements are considered with respect to property rights in inventions: "patent thicket" and "anticommons effects."[158] The term "anticommons effect" is used to describe the phenomenon induced by "fragmented property rights that must be aggregated to make effective use of the property".[159] In other words, it takes places when the development of a new invention requires the licensing of complementary patents from different patent holders. The problem here is that "too many owners can block each other": property rights might restrict access to research information and data in the name of enforcing a nonfunctional setting of property rights.[160] As observed in the Heller and Eisenberg's seminal article, "by conferring monopolies in discoveries, patents necessarily increase prices and restrict use".[161] Although empirical studies on this topic are not unanimous in their conclusions,[162] the anti-commons could result in a potential degeneration in scientific research as researchers are prevented from access to fundamental information. A closely related effect is the phenomenon of the "patent thicket".[163] It is generated by an overlapping of patent claims covering the same technology or process.[164] In a very similar manner as for the anticommons problem, "the patent thicket has the potential to prevent

---

[157] See Jerome H. Reichman, Of Green Tulips and Legal Kudzu: Repackaging Rights in Subpatentable Innovation, 53 Vand. L. Rev. 1743, 1745 (2000).

[158] See Dan Burk and Mark Lemley, The Patent Crisis and How the Courts Can Solve It, cit., at 76; Michael A. Heller, The Tragedy of the Anticommons: Property in the Transition from Marx to Markets, cit., at 670; Carl Shapiro, Navigating the Patent Thicket: Cross Licenses, Patent Pools, and Standard-Setting, in 1 Innovation Policy and the Economy 119–150 (Adam Jaffe, Joshua Lerner, & Scott Stern, eds., 2001).

[159] Burk & Lemley, The Patent Crisis and How the Courts Can Solve It, cit., at 76.

[160] The problem could be particularly troublesome when the development of a new product requires licensing of several complementary patents, held by different patentees.

[161] Michael A. Heller & Rebecca S. Eisenberg, Can Patents Deter Innovation? The Anticommons in Biomedical Research, cit., at 699.

[162] See infra ch. 4, § 2.

[163] For a general discussion on the problem of the patent thicket, see Carl Shapiro, Navigating the Patent Thicket: Cross Licenses, Patent Pools, and Standard-Setting, cit.; for a better idea of how patent thickets can work to prevent use of patented information in innovation, see James Besson, Patent Thickets: Strategic Patenting of Complex Technologies (Research on Innovation Working Papers, March 2003), available at http://www.researchoninnovation.org/thicket.pdf (last accessed 28 April 2016).

[164] See Carl Shapiro, Navigating the Patent Thicket: Cross Licenses, Patent Pools, and Standard-Setting, cit., at 121.

all parties from making a final product that incorporates multiple inventions".[165] Both the phenomena of "patent thicket" and "anticommons" are considered problematic for the biotechnology sector because they may hinder the development of new products, restricting access to research and to medicines. Human rights norms can be used to improve access rights by decreasing the strength of barriers created by property rights. The recent "Myriad Genetics case" is an emblematic representation of all of these concerns, ultimately resulting in negative consequences for patients and health care systems.[166] This much debated US case challenged the patentability of genes and DNA. The case refers specifically to patents covering two genes (BRCA-1 and BRCA-2) and the related genetic screening for susceptibility to breast and ovarian cancer developed by the Myriad Genetic laboratories.[167] According to the first-instance judgment, "isolated DNA is not markedly different from native DNA as it exists in nature" and consequently it represents unpatentable subject matter.[168] In this regard, the case invigorated the debate on policy issues involving the patenting of diagnostic methods based on the use of human genetic material.[169] The increasing importance of molecular biology in the prevention and diagnostics of human pathologies amplified the issue of access to genomic information for the development of drugs and therapies.[170] The Myriad case also suggests that, when basic genetic information is protected by patents, access to necessary diagnostics may interfere with health care treatment and access to medicine.

In order to facilitate the adaptation of patent law to an environment dominated and shaped by science and technology, it is recognized as necessary to rebalance and flexibilize the range of the patent system.[171] These various measures include the introduction or extension of restrictions and exceptions to property rights in the interest of other fundamental legal rights. For example, it was suggested to introduce a diagnostic-use exemption, protecting diagnostic testing from patent

[165] Burk & Lemley, The Patent Crisis and How the Courts Can Solve It, cit., at 78 (observing that while the anticommons analysis focuses on the need to aggregate fragmentary property rights owned by many different players and the difficulty of assembling those fragments into a coherent product, the patent thicket analysis focuses on the overlap of existing rights).

[166] Ass'n for Molecular Pathology v. U.S. Patent & Trademark Office, 702F. Supp. 2d 181 (S.D.N.Y. 2010).

[167] See Geertrui Van Overwalle, Turning Patent Swords into Shares, cit.

[168] Ass'n for Molecular Pathology v. U.S. Patent & Trademark Office, 702F. Supp. 2d 181, 232 (S.D.N.Y. 2010), as amended (Apr. 5, 2010) ("Because the claimed isolated DNA is not markedly different from native DNA as it exists in nature, it constitutes unpatentable subject matter under 35 U.S.C. § 101.").

[169] Geertrui Van Overwalle, Turning Patent Swords into Shares, cit. at 1630.

[170] Brian A. Jackosn, Innovation and Intellectual Property: The Case of Genomic Patenting, 22 J. Pol'y Analysis & Mgmt 5, 9–12 (2003).

[171] See Geertrui Van Overwalle et al., Models for Facilitating Access to Patents on Genetic Invention, 7 Nature Review Genetics 143 (2006); Geertrui Van Overwalle, Turning Patent Swords into Shares, cit., at 1630–31; Hazel V.J. Moir, Patent Policy and Innovation. Do Legal Rules Deliver Effective Economic Outcomes? 166–170 (2013).

infringement.[172] In addition, it is proposed that patents should grant less protection: in particular they should protect an innovation only in relation to a specific application, clearly indicated in the patent application.[173] Other possible measures of flexibilization include: compulsory licenses (for public health) and patent pools.[174] In general, intellectual property rights should be considered not as an absolute right, but as a bundle of rights with some specific social limits.[175]

4.7.2 *The Patentability of Expressed Sequence Tags*

The most striking example of the dilemma of patent proliferation in biotech can be found in the controversial debate over patenting of expressed sequence tags (ESTs).[176] Here the specific question is, "how much does a patentee have to know about the function and role of ESTs to actually patent them?"[177]

Expressed Sequence Tags are short single-pass sequence reads from complementary DNA (cDNA).[178] They are a fragment or a sequence of DNA which may or may not code for functional proteins.[179] Typically, they are produced in large batches. They represent the genes expressed in a given tissue or at a given developmental stage.[180] They are tags of expression for a given cDNA library.[181] A "gene" is a piece of DNA encoding a protein that is found amongst at least a million other

---

[172] See Geertrui Van Overwalle, Turning Patent Swords into Shares, cit., at 1630.

[173] Id. at 1631.

[174] See Geertrui Van Overwalle et al., Models for Facilitating Access to Patents on Genetic Invention, cit. at 144.

[175] See Josef Kohler, Das Autorrecht, eine zivilistische Abhandlung: Zugleich ein Beitrag zur Lehre vom Eigenthum, vom Miteigenthum, vom Rechtsgeschäft und vom Individualrecht 141 (1880) (arguining the necessity to set external limits for intellectual property rights).

[176] See e.g. Mark D. Adams et al., Complementary DNA Sequencing: Expressed Sequence Tags and Human Genome Project, 252 Science 1651 (1991); Arti K. Rai, Regulating Science Research: Intellectual Property Rights and the Norms of Science, 94 Nw. U.L. Rev. 77, 104 (1999); Molly A. Holman & Stephen R. Munzer, International Property Rights in Genes and Gene Fragments: A Registration Solution for Expressed Sequence Tags, 85 Iowa L. Rev. 735, 750 (2000); Matthew Rimmer, The New Conquistadors: Patent Law and Expressed Sequence Tags, 16 J. Law Inform. Sci. 10 (2007).

[177] See Stacy Lawrence, US Court Case to Define EST Patentability, 23 Nature Biotech. 513 (2005).

[178] A DNA sequence obtained by reverse transcription of a messenger RNA (mRNA) sequence. See The National Library of Medicine, The NCBI Handbook, Expressed Sequence Tags (ESTs), available at http://www.ncbi.nlm.nih.gov/books/NBK21083/#A858 (last accessed 28 April 2016).

[179] See Matthew Rimmer, The New Conquistadors: Patent Law and Expressed Sequence Tags, cit., at 11; Stacy Lawrence, US Court Case to Define EST Patentability, cit., at 513.

[180] See The National Library of Medicine, The NCBI Handbook, Expressed Sequence Tags (ESTs), cit.

[181] Id.

pieces of DNA, and the act of isolating a gene is a very complex and costly task with uncertain results.[182]

The National Center for Biotechnology Information (NCBI) explains in more detail the process of sequencing.[183] Specifically, ESTs are obtained

> by sequencing a short stretch of a DNA clone obtained from a complimentary DNA (cDNA) library. cDNA libraries are created by reverse transcribing mRNAs from a given cell into cDNA and then inserting the cDNA clones into vectors for transformation of bacteria. Each bacterial colony (clone) in the library contains a plasmid with a single cDNA and thus represents a single mRNA from a single gene that was expressed at the time the cDNA library was created. ESTs are useful in identifying genes expressed by a particular type of cell, especially diseased cells.[184]

From a practical point of view, ESTs are useful in identifying full-length genes and in mapping.[185] In particular, ESTs are found to be an invaluable resource for the discovery of new genes.[186] They can be used as probes[187] to locate and characterize complete genes or as diagnostic tools.[188] They are also used as research tools for studying and isolating other molecules. Often ESTs correspond to genes of unknown function. In such cases they do not satisfy the utility requirement for patent protection, even though they are useful as research tools. As tools their economic value is merely in assisting the discovery of pharmaceutical products. However, their patenting is justified by the traditional reason to encourage their identification and effective use. The principle of conferring exclusive rights on some fundamental elements for basic research raises the risk of slowing down the innovation process.[189] For this reason, concerns have been raised that patents covering expressed sequence tags might result in restricted access to research and health care. Due to the large number of patent applications on hundreds of thousands of ESTs, patent

---

[182] James A. Cowan, Inorganic Biochemistry: An Introduction 49 (1997); Rebecca Eisemberg, Patenting the Human Genome, 39 Emory L.J. 721, 735–36 (1990).

[183] The National Center for Biotechnology Information (NCBI) is a US government-funded national resource for molecular biology information. Information regarding the NCBI is available at http://www.ncbi.nlm.nih.gov/ (last accessed 28 April 2016).

[184] See The National Library of Medicine, The NCBI Handbook, Expressed Sequence Tags, cit.

[185] Id.

[186] See James M. Sikela & Charles Auffray, Finding new genes faster than ever, 3 Nature Genetics 189 (1993).

[187] A probe is a "dna sequence that is used to detect the presence of a complementary sequence by hybridization with a nucleic acid sample". See B. W. Old and S. B. Primrose, Principles of gene manipulation: an introduction to genetic engineering (1980) at 124.

[188] See Arti K. Rai, Regulating Science Research: Intellectual Property Rights and the Norms of Science, cit., at 104.

[189] See Andrea Ottolia, Riflessioni sulla Brevettabilità delle Sequenze Parziali di Geni, Riv. Dir. Ind. 457 (2005). EST public libraries can be used to identify unknown genes as well as to compare the expression of genes in different cells or tissues. See Arti K. Rai, Regulating Science Research: Intellectual Property Rights and the Norms of Science, cit., at 105 (observing how many EST applications are notable for the broad scope of their patent claims: the applications claim not only the EST but also the full gene of which it is a part and future uses of the gene).

owners can have significant influence over future research related to the gene of which the EST is a part.[190]

For a long time, the common practice was to file patent applications on various ESTs of unknown function. But, the mere mention of possible uses "is not sufficient to establish a definite utility".[191] This argument was also accepted by the United States Court of Appeals for the Federal Circuit in the case of *In re Fisher* because the applicant did not identify the function of the gene from which the ESTs were obtained.[192] Prior to this judicial decision, a claimed EST could be patentable in the US by affirming that it encoded a certain protein, even though the specific function or application of that protein was undetermined at the moment of filing the application. The European position on the matter does not appear to be significantly different. In fact, the patentability of expressed sequence tags has generated similar controversy also in Europe. Even though there is no substantial case law available, "it is generally accepted that ESTs are not patentable in Europe as long as their functions are credibly disclosed in order to fulfill the requirements for industrial application"[193] as required by Article 57 of the European Patent Convention (EPC).[194] In other words, utility is defined as "industrial applicability". To satisfy this requirement, the European Patent Office (EPO) issued revised examination guidelines explaining how the 'industrial applicability' condition should be applied to sequences and partial sequences of genes. While the US Patent's Act "utility requirement" approach implies that the application must disclose a "specific, substantial, and credible utility",[195] the European approach seems to be more structured. In particular the EPO Examination Guidelines clarify that:

> The invention claimed must have such a sound and concrete technical basis that the skilled person can recognize that its contribution to the art could lead to practical exploitation in industry (T 898/05). In relation to sequences and partial sequences of genes, this general requirement is given specific form in that the industrial application of a sequence or a partial sequence of a gene must be disclosed in the patent application. A mere nucleic acid sequence without indication of a function is not a patentable invention (EU Dir. 98/44/EC, rec. 23). In cases where a sequence or partial sequence of a gene is used to produce a protein or a part of a protein, it is necessary to specify which protein or part of a protein is produced and what function this protein or part of a protein performs. Alternatively, when a nucleotide

[190] On the argument, see Arti K. Rai, Regulating Science Research: Intellectual Property Rights and the Norms of Science, cit. at 104–105. See also generally Joseph P. Pieroni, The Patentability of Expressed Sequence Tags, 9 Fed. Cir. B.J. 401, 412 (2000).

[191] See Rebecca S. Eisenberg & Robert P. Merges, Opinion Letter as to the Patentability of Certain Inventions Associated with the Identification of Partial cDNA Sequences, 23 AIPLA Q.J. 1 (1995) (quoting the observation of the United States Patent and Trademark Office).

[192] In re Fisher, 421F.3d 1365 (Fed. Cir. 2005). For a detailed investigation of the case, see Yann Joly, Winds of Change: In re Fisher and the Evolution of the American Biotechnology Patent Law, 25 Law in Context 67 (2007).

[193] See Martin Grund et al., Patenting of Biotech Inventions in Europe: New Developments, 6 Bio-Science Law Review 6, 9 (2004).

[194] EPC, art. 57.

[195] See Utility Examination Guidelines, 66 Fed. Reg. 1092, cmt. 7 at 1093 (Jan. 5, 2001).

> sequence is not used to produce a protein or part of a protein, the function to be indicated could e.g. be that the sequence exhibits a certain transcription promoter activity.[196]

However, as observed by commentators, "the net effect of Article 5 and Recitals 16 and 38" of the European Biotechnology Directive[197] "is that genes and biological products that originate from humans are patentable so long as they have been isolated and the patent has industrial applicability".[198]

The core of the question stands in the fact that DNA sequences are not simply molecules, but they are also information.[199] This observation implies that "knowing the DNA sequence for the genome of an organism provides valuable scientific information that can open the door to future discoveries".[200] This materialized information, when detached from the control of the human body, can be converted into an intellectual patented product providing a form of control over life. It consequently seems reasonable to argue that there is "biological information, and the biological material (cell or tissue) from which the information is derived, material that subsequently becomes the substrate of experiments that validate the leads suggested by the information".[201] In this particular process, "information is detached from its biological material originator to the extent that it does have a separate social life, but the 'knowledge' provided by the information is constantly relating back to the material biological sample".[202] Therefore, innovative knowledge is the result of the relationship between biological information and biological materiality.

[196] See European Patent Office, Guidelines for Examination in the European Patent Office (2010) Part C, c. IV, s. 5.4, available at http://www.epo.org/law-practice/legal-texts/guidelines.html (last accessed 28 April 2016).

[197] Council Directive 98/44/EC, 1998 O.J. (L 213) 13 (EC).

[198] See Timothy Sampson, Achieving Ethically Acceptable Biotechnology Patents: A Lesson from the Clinical Trials Directive? 25 Eur. Intell. Prop. Rev. 419, 421 (2003) (noting also that "The "utility" provision of the US patent code and the USPTO Utility Guidelines achieve the same end by requiring that a patent application must disclose a "specific, credible and substantial" use or a "well established use" for the claimed invention); Denis Schertenleib, The Patentability and Protection of DNA-based Inventions in the EPO and the European Union, 25 Eur. Intell. Prop. Rev 125 (2003).

[199] See Rebecca S. Eisemberg, Patents on DNA Sequences: Molecules and Information, in The Commodification of Information 417, 418 (Niva Elkin-Koren & Neil Weinstick Netanel, eds., Kluwer Law 2002). The notion of DNA as information was originally introduced by Watson and Crick's 1953 article. See J.D. Watson & F.H.C. Crick, Molecular Structure of Nucleic Acids: A Structure for Deoxyribose Nucleic Acid, 171 Nature 737, (1953).

[200] See Eisemberg, Patents on DNA Sequences: Molecules and Information, cit., at 418.

[201] Kaushik Sunder Rajan, Biocapital: The Constitution of Postgenomic life 42 (Duke University Press 2006).

[202] Ibidem.

4.7.3 Property Rights and Human Genes

As previously mentioned, a recent study shows that about 20 % of human genes have been patented in the United States, mainly by private firms and universities.[203] These data have led to a heated debate among scientists, organizations advocating individual rights and governments on whether special regulation of biotech patents is warranted. The problem is that modern methods of gene identification and isolation have raised new legal, ethical and social questions. The widespread patenting of research tools – DNA sequences such as ESTs or SNPs (single nucleotide polymorphisms) – is now a common practice among pharmaceutical corporations and specialized biotech companies. Their global strategy is quite clear: building a sort of defensive patent portfolio to increase their monopoly power over markets, maintaining control over commercial research activities. As already pointed out, here the policy question is that the advent of high-throughput DNA sequencing technologies[204] has revolutionized the identification process of ESTs, which is now completely automatic.[205] These new technologies have encouraged the filing of patenting sequences without patenting the corresponding protein or its function.[206]

For these reasons, to find an EST sequence automated sequencing systems are commonly used. The real work is to identify the gene and study its function. But, despite the ease with which this can be achieved, the rewards can be significant and without the need of particular efforts. For example, let us suppose that someone patents an Expressed Sequence Tag. At the same time, someone else patents the entire gene, while a third party obtains intellectual property rights on a genetic variant that predisposes an individual to a given disease. In a similar (not merely hypothetical) situation, anyone wishing to develop a diagnostic test and place it on the market should be obliged to obtain licenses from all these people.

The conclusions that can be drawn is that the role of intellectual property rights in science and technology matters is gradually being supplanted by a wide-ranging control of all the uses of intellectual works or inventions. The upwards trend toward ownership is also evident in the area of genetic information. This leads to numerous

[203] See Kyle Jensen & Fiona Murray, Intellectual Property Landscape of the Human Genome, 310 Science 239 (2005) (referencing a study of 4382 of the 23,688 genes in the National Center for Biotechnology Information's database that showed that 63 % of the patents are assigned to private firms and that, of the top ten gene patent assignees, nine were based in the United States).

[204] High-throughput screening (HTS) is a method of scientific experimentation widely used in drug discovery and relevant to the fields of biology and chemistry. A screen is a large experiment designed to test for the presence or absence of particular chemical compounds or biological markers. See Jongin Hong and Jennifer R. Lukes, Microfluidic Systems for High-Throughput Screening, in Encyclopedia of Microfluidics and Nanofluidics 1230 (Dongqing Li, 2008).

[205] See Pramod K. Gupta, Ultrafast and low-cost DNA sequencing methods for applied genomics research, 78 Proc. Natl. Acad. Sci. India sect. B. Biol. Sci. 91 (2008); Elaine R. Mardis, The impact of next-generation sequencing technology on genetics, 24 Trends Genet. 133 (2008).

[206] Debra Greenfield, Intangible or Embodied Information: The Non-Statutory Nature of Human Genetic Material, cit. at 470.

concerns related to the collection and analysis of genetic data and to their private manipulation, impeding their use for non-commercial purposes.

This approach is pursued both by national or supranational governments and by private corporations (transnational corporations). Should this vision be realized, it might constitute an "internal limit to research activity" and access to scientific knowledge, with detrimental effects on society, freedom of expression and research.[207] Restricting the free reuse of information and ideas could also have a negative impact on a broad spectrum of existing fundamental legal rights.[208]

In particular, the granting of exclusionary patents to human genes and the information they embody might restrict and infringe the guarantees of the freedom of thought and expression, limiting research activity and the disclosure of experimental information.[209]

The current process of DNA sequencing usually results in patents on the informational content of DNA. This practice can have possible fundamental rights implications, since DNA is, in essence, information.[210] This observation indicates that "when a patent has been granted on the exclusive use of genetic information, the ability to use the information has been removed from the public domain" restricting – *de facto* – the freedom of thought.[211] A tolerant attitude towards the patenting and control of genetic information can have the adverse effect of weakening the public benefit of patents by undermining the disclosure requirement.[212] As noted in the seminal US Supreme Court decision Sweezy v. New Hampshire "Freedom to reason and freedom for disputation on the basis of observation and experiment are the necessary conditions for the advancement of scientific knowledge".[213] It is therefore necessary to protect this freedom rather than restrict it.

Such legal issues underlie conflicts of rights where, normally, freedom of speech has a prevalent position. In fact, in most democracies the freedom of scientific research is not directly protected at the constitutional level, but it is essentially safeguarded through the extension of other fundamental legal rights.[214] The notions of scientific and academic freedoms are particularly relevant in open societies, and in some countries these freedoms are directly or indirectly recognized as constitutional

---

[207] See Amedeo Santosuosso et al., What Constitutional Protection for Freedom of Scientific Research? cit., at 343.

[208] See Robin Gross, Intellectual Property Rights and the Information Commons, in Human Rights in the Global Information Society 107,119 (Rikke Frank Jorgenson ed., 2006).

[209] See Debra Greenfield, Intangible or Embodied Information: The Non-Statutory Nature of Human Genetic Material, 25 Santa Clara Computer & High Technology Law Journal 467 (2009).

[210] Id. at 477.

[211] Id. at 536.

[212] See Rebecca S. Eisenberg, How Can You Patent Genes? Am J. Bioethics, Summer 2002, at 3.

[213] See Sweezy v. New Hampshire, 354 U.S. 234, 262–63 (1957) (Frankfurter, J., concurring).

[214] See Amedeo Santosuosso et al., What Constitutional Protection for Freedom of Scientific Research?, cit., at 342; Id., Freedom of Research and Constitutional Law, in Simona Giordano, John Coggon and Marco Cappato (eds.), Scientific Freedom 73, 74 (2012).

rights.[215] For example, in Canada and in the US, this type of freedom is generally protected as a specific aspect of the wider freedom of thought and expression (respectively by article 2 of Canadian Charter of Rights and Freedom[216] and by the First and Fourteenth amendments of the US Constitution[217]). A similar approach is also evident in the constitutional provisions of some European countries where freedom of scientific research is recognized within the freedom of research and teaching or within the freedom of art and science.[218] In addition, Article 13 of the Charter of Fundamental Rights of the European Union explicitly provides for the freedom of the arts and sciences stating that "the arts and scientific research shall be free of constraint" and that "academic freedom shall be respected".[219] The right to benefit from the results of scientific research has also received renewed attention from international human rights institutions. In particular, the United Nations Human Rights Council recently issued three reports by the Special Rapporteur for cultural diversity carrying several critiques and concerns about the continuous expansion of intellectual property rights emphasizing the need of expanding opportunities for participation in cultural life.[220]

It is therefore clear that the question is of a controversial nature because "academic freedom is not a blanket permission to use any and all means to investigate any vaguely interesting problem".[221] Experimental approaches used for research activities must be confined within reasonable limits. But for now – as it has been rightly observed by others – "there are few if any restrictions on the questions that scientists might ask"[222]; most of the time, scientists must simply provide guidance to "balance the risks inherent in their experimental protocols – risks to humans or

---

[215] See Michele Garfinkel, Stem Cells, Morals and the Courts, 13 Eur. Molecular Biology Org. 2, 2 (2012).

[216] Canadian Charter of Rights and Freedom, art. 2.

[217] U.S. Const., amends. I, XIV.

[218] For example, article 5 of the German Constitution provides that "Art and science, research and teaching are free"; article 33 of the Italian Constitution states that "The arts and sciences as well as their teaching are free" and article 59 of the Slovenian Constitution establishes that "Freedom of scientific research and artistic endeavor shall be guaranteed". See Amedeo Santosuosso et al., What Constitutional Protection for Freedom of Scientific Research?, cit., at 342; Id., Freedom of Research and Constitutional Law, cit. at 75.

[219] Charter of Fundamental Rights of the European Union art. 13, 2000 O.J. (C 364) 1. On this, see also Christine Godt, Intellectual Property and European Fundamental Rights, cit., at 223.

[220] See United Nations General Assembly, Human Rights Council, Report of the Special Rapporteur in the Field of Cultural Rights: The Right to Enjoy the Benefits of Scientific Progress and its Applications, Farida Shaheed, U.N. Doc. UA/HRC/20/26 (14 May 2012) at 15; United Nations General Assembly, Human Rights Council, Report of the Special Rapporteur in the Field of Cultural Rights: Copyright policy and the right to science and culture, Farida Shaheed, U.N. Doc. A/HRC/28/57 (24 Dec. 2014); United Nations General Assembly, Human Rights Council, Report of the Special Rapporteur in the Field of Cultural Rights: Patent policy and the right to science and culture, Farida Shaheed, U.N. Doc. A/70/279 (4 Aug. 2015).

[221] See Michele Garfinkel, Stem Cells, Morals and the Courts, cit.

[222] Id.

animals, risks to the environment or, in some cases, non-physical risks such as to community values – with the value of their research".[223]

References

Adelman, David E. 2005. A fallacy of the commons in biotech patent policy. *Berkeley Technology Law Journal* 20: 985.

Adelman, David E., and Kathryn L. DeAngelis. 2007. Patent metrics: The mismeasure of innovation in the biotech patent debate. *Texas Law Review* 85: 1677.

Allan, Trevor R.S. 2003. *Constitutional justice: A liberal theory of the rule of law*. Oxford/New York: Oxford University Press.

Allison, Malorye. 2011. Myriad decision reassures biotechs but diagnostics still murky. *Nature Biotechnology* 29: 771.

Ancarani, Vittorio. 2008. *The politics of the human genome project. Do institutions matter?* Roma: Aracne.

Andrews, Lori B., and Jordan Paradise. 2005. Essay, gene patents: The need for bioethics scrutiny and legal change. *Yale Journal of Health Policy, Law & Ethics* 5: 403–404.

Bakshi, Ashish M. 2014. Gene patents at the supreme court: Association for molecular pathology v.myriad genetics. *Journal of Law & The Biosciences* 1: 183.

Balmer, Brian. 1996. Managing mapping in the human genome project. *Social Studies of Science* 26: 531.

Benkler, Yochai. 2006. *The wealth of networks: How social production transforms markets and freedom*. New Haven: Yale University Press.

Bernier, Louise. 2010. *Justice in genetics: Intellectual property and human rights from a Cosmopolitan Liberal Perspective*. Northampton: Edward Elgar Publishing.

Bessen, James, and Michael J. Meurer. 2008. *Patent failure: How judges, bureaucrats, and lawyers put innovators at risk*. Princeton: Princeton University Press.

Bin, Roberto. 2006. La Corte e la Scienza. In *Bio-Tecnologie e Valori Costituzionali. Il Contributo della Giustizia Costituzionale*, ed. Atonio D'Aloia. Torino: Giappichelli.

Bin, Roberto, et al. (eds.). 2011. *Biotech innovations & fundamental rights*. Milan/New York: Springer.

Boldrin, Michele, and David K. Levine. 2010. *Against intellectual monopoly*. Cambridge: Cambridge University Press.

Bonadio, Enrico. 2012. Biotech patents and morality after Brüstle. *European Intellectual Property Review* 34: 433.

Boschiero, Nerina (ed.). 2006. *Bioetica e Biotecnologie nel Diritto Internazionale e Comunitario*. Torino: Giappichelli.

Boyle, James. 2003. The second enclosure movement and the construction of the public domain. *Law & Contemporary Problems* 66: 33.

Bozeman, Barry (ed.). 2003. *Knowledge flows and knowledge collectives: Understanding the role of science and technology policies in development*. New York: Rockefeller Foundation.

Braman, Sandra. 2002. Information technologies and global politics: The changing scope of power and governance. In *Informational meta-technologies and international relations: The case of biotechnologies*, vol. 91, ed. James N. Rosenau and J.P. Singh. New York: State University of New York Press.

Braman, Sandra (ed.). 2004a. *Biotechnology and communication: The meta-technologies of information*. Mahwah: Lawrence Erlbaum Associates.

Braman, Sandra. 2004b. Technology. In *The sage handbook of media studies*, ed. John D.H. Downing, 123. Thousand Oaks: Sage Publications.

[223] Id.

Bratton, Mark (ed.). 2009. *God, ethics and the human genome*. London: Church House Publishing.
Brownsword, Roger. 2008. *Rights, regulation, and the technological revolution*. Oxford: Oxford University Press.
Brownsword, Roger, and Morag Goodwin. 2012. *Law and technologies of the twenty-first century*. Cambridge: Cambridge University Press.
Burk, Daniel L. 2013a. Are human genes patentable? *International Review of Intellectual Property and Competition Law* 44: 747.
Burk, Daniel L. 2013b. Edifying thoughts of a patent watcher: The nature of DNA. *UCLA Law Review Discourse* 60: 92.
Burk, Daniel L., and Mark A. Lemley. 2009. *The patent crisis and how the courts can solve it*. Chicago: University of Chicago Press.
Caulfield, Timothy, et al. 2007. Myriad and the mass media: The covering of a gene patent controversy. *Genetics in Medicine* 9: 850.
Center for Responsible Genetics Consumer Genetic Privacy Manual. 2010. Available at http://www.councilforresponsiblegenetics.org/geneticprivacy/.
Chandra, Rajshree. 2012. *Knowledge as property. Issues in the moral grounding of intellectual property rights*. Oxford: Oxford University Press.
Chandrasekharan, Subhashini, et al. 2009. Proprietary science, open science and the role of patent disclosure: The case of zinc-finger proteins. *Nature Biotechnology* 27: 140.
Chapman, Audrey R. 2009. Towards an understanding of the right to enjoy the benefits from scientific progress and its applications. *Journal of Human Rights* 8: 1.
Claude, Richard Pierre. 2002. *Science in the service of human rights*. Philadelphia: University of Pennsylvania press.
Cook-Deegan, Robert, et al. 2009. The dangers of diagnostic monopolies. *Nature* 458: 405.
Cutcliffe, Stephen H. 2000. *Ideas, machines and values: An introduction to science, technology and social studies*. Lanham: Rowman & Littlefield Publishers.
D'Antonio, Virgilio. 2004. *Invenzioni Biotecnologiche e Modelli Giuridici: Europa e Stati Uniti*. Napoli: Jovene.
David, Pail, and Dominique Foray. 1995. Accessing and expanding the science and technology knowledge base. *Science Technology Industry Review* 16: 13.
David, Paul A. 2002. The political economy of public science: A contribution to the regulation of science and technology. In *The regulation of science and technology*, vol. 33, ed. Helen Lawton Smith. New York: Palgrave Publishers.
David, Paul A. 2003. The economic logic of "Open Science" and the balance between private property rights and the public domain in scientific data and information: A primer. In *The role of scientific and technical data and information in the public domain*, ed. M. Esanu and F. Uhlir, 19. Washington, DC: National Academy Press.
Den Exter, André. 2010. Personalized medicine and access to genetic technologies. *Revista de Derecho y Genoma Humano* 33: 49.
Devlin, Patrick. 1965. *The enforcement of morals*. Oxford: Oxford University Press.
Doll, John J. 1998. The patenting of DNA. *Science* 280: 689.
Donders, Yvonne. 2011. The right to enjoy the benefits of scientific progress: In search of state obligations in relation to health. *Medicine Health Care & Philosophy* 14: 371.
Eisenberg, R.S. 1987. Proprietary rights and the norms of science in biotechnology research. *Yale Law Journal* 97: 177.
Eisenberg, Rebecca S. 1989. Patents and the progress of science: Exclusive rights and experimental use. *University of Chicago Law Review* 56: 1017.
Eisenberg, Rebecca S. 1992. Genes, patents, and product development. *Science* 257: 903.
Elkin-Koren, Niva, and Neil Netanel (eds.). 2002. *The commodification of information*. The Hague: Kluwer Law.
Feenberg, Andrew. 1999. *Questioning technology*. London/New York: Routledge.
Feldman, Robin. 2009a. *The role of science in law*. Oxford: Oxford University Press.
Feldman, Robin. 2009b. Historic perspectives on law & science. *Stanford Technology Law Review* 12: 1.

Frischmann, Brett (ed.). 2014. *Governing knowledge commons*. Oxford: Oxford University Press.
Gaisser, Sibylle, et al. 2009. The phantom menace of gene patents. *Nature* 458: 407.
Geiger, Christophe. 2006. Constitutionalising' intellectual property law? The influence of fundamental rights on intellectual property in the European Union. *International Review of Intellectual Property and Competition Law* 37: 371.
Geiger, Christophe (ed.). 2014. *Research handbook on human rights and intellectual property*. Cheltenham: Edward Elgar Publishing.
Ghosh, Shubba. 2012. *Identity, invention and the culture of personalized medicine patenting*. Cambridge: Cambridge University Press.
Ghosh, Samantak. 2014. The taking of human biological products. *California Law Review* 102: 511.
Giordano, Simona (ed.). 2012. *Scientific freedom*. London: Bloomsbury Publishing.
Girotto, Sabina. 2010. Il Trattamento dei Dati Biometrici. In *Trattato di Biodiritto*, vol. I, ed. Stefano Rodotà and Mariachiara Tallacchini, 1237. Milano: Giuffrè editore.
Gitter, Donna M. 2001. International conflicts over patenting human DNA sequences in the United States and the European Union: An argument for compulsory licensing and a fair-use exemption. *New York University Law Review* 76: 1623.
Goggin, L. Malcom. 1986a. Governing science and technology: Reconciling science and technology and democracy. In *Governing science and technology in a democracy*, ed. Malcom Goggin. Knoxville: University of Tennessee Press.
Goggin, L. Malcom. 1986b. *Governing science and technology in a democracy*. Knoxville: University of Tennessee Press.
Gold, Richard E., and Julia Carbone. 2010. Myriad genetics: In the eye of the policy storm. *Genetics in Medicine* 12: S39.
Greenfield, Debra. 2009. Intangible or embodied information: The non-statutory nature of human genetic material. *Santa Clara Computer & High Technology Law Journal* 25: 467.
Grodin, Michael (ed.). 2013. *Health and human rights in a changing world*, 3rd ed. New York: Routledge.
Grosheide, Willem (ed.). 2010. *Intellectual property and human rights. A paradox*. Cheltenham/Northampton: Edward Elgar.
Guellec, Dominique, and Bruno van Pottelsberghe de la Potterie. 2007. *The economic of the european patent system: IP policy for innovation and competition*. Oxford: Oxford University Press.
Hamelink, Cees. 2003. Human rights for the information society. In *Communicating in the information society*, ed. Bruce Girard and Seán Ó. Siochrú. Geneva: United Nations Research Institute for Social Development.
Hanson, Mark J. 1997. Religious voices in biotechnology: The case of gene patenting. *Hastings Center Report* 27: 1.
Hardin, Garret. 1968. The tragedy of the commons. *Science* 162: 1243.
Haunss, Sebastian. 2013. *Conflicts in the knowledge society. The contentious politics of intellectual property*. Cambridge: Cambridge University Press.
Helfer, Laurence, and W. Austin Graeme. 2011. *Human rights and intellectual property: Mapping the global interface*. Cambridge: Cambridge University Press.
Heller, Michael A. 1998. The tragedy of the anticommons: Property in the transition from Marx to Markets. *Harvard Law Review* 111: 621.
Heller, Michael. 2008. *The gridlock economy: How too much ownership wrecks markets, stops innovation, and costs lives*. New York: Basic Books.
Heller, Michael A., and Rebecca S. Eisenberg. 1998. Can patents deter innovation? The anticommons in biomedical research. *Science* 280: 698.
Hess, Charlotte, and Elinor Ostrom (eds.). 2006. *Understanding knowledge as a commons: From theory to practice*. Cambridge, MA: MIT Press.
Hestermeyer, Holger. 2007. *Human rights and the WTO: The case of patents and access to medicines*. Oxford: Oxford University Press.
Holman, Christopher M. 2008. Trends in human gene patent litigation. *Science* 322: 198.

Holman, Christopher M. 2013. In myriad the supreme court has, once again, increased the uncertainty of U.S. patent law. *Biotechnology Law Report* 32: 1.
Holman, Molly A., and Stephen R. Munzer. 2000. Intellectual property rights in genes and gene fragments: A registration solution for expressed sequence tags. *Iowa Law Review* 85: 735.
Hveem, Helge, and Lelio Iapadre (eds.). 2011. *The global governance of knowledge creation and diffusion*. New York: Routledge.
Irwin, Alan. 2001. Constructing the scientific citizen: Science and democracy in the biosciences. *Public Understanding of Science* 10: 1.
Jackson, Jonah D. 2011. Something like the sun: Why even "Isolated and Purified" genes are still products of nature. *Texas Law Review* 89: 1453.
Jasanoff, Sheila. 1995. *Science at the bar. Law, science and technology in America*. Cambridge, MA: Harvard University Press.
Jasanoff, Sheila. 2004. Science and citizenship: A new synergy. *Science and Public Policy* 31: 90.
Jasanoff, Sheila. 2005. *Designs on nature: Science and democracy in Europe and the United States*. Princeton: Princeton University Press.
Jasanoff, Sheila. 2011a. Constitutional moments in governing science and technology. *Science and Engineering Ethics* 17: 621.
Jasanoff, Sheila (ed.). 2011b. *Reframing rights: Bioconstitutionalism in the genetic age*. Cambridge, MA: MIT Press.
Jensen, Kyle, and Fiona Murray. 2005. Intellectual property landscape of the human genome. *Science* 310: 239.
Jørgensen Rikke, Frank (ed.). 2006. *Human rights in the global information society*. Cambridge, MA: MIT press.
Kauble, Krysta. 2011. Patenting everything under the sun: Invoking the first amendment to limit the use of gene patents. *UCLA Law Review* 58: 1123.
Kaye, Jane, et al. 2007. Patents and translational research in genomics. *Nature Biotechnology* 25: 739.
Kevles, Daniel J. 2013. Can they patent your genes? *The New York Review of Books*, March 7.
Kevles, Daniel J., and Ari Berkowitz. 2001. The gene patenting controversy: A convergence of law, economic interests, and ethics. *Brooklyn Law Review* 67: 233.
Kleinman, Daniel Lee (ed.). 2000a. *Science, technology, and democracy*. Albany: State University of New York Press.
Kleinman, Daniel Lee. 2000b. Democratizations of science and technology. In *Science, technology, and democracy*, ed. Daniel Lee Kleinmann, 139. Albany: State University of New York Press.
Krimsky, Sheldon. 1982. *Genetic alchemy: The social history of the recombinant DNA controversy*. Cambridge, MA: MIT University Press.
Krimsky, Sheldon, and Peter Shorett (eds.). 2005. *Rights and liberties in the biotech age: Why we need a genetic bill of rights*. Lanham: Rowman & Littlefield Publishers.
Kur, Annette, and Marianne Levin. 2011. *Intellectual property rights in a fair world trade system: Proposals for reform of trips*. Cheltenham/Northampton: Edward Elgar.
Laurie, Graeme. 2004. *Genetic privacy. A challenge to medico-legal norms*. Cambridge: Cambridge University Press.
Lawton Smith, Helen (ed.). 2002. *The regulation of science and technology*. New York: Palgrave Publishers.
Leenes, Ronald E. et al. (eds.). 2008. *Constitutional rights and new technologies. A comparative study*. The Hague: T.M.C. Asser Press.
Liivak, Oskar. 2007. Maintaining competition in copying: Narrowing the scope of gene patents. *U.C. Davis Law Review* 41: 177.
Marks, Stephen. 2010. Out of obscurity: The right to benefit from advances in science and technology and its implications for Global Health. In *Proceedings of the 3rd conference on law, science, and technology: health and science: human rights and legal issues*. Taipei: Academia Sinica.

Matthijs, Gert. 2011. Gene and genetic diagnostic method patent claims: A comparison under current European and US Patent Law. *European Journal of Human Genetics* 19: 1.

Michaels, Dennis. 1999. Bioprospecting agreements: Forging a comprehensive strategy for managing genetic resources on public lands. *Environs: Environmental Law & Policy Journal* 22: 3.

Mills, Oliver. 2010. *Biotechnological inventions. Moral restraints and patent law*. Farnham/Burlington: Ashgate.

Minssen, Timo, and David Nilson. 2011. Standing on shaky ground: US patent-eligibility of Isolated DNA and genetic diagnostics after AMP v USPTO – Part I. *Queen Mary Journal of Intellectual Property* 1: 223.

Minssen, Timo, and David Nilson. 2012a. Standing on shaky ground: US patent-eligibility of isolated DNA and genetic diagnostics after AMP v USPTO – Part III. *Queen Mary Journal of Intellectual Property* 1: 225.

Minssen, Timo, and David Nilson. 2012b. Standing on shaky ground: US patent-eligibility of isolated DNA and genetic diagnostics after AMP v USPTO – Part II. *Queen Mary Journal of Intellectual Property* 1: 136.

Moir, Hazel V.J. 2013. *Patent policy and innovation. Do legal rules deliver effective economic outcomes?* Cheltenham: Edward Elgar Publishing.

Moore, Adam D. 2003. Intellectual property, innovation, and social progress: The case against incentive based arguments. *Hamline Law Review* 26: 601.

Moore, Jocob D. 2011. The forgotten victim in the human gene patenting debate: Pharmaceutical companies. *Florida Law Review* 63: 1277.

Murphy, Thérèse (ed.). 2009. *New technologies and human rights*. Oxford: Oxford University Press.

Murray, Fiona, and Scott Stern. 2007. Do formal intellectual property rights hinder the free flow of scientific knowledge? An empirical test of the anti-commons hypothesis. *Journal of Economic Behavior and Organization* 63: 648.

Murray, Kali, and Esther van Zimmeren. 2011. Dynamic patent governance In Europe and the United States: The Myriad example. *Cardozo Journal of International & Comparative Law* 19: 287.

Ostrom, Elinor. 1990. *Governing the commons: The evolution of institutions for collective action*. Cambridge: Cambridge University Press.

Ouellette, Lisa Larrimore 2010. Access to bio-knowledge: From gene patents to biomedical materials. *Stanford Technology Law Review* N1.

Ozolina, Zaneta et al. 2012. *Ethical and regulatory challenges to science and research policy at the global level*. Expert group report, directorate-general for research and innovation of the European Commission. Publication Office of the European Union.

Paradise, Jordan, et al. 2005. Patents on human genes: An analysis of scope and claims. *Science* 307: 1566.

Parkinson, John (ed.). 2009. *Expressed Sequence Tags (ESTs). Generation and analysis*. New York: Humana Press.

Pascuzzi, Giovanni, Izzo, and Matteo Umberto e Macilotti (eds.). 2013. *Comparative issues in the Governance of Research Biobanks: Property, privacy, intellectual property and the role of technology*. Berlin/New York : Springer.

Pestre, Dominique. 2008. Challenges for the democratic management of technoscience: Governance, participation and the political today. *Science as Culture* 17: 101.

Pierce, Brandon L. 2009. The impact of patents on the development of genome-based clinical diagnostics: An analysis of case studies. *Genetics in Medicine* 11: 202.

Pizzoferrato, Alberto. 2002. *Brevetto per Invenzioni e Biotecnologie*. Padova: Cedam.

Plomer, Aurora. 2005. *The law and ethics of medical research: International bioethics and human rights*. London/Portland: Cavendish Publishing.

Plomer, Aurora. 2012. After Brüstle: EU accession to the ECHR and the future of European Patent Law. *Queen Mary Journal of Intellectual Property* 2: 110.

Plomer, Aurora. 2013. The Human rights paradox: Intellectual property rights and rights of access to science. *Human Rights Quarterly* 35: 143.

Plomer, Aurora, and Paul Torremans (eds.). 2009. *Embryonic stem cell patents. European law and ethics*. Oxford: Oxford University Press.
Plomer, Aurora, et al. 2008. Challenges to human embryonic stem cell patents. *Cell Stem Cell* 2: 13.
Rai, Arti K. 1999. Regulating scientific research: Intellectual property rights and the norms of science. *Northwestern University Law* 94: 77.
Rai, Arti K. 2013. Biomedical patents at the supreme court: A path forward. *Stanford Law Review Online* 66: 111.
Rai, Arti K., and Rebecca S. Eisenberg. 2003. Bayh-dole reform and the progress of biomedicine. *Law Contemporary Problems* 66: 289.
Reichman, Jerome, and Rochelle Dreyfuss. 2007. Harmonization without consensus: Critical reflections on drafting a substantive patent law treaty. *Duke Law Journal* 57: 85.
Reichman, Jerome H., and Paul Uhlir. 2003. Contractually reconstructed research commons for scientific data in a highly protectionist intellectual property environment. *Law and Contemporary Problems* 66: 315.
Resnik, David B. 2001. DNA patents and human dignity. *Journal of Law Medicine & Ethics* 29: 152.
Resnik, David. 2004. *Owning the genome. A moral analysis of DNA patenting*. New York: SUNY Press.
Resta, Giorgio. 2009. Proprietà Intellettuale e Diritti Fondamentali: Una Relazione Ambigua. In *Persona, Derecho y Libertad: Nuevas Perspectivas. Escritos en Homenaje al Profesor Carlos Fernández Sessarego*, ed. Carlos Alberto and Calderón Puertas, 787. Lima: Motivensa Editora Jurídica.
Resta, Giorgio. 2011. The case against the privatization of knowledge: Some thoughts on the Myriad genetics controversy. In *Biotech innovations & fundamental rights*, eds. Bin Roberto et al., 34. Milan/New York: Springer.
Rimmer, Matthew. 2008. *Intellectual property and biotechnology. Biological inventions*. Cheltenham/Northampton: Edward Elgar.
Rimmer, Matthew, and Alison McLennan. 2012. *Intellectual property and emerging technologies: The new biology*. Cheltenham: Edward Elgar Publishing.
Robinson, Douglas, and Nina Medlock. 2005. Diamond v. Chakrabarty: A retrospective on 25 years of biotech patents. *Intellectual Property & Technology Journal* 17: 12.
Roffe, Pedro, and Maximiliano Santa Cruz. 2007. *Intellectual property rights and sustainable development: A survey of major issues*. New York: United Nations Publication.
Saladino, Tina. 2011. Seeing the forest through the trees: Gene patents & the reality of the commons. *Bekeley Technology Law Journal* 26: 301.
Santosusso, Amedeo. 2011. *Diritto, scienza e nuove tecnologie*. Padova: Cedam.
Santosuosso, Amedeo, et al. 2007. What constitutional protection for freedom of scientific research? *Journal of Medical Ethics* 33: 342.
Sarnoff, Joshua. 2011. Patent eligible medical and biotechnology inventions after Bilski, Prometheus and Myriad. *Texas Intellectual Property Law Journal* 19: 393.
Shaver, Lea. 2010. The right to science and culture. *Wisconsin Law Review* 2010: 121.
Shiva, Vandana. 1997. *Biopiracy: The plunder of nature and knowledge*. Boston: South End Press.
Sinjela, Mpazi (ed.). 2007. *Human rights and intellectual property rights: Tensions and convergences*. Leiden: Martinus Nijhoff Publishers.
Soini, Sirpa, et al. 2008. Patenting and licensing in genetic testing: Ethical, legal and social issues. *European Journal of Human Genetics* 16: S10.
Spinello, Richard A., and Maria Bottis. 2009. *A defense of intellectual property rights*. Cheltenham/Northampton: Edward Elgar.
Stazi, Andrea. 2015. *Biotechnological inventions and patentability of life: The US and European experience*. Cheltenham: Edward Elgar.
Stemerding, Dirk. 1993. How to deal with the implications of human genome research? On the bounds of a politics of regulation. In *Ethics of human genome analysis. European perspectives*, ed. Hille Haker, Richard Hearn, and Klaus Steigleder, 217. Tübingen: Attempto Verlag.

Sterckx, Sirid, and Julian Cockbain. 2012. *Exclusions from patentability: How far has the European patent office eroded boundaries?* Cambridge: Cambridge University Press.
Straus, Joseph. 2004. *Genetic inventions and patent law, an empirical survey of selected German R&D Institutions*. München: Verlag Medien Design.
Tallacchini, Mariachiara. 2003. La Trappola e il Topo: La Brevettabilità della Materia Vivente. In *Le tecniche della Biologia e gli Arnesi del Diritto* 203, ed. Amedeo Santosuosso. Pavia: Ibis.
Tallacchini, Mariachiara. 2013. Human tissues in the 'Public Space': Beyond the property/privacy dichotomy. In *Comparative issues in the governance of research biobanks: Property, privacy, intellectual property and the role of technology*, ed. Giovanni Pascuzzi, Umberto Izzo, and Matteo Macilotti. Berlin/New York: Springer.
Torremans, Paul L.C. (ed.). 2008. *Intellectual property and human rights*. The Hague: Kluwer Law International.
Vallas, Steven P., Daniel Lee Kleinman, and Dina Biscotti. 2011. Political structures and the making of U.S. biotechnology. In *State of innovation: The U.S. Government's role in technology development*, ed. Fred Block and Matthew Keller, 57. Boulder: Paradigm.
van den Hoven, Jeroen. 2010. The use of normative theories in computer ethics. In *The Cambridge handbook of information and computer ethics*, ed. Floridi Luciano, 59. Cambridge: Cambridge University Press.
Van Overwalle, Geertrui (ed.). 2009. *Gene patents and collaborative licensing models. Patent pools, clearinghouses, open source models and liability regimes*. Cambridge/New York: Cambridge University Press.
Van Overwalle, Geertrui, et al. 2006. Models for facilitating access to patents on genetic inventions. *Nature Reviews Genetics* 7: 143.
Varju, Marton. 2014. *European Union Human Rights Law: The dynamics of interpretation and context*. Northampton: Edward Elgar Publishing.
Verbeure, Birgit, et al. 2006. Analysing DNA patents in relation with diagnostic genetic testing. *European Journal of Human Genetics* 14: 26.
Vila De Azevedo Cunha, Mario (ed.). 2013. *New technologies and human rights*. Farnham: Ashgate Publishing.
Warren-Jones, Amanda. 2001. *Patenting rDNA. Human and animal biotechnology in the United Kingdom and Europe*. Witney: Lawtext Publishing.
Weeramantry, Christopher Gregory. 1990. *Human rights and scientific and technological development*. Tokyo: United Nations University Press.
Wright, Susan. 1994. *Molecular politics: Developing American and British regulatory policy for genetic engineering*. Chicago: University of Chicago Press.

Chapter 5
Legal Controversies in the Biosciences

Abstract The chapter – drawing upon comparative materials and case law analysis – investigates the potential risks and vulnerabilities related to the commodification of essential public knowledge assets in the life sciences focusing on the controversy over gene patenting and the possible implications for individual rights and conservation of natural resources.

5.1 Legal Controversies in Genetics and Genomics

Now that we have laid down some basic rules of DNA patenting and explored the growing field of biotech, we can start to face in details the multifaceted and controversial issues concerning the protection of genetic information and inherent rights implications. In the following pages we address this dispute though the analysis of some recent court cases. This "case based" approach will permit us to evaluate the coherence between the law in the books and the law in action.[1]

As already discussed above, one of the most debated aspects in this complicated field relates to the question of whether it is acceptable to hold human DNA sequences and whether their applications can be considered patent-eligible.[2] Here the theme revolves around patent eligibility and the identification of the boundaries within which patentable subject matter should be limited. Most of the controversy in the patenting of DNA-based materials has revolved around the question of whether DNA can be defined a patentable subject matter. In other words, the point is whether it is possible and reasonable to recognize property rights in DNA information.[3] As previously reported, this is also a central issue that combines the jurisdictions of different countries, mainly Europe and North America. In particular, recent patent law decisions in United States courts have exacerbated the confusion surrounding the function and value of biotech patents.

[1] See Roscoe Pound, Law in Books and Law in Action, 44 Am. L. Rev., 12 (1910).

[2] Timo Minssen & David Nilson, Standing on shaky ground: US patent-eligibility of isolated DNA and genetic diagnostics after AMP v USPTO – Part I, 1 Queen Mary J. of Intell. Prop., 223, 224 (2011).

[3] David B. Resnik, Owning the Genome 50 (2004)

N. Lucchi, *The Impact of Science and Technology on the Rights of the Individual*, Law, Governance and Technology Series 26,
DOI 10.1007/978-3-319-30439-7_5

In United States patent law, an invention must be of a proper subject matter in order to be considered for a patent. In addition, patents have a constitutional and a statutory basis.[4] The statutory basis for patents is 35 U.S.C. § 101, which states that "whoever invents or discovers any *new* and useful process, machine, manufacture, or composition of matter, or any new and useful improvement thereof, may obtain a patent therefor, subject to the conditions and requirements of this title".[5] Therefore, suitable subject matter includes – by statutory definition – one or more of the following statutory claims: a machine, article of manufacture, composition of matter, or process.[6] For most of the inventions conceived by individual inventors, the question of patent eligibility is generally of easy determination. However, in some areas of science or technology, this question could become extremely challenging. On the other hand, the constitutional basis for patents is provided by Article I, Section 8, Clause 8 of the U.S. Constitution (the so called "Patent Clause").[7] This provision gives Congress the power to "promote the Progress of Science and useful Arts, by securing for limited Times to Authors and Inventors the exclusive Right to their respective Writings and Discoveries". [8]

Historically US courts have scrutinized patent eligibility criteria under US patent statutes with reference to the 'Patent Clause' of the US Constitution.[9] Theoretically, patents should promote and encourage the free flow of information as well as intellectual production.[10] The inventor agrees to reveal information about his invention to the public, who probably will benefit from this new knowledge. In return, the government grants the inventor the right to exclude others from using the invention for a limited time.[11] The U.S. Supreme Court has articulated this basic *quid pro quo*[12] of the patent system as follows:

---

[4] See Douglas L. Rogers, After Prometheus, Are Human Genes Patentable Subject Matter?" 11 Duke L. & Tech. Rev. 434, 439 (2013).

[5] 35 U.S.C. § 101 (2002)

[6] Id.

[7] Article I, § 8, Clause 8 of the U.S. Constitution authorizes Congress to "promote the Progress of Science and useful Arts, by securing for limited Times to Authors and Inventors the exclusive Right to their respective Writings and Discoveries." See Edward C. Walterscheid, To Promote the Progress of Useful Arts: American Patent Law and Administration 1787–1836, at 19 (1998) (observing how the "intellectual property clause clearly encompassed two separate powers packaged together; one to promote the progress of science, i.e., knowledge, through the exclusive grant known as a copyright, and the other to promote the progress of useful arts through the exclusive grant known as a patent."

[8] See U.S. Const. art. 1, §8, cl. 8.

[9] Minssen & Nilson, Standing on shaky ground: US patent-eligibility of isolated DNA and genetic diagnostics after AMP v USPTO – Part I, cit., at 224; Douglas L. Rogers, After Prometheus, Are Human Genes Patentable Subject Matter?", cit. at 440.

[10] See Rochelle Cooper Dreyfuss, Does IP Need IP? Accomodating Intellectual Production Outside the Intellectual Paradigm, 31 Cardozo L. Rev. 1437, 1444 (2010) (discussing how intellectual production can occur also in absence of intellectual property rights).

[11] See Lionel Bently & Brad Sherman, Intellectual Property Law, 3rd ed., 339 et seq. (OUP 2009).

[12] See Enzo Biochem, Inc. v. Gen-Probe Inc., 323 F.3d 956, 970 (Fed. Cir. 2002) (reporting how the description of the patent "is the quid pro quo of the patent system; the public must receive mean-

> First, patent law seeks to foster and reward invention. Second, it promotes disclosure of inventions to stimulate further innovation and to permit the public to practice the invention once the patent expires. Third, the stringent requirements for patent protection seek to assure that ideas in the public domain remain there for the free use of the public.[13]

Therefore, the inventor is given exclusive rights in exchange for disclosing his invention to the public. However, some recent court cases challenging the patentability of genetic material seem to support a different interpretation or perspective than the traditional one.

5.2 Patent Litigation in the Biosciences: From Brüstle to Myriad

Legal questions concerning the interpretation and application of patent laws to the scientific area have started to be challenged more frequently also in courts in different countries. In particular, the effects and consequences of these controversial judgments have been intensively discussed both in academia and policy circles. Courts and scholars have reopened and fueled the debate over the benefits and risks associated with patent protection to diagnostic methods and other scientific research techniques. For the most part, these discussions are focused on patent applications with the aim to determine the patentability of a particular invention related to human DNA sequences or stem cells developed in vitro and used for scientific research. A key example is the recent controversy surrounding Myriad Genetics' BRCA patents involving a human gene associated with breast cancer.[14] On the same footing – but

ingful disclosure in exchange for being excluded from practicing the invention for a limited period of time.").

[13] Aronson v. Quick Point Pencil Co., 440 U.S. 257, 262 (1979).

[14] For a complete chronology of the legal controversy, see Ass'n for Molecular Pathology v. U.S. Patent & Trademark Office (Myriad I), 702 F. Supp. 2d 181, (S.D.N.Y. 2010), aff'd in part, rev'd in part, 653 F.3d 1329 (Fed. Cir. 2011); Ass'n for Molecular Pathology v. U.S. Patent & Trademark Office (Myriad II), 689 F.3d 1303, (Fed. Cir. 2012), cert. granted sub nom. Myriad Genetics, 133 S. Ct. 694 (2012) (granting certiorari); Petition for Writ of Certiorari at i, Myriad Genetics, 133 S. Ct. 694 (No. 11-725), 2011 WL 6257250; Ass'n for Molecular Pathology v. Myriad Genetics, Inc., 133 S. Ct. 2107, 2111 (2013) (holding that "a naturally occurring DNA segment is a product of nature and not patent eligible merely because it has been isolated, but that cDNA is patent eligible because it is not naturally occurring"). For a complete analysis and discussion of the case, see Timo Minssen and David Nilson, "Standing on shaky ground: US patent-eligibility of isolated DNA and genetic diagnostics after AMP v USPTO – Part I", 1 Queen Mary J. of Intell. Prop. 223 (2011); Idd., Standing on shaky ground: US patent-eligibility of isolated DNA and genetic diagnostics after AMP v USPTO – Part II, 1 Queen Mary J. of Intell. Prop., 136 (2012); Idd., Standing on Shaky Ground: US patent-Eligibility of Isolated DNA and genetic diagnostics after AMP v USPTO – Part III", 1 Queen Mary J. of Intell. Prop. 225 (2012). For the most recent developments and comments, see e.g.. Dan Burk, Anticipating Patentable Subject Matter,65 Stanford L. Rev. Online 109 (2013); Rochelle C Dreyfuss, The Patentability of Genetic Diagnostics in U. S. Law and Policy, in Pharmaceutical Innovation, Competition and Patent Law: A Trilateral Perspective 7 (Josef Drexl and Nari Leei eds. 2013); Samantak Ghosh, The Taking of Human

on the other side of the Atlantic – is also the so called "Brüstle case" decided by the Court of Justice of the European Union (CJEU) and linked to a patent concerning the production of neural precursor cells, (used for the treatment of neurological diseases) derived from human embryonic stem cells.[15] In this decision, the CJEU held that processes that require the use of stem cells gathered from a human embryo involving the destruction of that embryo cannot be subject to a patent. In particular, the Court recognized that "any human ovum after fertilization, any non-fertilized human ovum into which the cell nucleus from a mature human cell has been transplanted, any non-fertilized human ovum whose division and further development have been stimulated by parthenogenesis constitute a "human embryo"[16] thus constituting an unpatentable subject matter within the meaning of Article 6(2)(c) of the Biotech Directive.[17] The decision prompted intriguing questions, in particular about the freedom of research versus concerns about the morality of a technology. The use of morality (or *ordre public*) tests for the appropriateness of a patent is a very sensitive matter and it could be difficult to evaluate which criteria are relevant. In this case the plaintiff raised concerns about commodification. In other words, the main argument against the validity of the patent was that the effect of the patent was to transform a good originally considered inalienable into a commodity available on the market.[18] At present, it remains uncertain whether concerns regarding commodification and dignity can be limited to stem cells or can be used in other cases including commercial uses of other human tissue products. Furthermore, the concept of human dignity reveals itself as equally complicated and multifaceted in particular when applied to the field bioethics and human genetics.[19] In the wake of the Brüstle

Biological Products, 102 Cal. L. Rev., 511 (2014); Arti K. Rai, Diagnostic Patents at the Supreme Court, 18 Marq. Intell. Prop. L. Rev., 1 (2014); Ashish M. Bakshi, Gene Patents at the Supreme Court: Association for Molecular Pathology v. Myriad Genetics, 1 J.Law Biosci. 183 (2014).

[15] See Oliver Brüstle v Greenpeace eV (C-34/10) [2012] 1 C.M.L.R. 41. For a more detailed analysis, see: For a more detailed analysis, see: Enrico Bonadio, Biotech patents and morality after Brustle", 34 Eur. Intell. Prop. Rev. 433 (2012); Aurora Plomer, After Brüstle: EU accession to the ECHR and the future of European patent law, 2 Queen Mary J. of Intell. Prop., 110 (2012); Martina Ines Schuster, The Court of Justice of the European Union's ruling on the patentability of human embryonic stem-cell-related inventions (case C-34/10), 43 Int'l Rev. Intell. Prop. & Competition L., 626 (2012); Aidan Courtney, Dignity, plurality and patentability: the unfinished story of Brustle v Greenpeace, 38 Eur. L. Rev., 92 (2013).

[16] See Oliver Brüstle v Greenpeace eV (C-34/10) [2012] 1 C.M.L.R. 41, at § 38.

[17] Directive 98/44/EC of the European Parliament and of the Council of 6 July 1998 on the legal protection of biotechnological inventions, OJ EC L 213, 30 July 1998, 13–21.

[18] See Timothy Caulfield & Ubaka Ogbogu, Stem Cell Research, Scientific Freedom and the Commodification Concern, 13 Eur. Molecular Biology Org. 12, 12 (2011).

[19] See Jeff Malpas and Norelle Lickiss, Introduction to a Conversation, in Perspectives on Human Dignity: A Conversation 1 (Jeff Malpas and Norelle Lickiss eds., 2007). For more on this topic, see e.g. Charles Foster, Human Dignity in Bioethics and Law (2011); Miguel Nogueira de Brito, Human Reproduction and Human Dignity as a Constitutional Concept, in New Technologies and Human Rights 169 (Mario Viola de Azevedo Cunha et. Al. eds., 2013); Paolo Veronesi, La Dignità Umana tra Teoria dell'Interpretazione e Topica Costituzionale, 34 Quaderni Costituzionali 315 (2014).

decision, the CJEU has recently had an opportunity to clarify and further define the notion of 'human embryo' as well as the patentability of inventions involving uses of human embryos for industrial or commercial purposes. It was in fact necessary to dispel a doubt left open after the Brüstle decision, namely whether "organisms which the embryonic stem cells are derived from and which do not have the inherent capacity of developing into a human being" are patentable or not. This new case – proposed by the UK High Court of Justice – involves a dispute between International Stem Cell Corporation and the United Kingdom intellectual property office concerning the patentability of methods of "parthenogenetic activation"[20] of human ova.[21] At issue was the patentability of a process for the production of pluripotent human stem cell lines derived from unfertilized oocytes whose division and further development have been stimulated by parthenogenesis. The High Court asked to the CJEU if the notion of "Human embryo" – as intended in the Brüstle case – can be limited or not to organisms capable of leading to a human being.[22] Specifically, the UK court referred the following question to the CJEU:

> Are unfertilized human ova whose division and further development have been stimulated by parthenogenesis, and which, in contrast to fertilized ova, are incapable of developing into human beings, included in the term "human embryo" under Article 6(2)(c) of the Biotechnology Directive?[23]

On 17 July 2014, the Advocate General Cruz Villalon presented his opinion before the Court of Justice of the European Union[24] observing that "unfertilized human ova whose division and further development have been stimulated by parthenogenesis" should be excluded from the notion of 'human embryos' in the context of Article 6(2)(c) of the Biotech Directive.[25] Following the approach proposed by the Advocate General, the CJEU held that an organism that is not able of developing into a human being does not represent a human embryo within the meaning

[20] "Parthenogenesis consists in the activation of an oocyte, in the absence of sperm, by a variety of chemical and electrical techniques and the organism thus created is called a parthenote." See Court of Justice of the European Union, Press release No. 181/14, (2014).

[21] International Stem Cell Corp v Comptroller General of Patents (2013) EWHC 807 (Ch); (2013) 3 C.M.L.R. 14.

[22] For extended comments on this case, see e.g. Ella O'Sullivan, International Stem Cell Corp v Comptroller General of Patents: the debate regarding the definition of the human embryo continues, 36 Eur. Intell. Prop. Rev. 155 (2014); Charles Brabin, Intellectual Property Law in the Realm of Biology – Striking the Right Balance, 36 Eur. Intell. Prop. Rev. 687 (2014); Sebastian Moore, Clarification of European Law Relating to Stem Cell Patents, 37 Eur. Intell. Prop. Rev. 258 (2015).

[23] International Stem Cell Corp v Comptroller General of Patents (2013) EWHC 807 (Ch); (2013) 3 C.M.L.R. 14, at 59.

[24] Opinion of Advocate General Cruz Villalón in the Cases C-364/13 International Stem Cell Corporation v. Comptroller General of Patents delivered on 17 July 2014 (2014).

[25] For an expanded comment on the Advocate General's opinion, see Aurora Plomer, Case Comment: Opinion of Advocate General Cruz Villalon in International Stem Cell Corporation (C-364/13), EUtopia law, available at <http://eutopialaw.com/2014/08/11/case-comment-opinion-of-advocate-general-cruz-villalon-in-international-stem-cell-corporation-c-36413/> (last accessed 28 April 2016); Christopher Hayes, Stem cell patents: limiting the application of Brüstle?, 9 J. Intell. Prop. L. & Pract. 951 (2014).

of the Directive on the legal protection of biotech inventions.[26] As a consequence, uses of similar organism for industrial or commercial applications may be patented. On this point, the decision seemed to design new boundaries for patentability of stem cells offering a higher level of certainty compared to unclear situation resulting from the Brüstle judgment.

All these cases are just a few of the growing number of elements that would seem to argue that some forms of patents can really have the ability of hampering the development of potentially life-saving medical treatment restricting the access to scientific knowledge and to affordable health care. This issue is even more critical in light of the possible asymmetries that may arise when patent offices in different countries apply different standards for patent eligible subject matter in the genetic context.

Within the framework of the present part of the book, the Myriad controversy deserves special attention and a more central place in this debate since – in our opinion – it can be considered the most significant human gene patent case in recent history. In many ways, much of the current debate surrounding the patentability of genetic material – with respect to genetic diagnostic methods – revolves exactly around the patents held by the US biotech company Myriad Genetics. Myriad's patents have generated transnational attention and discussions, affecting local authorities in the European Union, Canada, and most recently, the United States.[27] Moreover, as argued by many authors, the Myriad controversy can be considered "a test case on how the public discourse on constitutional rights gets transformed into a more narrow epistemic IP discourse".[28] For all these motivations, in the following pages particular attention will be devoted to the analysis of this legal dispute.

[26] International Stem Cell Corporation v Comptroller General of Patents, Designs and Trade Marks (C-364/13). Judgment of December 18, 2014, at 38. The full reasoning of the Court was as follows: "Article 6(2)(c) of Directive 98/44 must be interpreted as meaning that an unfertilised human ovum whose division and further development have been stimulated by parthenogenesis does not constitute a 'human embryo', within the meaning of that provision, if, in the light of current scientific knowledge, that ovum does not, in itself, have the inherent capacity of developing into a human being, this being a matter for the national court to determine".

[27] See E. Richard Gold & Julia Carbone, Myriad Genetics: In the Eye of the Policy Storm, 12 Genetics Med. S39 (2010) (discussing the global impact of the BRCA1 and BRCA2 patents on scientific research). Apart from the above-mentioned case, there are at least other two important cases related to the patent eligibility of biotech inventions with respect to genetic diagnostic methods: Prometheus Labs. Inc. v. Mayo Collaborative Servs. & Mayo Clinic Rochester, 628 F.3d 1347 (Fed. Cir. 2010) and Classen Immunotherapies v. Biogen Idec, Case no. 2006-1634 (Fed. Cir. August 31, 2011).

[28] See Christine Godt, Intellectual Property and European Fundamental Rights, cit., at 222.

5.3 Biosciences and Patentable Subject Matter

The general conditions for patentability under modern international patent law are substantially similar to those of the TRIPS Agreement and include the criteria of novelty, inventiveness and industrial applicability. As we have seen before, these requirements alone can "leave certain subject matter capable of being patented that may nonetheless be inappropriate for patenting".[29] In particular, the patenting of life raises the most troublesome questions. The growing extension of the patent protection to genetic information grants an unnatural exclusive control to property holders – normally international corporations – over what uses are and are not permitted restricting individual rights and jeopardizing other potential directions of "genomics research and application".[30] The current extension of the concept of patentability (encompassing subjects previously considered to be in the public domain) emphasizes the importance of the existence of limitations and the need to create new boundaries to patenting.[31]

In the context of patent eligibility of medical methods, the principle upon which the whole question turns is the failure to meet these conditions for patentability.[32] In the European patent system, the European Patent Convention (EPC) sets up patentability standards stipulating what matter shall be excluded as patentable subject matter and to what extent.[33] On the other hand, in the United States patent eligibility is essentially grounded on Section 101 of Title 35 of the United States Code, as currently interpreted by the Federal courts.[34] Section 101 of Title 35 reads as follows:

---

[29] See Sigrid Sterckx and Julian Cockbain, Exclusions from patentability: How far has the European Patent Office eroded boundaries? 1 (2012).

[30] See Bita Amani, State Agency and the Patenting of Life in International Law: Merchants and Missionaries in a Global Society 333 (2009).

[31] Sigrid Sterckx and Julian Cockbain, Exclusions from patentability, cit. (observing that exceptions to patentability, as well as restrictions on patent holders' ability to enforce their patents, have long provided important safeguards to society, nascent industries, academics, farmers, members of the medical professions etc.)

[32] See Spinello & Bottis, A Defense Of Intellectual Property Rights, cit. at 52.

[33] Convention on the Grant of European Patents (European Patent Convention), Oct. 5, 1973, 1065 U.N.T.S. 199 (entered into force Oct. 7, 1977), as amended by the Act revising the Convention on the Grant of European Patents of Nov. 29, 2000 (entered into force Dec. 13, 2007).

[34] As interpreted by the Federal courts, 35 U.S.C. 101 has two purposes: "first, 35 U.S.C. 101 defines which categories of inventions are eligible for patent protection. An invention that is not a machine, an article of manufacture, a composition or a process cannot be patented. See Diamond v. Chakrabarty, 447 U.S. 303, 206 USPQ 193 (1980); Diamond v. Diehr, 450 U.S. 175, 209 USPQ 1 (1981). Second, 35 U.S.C. 101 serves to ensure that patents are granted on only those inventions that are "useful". This second purpose has a Constitutional footing – Article I, Section 8 of the Constitution authorizes Congress to provide exclusive rights to inventors to promote the "useful arts". See Carl Zeiss Stiftung v. Renishaw PLC, 945 F.2d 1173, 20 USPQ2d 1094 (Fed. Cir. 1991). Thus, to satisfy the requirements of 35 U.S.C. 101, an applicant must claim an invention that is statutory subject matter and must show that the claimed invention is "useful" for some purpose either explicitly or implicitly". See U.S. Dep't of Commerce Patent & Trademark Office, Manual of Patent Examining Procedure § 2107.01 (8th ed. rev. Jul. 2010).

> Whoever invents or discovers any new and useful process, machine, manufacture, or composition of matter, or any new and useful improvement thereof, may obtain a patent therefor, subject to the conditions and requirements of this title.[35]

Contrary to what happens in European patent legislation,[36] US patent statutes have not explicitly outlined what categories of inventions or discoveries are placed outside the umbrella of patentability.[37] It is thus left to the Courts to define – time by time – where the boundary of patentability lies, and they are bound only by the provisions of the legislation.

Another major distinction between the two systems concerns the "public morality argument". This aspect is not particularly strong within American patent law. On the contrary, in Europe the question of morality in the patenting of human genetic material "is not only a matter of common public discussion, but has entered the very text of the law".[38] The American approach is intrinsically "court-oriented" because frequently delegate to courts the task of deciding what elements are protectable by patent law. As remarked by some authors, "although several bills had attempted to exclude genes and proteins from patent protection", also the recent Patent Reform Act of 2011 (the so called *Leahy-Smith America Invents Act*)[39] corroborate this pragmatic approach.[40]

In recent years, the US Supreme Court has decided a number of patent cases also reversing the Federal Circuit decisions.[41] Much of the debate over the patent-eligibility

---

[35] 35 USC § 101.

[36] The European Patent Convention specifically enumerates the cases of unpatentability. See Convention on the Grant of European Patents art. 52(2), Oct. 5, 1973, available at http://www.epo.org/law-practice/legal-texts/html/epc/1973/e/ar52.html (last accessed 28 April 2016); Convention on the Grant of European Patents art. 53, Oct 5, 1973, available at http://www.epo.org/law-practice/legal-texts/html/epc/1973/e/ar53.html (last accessed 28 April 2016). See Richard A. Spinello & Maria Bottis, A Defense Of Intellectual Property Rights 67–68 (2009) (describing the differences between patent law in the US and Europe).

[37] See Minssen & Nilson, Standing on shaky ground: US patent-eligibility of isolated DNA and genetic diagnostics after AMP v USPTO – Part I, cit., at 224

[38] See Spinello & Bottis, A Defense Of Intellectual Property Rights, cit. at 68.

[39] Leahy-Smith America Invents Act, Pub. L. 112-029, 125 Stat. 284 (2011). Signed into law by President Barack Obama on September 16, 2011, it is considered the most significant amendment to the US patent laws since 1952.

[40] See Minssen & Nilson, Standing on shaky ground: US patent-eligibility of isolated DNA and genetic diagnostics after AMP v USPTO – Part I, cit., at 225.

[41] The debate over patent eligibility of processes and products has essentially centered around five United States Supreme Court cases and a decision of the Court of Appeals for the Federal Circuit: Funk Brothers Seed Co v Kalo Inoculant Co, 333 US 127 (1948) was decided before the 1952 Patent Act. As for subsequent decisions, see Gottschalk v Benson, 409 US 63 (1972); Parker v Flook, 437 US 584 (1978), Diamond v. Chakrabarty, 447 U.S. 303 (1980).; Diamond v Diehr, 450 US 175, 184 (1981); State Street Bank v Signature Financial Group, Inc 149 F 3d 1388 (Fed Cir 1998) cert denied 525 US 1093 (1999) abrogated by In re Bilski, 545 F 3d 943, 958–9 (Fed Cir 2008). See Minssen & Nilson, Standing on shaky ground: US patent-eligibility of isolated DNA and genetic diagnostics after AMP v USPTO – Part I, cit., at 225.

has focused on the three classical judicial exceptions: laws of nature, natural phenomena and abstract ideas.[42]

Among the most significant and recent decisions taken by the U.S. Supreme Court is that of Bilski v. Kappos.[43] Here the Court unanimously agreed that the "machine-or-transformation" test was not the exclusive test for patentable subject matter.[44]

The court also held that the Bilski's invention was not a patent eligible "process" under Section 101 of the Patent Act.[45] In particular, the Court recognized that the "machine-or-transformation test" is not the only test for determining the patent eligibility of a process, but rather "a useful and important clue, an investigative tool, for determining whether some claimed inventions are processes under § 101". In United States patent law, the "machine-or-transformation test" is a test for assessing patent eligibility. Under this test a claim to a process qualifies to be considered for patenting if "(i) it is tied to a particular machine or apparatus, or (ii) it transforms a particular article into a different state or thing".[46]

However, as already mentioned, the U.S. landmark case in biotechnology-related patent law is Diamond v. Chakrabarty.[47] Here, the Court held that a human-made microorganism was not excluded from patentability.[48] According to the Court, new microorganisms not found in nature (i.e. human made) were 'manufacture' or 'composition of matter' within the meaning of § 101 of the Patent Act.[49] They are also eligible for patent protection provided they are new, useful and non-obvious[50] and do not fall within the three categories of "patent-ineligible" subject matter: "laws of nature, physical phenomena, and abstract ideas".[51]

---

[42] These exceptions to eligibility for patent protection have been used to the many patent statutes "as a matter of statutory stare decisis going back 150 years." See Bilski, 130 S. Ct. at 3225; Chakrabarty, 447 U.S. at 309 (quoting Supreme Court precedents from 1978 to 1853). See also Bilski, 130 S. Ct. at 3221; Chakrabarty, 447 U.S. at 309; Gottschalk v. Benson, 409 U.S. 63, 67 (1972).

[43] Bilski v. Kappos, 130 S. Ct. 3218, 3222 (2010).

[44] Id.

[45] 35 U.S.C. § 101; Bilski v Kappos, 130 S Ct 3218 (2010).

[46] In re Bilski, 545 F.3d 943, 954 (Fed. Cir. 2008). The court observed that this test was already "articulated in Benson and reaffirmed in Diehr." Id. at 955. In effect the dates back to the nineteenth century and it articulated also in Gottschalk v. Benson, 409 U.S. 63 (1972); Parker v. Flook, 437 U.S. 584 (1978) and Diamond v. Diehr, 450 U.S. 175 (1981).

[47] Diamond v Chakrabarty, 447 U.S (holding that a genetically engineered bacterium created by the inventor's process was a patentable 'manufacture' under §101 of the US Patent Act). For a brief summary of the case, see See Kathrin Garforth, Life as Chemistry or Life as Biology? An Ethic of Patents on Genetically Modified Organisms", in Patenting Lives: Life Patents, Culture and Development 27, 39 (Johanna Gibson ed., 2008).

[48] Diamond v. Chakrabarty, 447 U.S. 303 (1980).

[49] Id.

[50] Id., at 309–10.

[51] Id. at 309 (1980) ("The laws of nature, physical phenomena, and abstract ideas have been held not patentable."). See also Gottschalk v. Benson, 409 U.S. 63, 67 (1972) ("Phenomena of nature,

In the years following the principle established in the Chakrabarty decision, the biotechnology field advanced as well as the number of patents issued in the biotech field. As a consequence, the European Patent Office (EPO) and the Japanese Patent Office also started granting patent protection for microorganisms.[52]

The new procedural patent rules largely take account of the previous case law and administrative practice. It has reinforced the concern that intellectual property protection restricts use of information rather than facilitate its creation.[53] But the fact remains that the use of genetic sequences or biological materials should be more balanced with the international human rights framework and the other Constitutional values at stake. The vast majority of the world's nations have acknowledged a right to health under international human rights law. Furthermore, all members of the UN recognize a right to health through the Universal Declaration of Human Rights. The right to health includes also the access to medicine and to other medical products. Patent protection, by granting monopolies in pharmaceutical and medical production, can hamper the access to medicine.[54] Patents can in fact increase the cost of the medicines or the treatments, making the access to them very difficult.[55] Patents can also provide a profit mechanism that boosts "private firm to research treatment for diseases prevalent in industrialized countries"[56] with the most lucrative markets for new drugs and medical treatments. Access to medicine is currently one of the main challenges of public health policies. The issue is particularly relevant when drugs are protected by patents or other instruments ensuring market exclusivity. This is also the rationale behind the increasing number of court decisions in countries like Asia, Africa and Latin America that have established a right of access to essential medicines in order to improve equitable access to essential pharmaceutical products.[57]

---

though just discovered, mental processes, and abstract intellectual concepts are not patentable, as they are the basic tools of scientific and technological work").

[52] In Europe, EPO granted is first patent on engineered plant in 1989, see Lubrizol Genetics, Inc., (Lubrizol II), EP-B1-122 791, 1990 O.J. E.P.O. 71 (Opp. Div.); then, in a 1995 human DNA patent case decided under the EPC, the EPO approved the grant of a patent for a DNA sequence encoding a human protein; see Case V 8/94, Relaxin/Howard Florey institute, 1995 O.J. E.P.O. 388 para. 6 (Opp. Div.).

[53] See Geertrui Van Overwalle, Human rights' limitations in patent law, in Intellectual Property And Human Rights. A Paradox 236, 262 (Willem Grosheide ed., 2010).

[54] Laurence Helfer and Graeme Austin, Human Rights and Intellectual Property: Mapping the Global Interface 90 (2011).

[55] Id., at 140 et seq.

[56] Id.

[57] On this debate, see e.g. Rochelle C. Dreyfuss, and César Rodríguez-Garavito (eds.), Balancing Wealth and Health: The Battle over Intellectual Property and Access to Medicines in Latin America (2014); Katharine G. Young and Julieta Lemaitre, The Comparative Fortunes of the Right to Health: Two Tales of Justiciability in Colombia and South Africa, 26 Harv. Hum. Rts. J. 179 (2013); Siri Gloppen & Mindy Jane Roseman, Introduction: Can Litigation Bring Justice to Health? in Litigating Health Rights: Can Courts Bring More Justice to Health? (Alicia Ely Yamin & Siri Gloppen eds., 2011).

Biotechnology is then an area in which the granting of a patent can theoretically involve freedom of expression concerns.[58] The patentability of genetic information – that is "pure information" – can have the adverse effect to exclude others from research on a particular genetic sequence and also preclude "some forms of genetic counselling".[59] These considerations are also relevant in respect of protection of the right to participate in culture and to benefit from scientific progress and its further application.[60]

For all these reasons, the debate on DNA-based inventions remains subject to intense discussions, in particular with regard to patent claims that are essentially focused on inventions based on informational elements (such as genes), or on techniques that extract and utilize such information (such as DNA-related diagnostics).[61]

5.4 The Myriad Genetics Controversy and Its Ramifications

The case study chosen for this analysis is a landmark and recent litigation filed by the American Civil Liberties Union (ACLU) alleging violation of constitutional rights and the legitimacy of patents on two human genes used to predict breast and ovarian cancer.[62] More specifically, the controversy has centered on the validity – under § 101 of the US Patent Code – of two patents on tumor suppressor genes known as BRCA1[63] and BRCA2.[64]

---

[58] Id. at 314.

[59] Id. at 315.

[60] See International Covenant on Economic, Social and Cultural Rights art. 15(1)(a) and (b) Dec. 19, 1966, 993 U.N.T.S. 3, S. Treaty Doc. No. 95-19; Universal Declaration of Human Rights (UDHR) art. 27, Dec. 10, 1948, 19 U.S.T. 6228, 999 U.N.T.S. 302. On this, see Audrey R. Chapman, Towards an Understanding of the Right to Enjoy the Benefits from Scientific Progress and Its Applications, 8 J. Hum. Rts. 1 (2009); Yvonne Donders, The Right to Enjoy the Benefits of Scientific Progress: In Search of State Obligations in Relation to Health, 14 Med Health Care and Philos 371 (2011).

[61] See Minssen & Nilson, Standing on shaky ground: US patent-eligibility of isolated DNA and genetic diagnostics after AMP v USPTO, cit., at 226.

[62] Assoc. for Molecular Pathology v US Patent and Trademark Office, 702 F Supp 2d 181 (SDNY 2010) [hereinafter Myriad I].

[63] U.S. Patent No. 5,747,282 (filed June 7, 1995). BRCA1 is a human gene expressed in the cells of breast and other tissues to repair damaged DNA and suppress tumor growth. See Tina Saladino, Seeing the Forest Through the Trees: Gene Patents & the Reality of the Commons, 26 Berkeley Tech. L.J. 301, 302 (2011).

[64] U.S. Patent No. 5,710,001 (filed Dec. 21, 1995). BRCA2 is a human gene that binds to and regulates a protein which fixes breaks in DNA. Although structurally different from BRCA1, BRCA2 serves a similar function and the two genes are often referred to collectively as "BRCA". See Saladino, Seeing the Forest Through the Trees: Gene Patents & the Reality of the Commons, cit. at 302.

The origins of the Myriad controversy date back to September 1994, when the U.S. Biotech Company Myriad Genetics,[65] in collaboration with the University of Utah and other research laboratories, was able to identify the nucleotide sequences linked to susceptibility for breast and ovarian cancer.[66] The oncogene was identified with the acronym BRCA that stands for "breast cancer". Following the isolation of the oncogene, Myriad also developed a diagnostic test intended to identify genetic predisposition to breast and ovarian cancer.[67] After the isolation of these two genes, Myriad filed for patent protection in both the United States and Europe.[68] These patents immediately raised questions for discussion among scientists and others concerned. Their controversial nature is reflected in their negative feedback received in different countries.[69] In Europe, unlike in the United States, the opponents contested the patent on the basis of the European Patent Convention's patentability criteria, claiming that the invention "lacked novelty, inventive step and industrial application, and that the patent failed to disclose the invention sufficiently for a person skilled in the art to carry it out."[70]

Negative reactions were particularly strong in France, where French public health organizations and genetics societies promoted opposition proceedings before the European Patent Office (EPO) against the Myriad' patents.[71] These oppositions have been mostly successfully affected in amendment of the opposed Myriad's

[65] See E. Richard Gold & Julia Carbone, Myriad Genetics: In the Eye of the Policy Storm, 12 Genetics Med. S39, S41 (2010) (observing how the continuing debate on Myriad's patents began in October, 1994 with the publication in "Science" of an article reporting the results about BRCA1). Myriad Genetics is a healthcare company founded in May 1991 specializing in developing and marketing molecular diagnostic products to perform such tasks as assessing a person's risk of developing a disease later in life. See Myriad Genetics – About, www.myriad.com/about (last visited Nov. 14, 2015). "Myriad is a for-profit corporation located in Salt Lake City, Utah [that does] business throughout the United States. Myriad is incorporated in Delaware. Myriad is a co-owner of patent 5,747,282, and formerly was a co-owner of several of the other patents challenged [by the Association for Molecular Pathology]."

[66] See Myriad I, cit., at 201-03 (S.D.N.Y. 2010); See also Yoshio Miki et al., A Strong Candidate for the Breast and Ovarian Cancer Susceptibility Gene BRCA1, 266 Science 66–71 (1994).

[67] See Myriad I, cit. at 201.

[68] Id. at 202.

[69] "Oppositions were filed against the European patent (EP 705902) on the isolated BRCA-1 gene by, among others, Switzerland's Social Democratic Party; Greenpeace Germany; the French Institut Curie; Assistance Publique-Hôpitaux de Paris; the Belgian Society of Human Genetics; the Netherlands, represented by the Ministry of Health; and the Austrian Federal Ministry of Social Security." See Anja von der Ropp and Tony Taubman, Bioethics and Patent Law: The Case of Myriad, WIPO MAG., Aug. 2006, at 8, available at <http://www.wipo.int/wipo_magazine/en/2006/04/article_0003.html> (last accessed 28 April 2016).

[70] Id.

[71] See E. Richard Gold & Julia Carbone, Myriad Genetics: In the Eye of the Policy Storm, 12 Genetics Med. S39, S45, S54 et seq. (2010); Joshua D. Sarnoff, Patent Eligible Medical and Biotechnology Inventions After Bilski, Prometheus, and Myriad, 19 Tex. Intell. Prop. L.J. 393, 416 (2011).

patents.[72] In particular, the claims of the gene sequence were held invalid for lack of novelty.[73]

The following sections present and consider the findings that both the district Court (Myriad I)[74] and the Federal Circuit (Myriad II)[75] reached on the Myriad case as well as the final outcome as decided by the US Supreme Court (Myriad III).[76] In particular, we analyze the conflicts, context and implications of the case outlining how they are relevant to other intimately connected sectors. Using the Myriad Genetics controversy as a paradigmatic example, we then discuss the significance of fundamental rights as an institutional boundary against the expansionary tendency of intellectual property law and the consequential privatization of knowledge. On this ground we also explore the role of the courts as "guardians" of fundamental rights supervising and revising unfair acts issued by other branches of government.[77] The case is offered to demonstrate that fundamental rights arguments can be successfully used to measure and interpret the effects of patent law.

[72] See von der Ropp & Taubman, Bioethics and Patent Law: The Case of Myriad, cit. (noting that the opposition proceedings led to the revocation in 2004 of European Patent 699754, which covered a method for diagnosis); See also Sarnoff, Patent Eligible Medical and Biotechnology Inventions After Bilski, Prometheus, and Myriad, cit. at 416; Gold & Carbone, Myriad Genetics: In the Eye of the Policy Storm, cit. at S45; Jordan K. Paradise, Lessons from the European Union: The Need for a Post-Grant Mechanism for Third-Party Challenge to U.S. Patents, 7 Minn. J.L. Sci. & Tech. 315, 320 (2005).

[73] The opposition procedure concerning the BRCA1 gene concluded in 2007, following an appeal procedure. European patents on the BRCA genes were partially revoked or amended for lack of conformity to the fundamental patentability requirements: novelty, inventive step, industrial application and disclosure of technical information. See Board of Appeal decision T1213/05 available at <http://www.epo.org/law-practice/case-law-appeals/pdf/t051213eu1.pdf> (last accessed 28 April 2016). For related European perspectives, see von der Ropp & Taubman, Bioethics and Patent Law: The Case of Myriad, cit. (arguing that "the proceedings found that errors in the original patent application had not been corrected until the gene sequences were in the public domain. This meant that, according to patentability criteria, the invention had not been fully disclosed in the application as originally filed; and was not novel by the time the invention was fully described in the amended application"). See also E. Richard Gold & Julia Carbone, Myriad Genetics: In the Eye of the Policy Storm, 12 Genetics Med. S39, S45, S54 (2010); Nayanah Siva, Myriad Wins BRCA1 Row, (2009) 27 Nat. Biotechnol. 8 (2009); Gert Matthijs, The European Opposition against the BRCA Gene Patents, 5 Fam. Cancer 95 (2006); Gertrui Van Overwalle, Analysing DNA patents in relation with diagnostic genetic testing, in 14 European J. Human Genetics, 26, 30 (2006).

[74] Ass'n for Molecular Pathology v US Patent and Trademark Office, 702 F Supp 2d 181 (SDNY 2010) [hereinafter Myriad I].

[75] Ass'n of Molecular Pathology v. U.S. Pat. & Trademark Office, 653 F.3d 1329 (Fed. Cir. 2011) [hereinafter Myriad II].

[76] Ass'n for Molecular Pathology v. Myriad Genetics, Inc., 133 S. Ct. 2107, 186 L. Ed. 2d. 124 (2013) [hereinafter Myriad III].

[77] See Giorgio Resta, The Case Against the Privatization of Knowledge: Some Thoughts on the Myriad Genetics Controversy in Biotech Innovations & Fundamental Rights 11 (Roberto Bin et al. eds, 2011).

5.4.1 The District Court's Decision: "Myriad I"

On May 12, 2009, the Association for Molecular Pathology along with individual patients and many other medical organizations filed suit in the Southern District of New York against the United States Patent and Trademark Office and Myriad Genetics Corporation.[78] The plaintiffs explicitly claimed – *inter alia* – the validity of Myriad's patents arguing that the subject matter of the claims was ineligible for patent protection under § 101 of the US Patent Code.[79]

In particular, the plaintiffs have asserted claims for violation of the First Amendment freedom of thought, a violation of patent law set forth in 35 USC 101 (requiring novelty and non-obviousness), as well as Constitution's mandate to

[78] See Myriad I, cit., at 186–89. Among the several works published on the controversy, see Timothy Caulfield et al., Myriad in the Mass Media: The Covering of a Gene Patent Controversy, 9 Genetics in Medicine 850 (2007). Among earlier commentators, see Jocob D. Moore, The Forgotten Victim in the Human Gene Patenting Debate: Pharmaceutical Companies, 63 Fla. L. Rev. 1277 (2011); Jonah D. Jackson, Something Like the Sun: Why Even "Isolated and Purified" Genes Are Still Products of Nature, 89 Tex. L. Rev. 1453 (2011); Krysta Kauble, Patenting Everything Under the Sun: Invoking the First Amendment to Limit the Use of Gene Patents, 58 UCLA L. Rev. 1123 (2011); Kali Murray & Esther van Zimmeren, Dynamic Patent Governance In Europe And The United States: The Myriad Example, 19 Cardozo J. Int'l & Comp. L. 287 (2011); Douglas L. Rogers, Coding For Life – Should Any Entity Have The Exclusive Right To Use And Sell Isolated Dna?, 12 Pgh. J. Tech. L. & Pol'y 1 (2011); Malorye Allison, Myriad Decision Reassures Biotechs but Diagnostics still Murky, 29 Nature Biotech. 771 (2011); Andrew Chin, Gene Probes As Unpatentable Printed Matter, 20 Fed. Cir. B.J. 527 (2011); Lamis G. Eli, When Myriad Genetics Prohibited a Myriad of Options: Association for Molecular Pathology V. USPTO, 21 DePaul. J. Art Tech. & Intell. Prop. L. 357 (2011); Jenny L. Maxey, A Myriad of Misunderstanding Standing: Decoding Judicial Review for Gene Patents, 113 W. Va L. Rev. 1033 (2011); Joshua D. Sarnoff, Patent Eligible Medical and Biotechnology Inventions After Bilski, Prometheus and Myriad, 19 Tex. Intell. Prop. L.J. 393 (2011); Matthew Poulsen, Jurisprudential and Economic Justifications for Gene Sequencing Patents, 90 Neb. L. Rev. 196 (2011); Peter Edwards, AMP v. Myriad: The Future of Medicine and Patent Law, 12 Minn. J.L. Sci. & Tech. 811 (2011); Tina Saladino, Seeing the Forest Through the Tees: Gene Patents and the Reality of the Commons, 26 Bekeley Tech. L. J. 301 (2011); Morgan Geller, Every Woman Deserves Her Own Pair of Genes: The Constitutionality of Patenting the BRCA Genes in Association for Molecular Pathology v. U.S. Patent & Trademark Office, 34 Nova L. Rev. 765 (2010); Alex Osterlind, Staking a Claim on the Building Blocks of Life: Human Genetic Material Within the United States Patent System, 75 Mo. L. Rev. 617 (2010); Lauren M. Dunne, "Come, Let Us Return to Reason": Association of Molecular Pathology v. USPTO, 20 DePaul J. Art Tech. & Intell. Prop. L. 473 (2010); Tiana Leia Russell, Unlocking the Genome: The Legal Case Against Diagnostic Genetic Patens, 16 Marq. Intell. Prop. L. Rev. 81 (2012); Ashish Bakshi, Gene Patents at the Supreme Court: Association for Molecular Pathology v.Myriad Genetics, 1 J. Law Biosci. 183 (2014).

For a comparative analysis of the BRCA debate in Europe and the US, see Isabelle Huys, Geertrui Van Overwalle and Gert Matthijs, Gene and Genetic Diagnostic Method Patent Claims: A Comparison under Current European and US Patent Law, 19 Eur. J. Hum. Genetics 1 (2011); see also Gert Matthijs, The European Opposition against the BRCA Gene Patents, 5 Fam. Cancer 95 (2006).

[79] See Myriad I, cit., at 184.

promote the progress of science set forth in Article I, Section, 8, clause 8.[80] In addition, plaintiffs emphasized that the BRCA1 and BRCA2 genes exist as naturally occurring products of nature. Consequently, according to the plaintiff's complaint, Myriad did not invent, create or in any way construct or engineer the human BRCA1 and BRCA2 genes, because these genes are existing products of nature, naturally occurring within the human body.[81] Myriad simply located them in nature and merely defined their informational content as it exists and functions in natural environment.[82]

In their opening brief, the plaintiffs emphasized an emerging and significant risk of a serious breach of fundamental rights. Specially, they developed their arguments as follows:

> Ease of access to genomic discoveries is crucial if basic research is to be expeditiously translated into clinical tests that benefit patients in the emerging era of personalized and predictive medicine. The patents make ease of access more restricted. Because of the patents, defendant Myriad has the right to prevent clinicians from independently looking at or interpreting a person's BRCA1 and BRCA2 genes to determine if the person is at a higher risk of breast and/or ovarian cancer. Because of the patents and because Myriad chooses not to license the patents broadly, woman who fear they may be at an increased risk of breast and/or ovarian cancer are barred from having anyone look at their BRCA1 and BRCA 2 genes or interpret them except for the patent holder.[83]

They also stressed how Myriad's gene patents were able to illegally limit the free exchange of information, scientific freedom, bodily integrity and, above all, women's health[84]:

> Women are thereby prevented from obtaining information about their health risks from anyone other than the patent holder, whether as an initial matter or to obtain a second opinion. The patents also prevent doctors or laboratories from independently offering testing to their patients, externally validating the test, or working cooperatively to improve testing. Many women at risk cannot even be tested because they are uninsured and/or cannot afford the test offered by Myriad.[85]

In the memorandum of law in support of its motion for summary judgment, the plaintiffs also argue that gene patents violate the First Amendment because these specific patents directly limit thought and knowledge, research activity as well as

---

[80] Complaint, Ass'n for Molecular Pathology v. U.S. Patent & Trademark Office, No. 09-4515 (S.D.N.Y. filed May 12, 2009) available at <http://www.aclu.org/files/images/asset_upload_file939_39568.pdf> (last accessed 28 April 2016). The defendants moved to dismiss the complaint for lack of standing. The petition was denied by an opinion dated November 1, 2009, see Assoc for Molecular Pathology v US Patent and Trademark Office, 669 F Supp 2d 365 (SDNY 2009).

[81] Id. at 18.

[82] Id. at 18.

[83] Id., at 2.

[84] See American Civil Liberties Union, Legal Challenge to Human Gene Patents 1, 5 (May 27, 2009), available at <http://www.aclu.org/pdfs/freespeech/brca_qanda.pdf> (last accessed 28 April 2016).

[85] Complaint, Ass'n for Molecular Pathology v. U.S. Patent & Trademark Office, cit., at 2.

the free flow of information[86]: "Providing a private company a monopoly that has the effect of inhibiting, even completely preventing scientific inquiry, into a field of knowledge is not permissible under the First Amendment".[87] Even in countries whose constitutions reserve special rules for the protection of science, there is an inevitable tendency to explain the problem by observing the question in the light of the traditional concept of the limits to freedom of speech.[88] It happens, because the freedom of research is generally perceived as a special and "privileged" aspect of the freedom of speech.[89] In those countries, such as in the U.S., where freedom of research activity does not have specific legal protection, this freedom turns out to be protected as a specific aspect of the wider freedom of thought and expression covered by the First Amendment of the US Constitution.[90] However, as stressed by other legal scholars, the extensive case law developed by many constitutional Courts on the limitations to freedom of expression can offer interesting indications "for reconstructing the judicial criteria to adopt when evaluating the limitations of freedom of research".[91] Accordingly even in countries whose constitutions reserve special rules for the protection of science, there is a natural inclination to interpret the problem by reviewing "the question in the light of the traditional concept of the limits to freedom of speech".[92]

In essence, this case brought before the U.S. District Court for the Southern District of New York the question of whether isolated human genes and the comparison of related DNA sequences are patentable.[93] Essentially, two are the main sets of claims at issue here, both related to two distinct levels of subject matter. The first claim concerns the compositions of matter involving isolated DNA sequences. The second concerns the techniques of using the isolated sequences to find alterations in BRCA1 and BRCA2 genes.

---

[86] See Plaintiff's Memorandum of Law in Support of Motion for Summary Judgment, Ass'n for Molecular Pathology v. U.S. Patent & Trademark Office, 669 F. Supp. 2d 365 (S.D.N.Y. 2009) at 32–33.

[87] Id., at 35.

[88] See Roberto Bin, Freedom of Scientific Research in the Field of Genetics, in in Biotech Innovations & Fundamental Rights 131, 133 (R. Bin, et al. eds., 2011).

[89] Id., at 142. On this point see also Amedeo Santosuosso et al., What Constitutional Protection for Freedom of Scientific Research? cit., at 342; Id., Freedom of Research and Constitutional Law, cit. at 75.

[90] See Amedeo Santosuosso et al., What Constitutional Protection for Freedom of Scientific Research, 33 Journal of Medical Ethics 342 (2007); Roberto Bin, Freedom of Scientific Research in the Field of Genetics, in Biotech Innovations & Fundamental Rights 131, 142 (R. Bin et al., eds. 2011).

[91] See Roberto Bin, Freedom of Scientific Research in the Field of Genetics, in Biotech Innovations & Fundamental Rights 131, 133 (R. Bin et al., eds. 2011). See also Natasha Lisman, Freedom of Scientific Research: A Frontier Issue in First Amendment Law, 35 Boston Bar J. 4 (1991).

[92] See Roberto Bin, Freedom of Scientific Research in the Field of Genetics, cit.

[93] Ass'n for Molecular Pathology v. U.S. Patent & Trademark Office, 702 F. Supp. 2d 181, 185 (S.D.N.Y. 2010).

Regarding the claims about the composition, the District Court noted that "the clear line of United States Supreme Court precedent and accompanying lower court authorities, establishes that purification of a product of nature, without more, cannot transform it into patentable subject matter. Rather, the purified product must possess markedly different characteristics in order to satisfy the requirements of 35 U.S.C.S. § 101."[94] With this principle in mind, the Court found that the isolated DNA set forth in Myriad's claims were not "markedly different" from native and non-isolated DNA. Furthermore, the Court highlights the informational aspects of DNA:

> In light of DNA's unique qualities as a physical embodiment of information, none of the structural and functional differences cited by Myriad between native BRCA1/2 DNA and the isolated BRCA1/2 DNA claimed in the patents-in-suit render the claimed DNA "markedly different." This conclusion is driven by the overriding importance of DNA's nucleotide sequence to both its natural biological function as well as the utility associated with DNA in its isolated form. The preservation of this defining characteristic of DNA in its native and isolated forms mandates the conclusion that the challenged composition claims are directed to unpatentable products of nature.[95]

Regarding the claims directed to the methods of comparing and analyzing DNA sequences, the Court concluded that the claims did not satisfy the "machine-or-transformation" test as defined by the earlier Federal Circuit precedent *In re Bilski*.[96] In particular, the Court observed how the claims did not incorporate a "transformation" phase.[97] According to the Court, even if the challenged method claims were interpreted to include the alterations connected with isolating and sequencing human genes, these alterations would constitute no more than "data-gathering step[s]" that are not "central to the purpose of the claimed process."[98]

In conclusion, the Court ruled that all the claims at issue were invalid because the human genes and the methods of detecting mutations in those genes were unpatentable subject matter under 35 U.S.C. § 101.[99]

Understandably, the court's decision has given rise to some serious concerns among biotech and pharma companies. *De facto*, the effect of the Court's decision was to declare that isolated human genes are product of nature, rather than man-made inventions and consequently they cannot be patented. However, the unquestionable merit of the decision of the US District Court for the Southern District of

---

[94] Id., at 227 (quoting Diamond v. Chakrabarty, 447 U.S. 303, 310 (1980)).

[95] Id., at 229.

[96] See In re Bilski, 545 F.3d 943 (Fed. Cir. 2008) (holding that a process is only patentable if "(i) it is tied to a particular machine or apparatus, or (ii) it transforms a particular article into a different state or thing"). It is important to note that since the district court issued its opinion, the Supreme Court has clarified the value of the test ruling that this test is a "useful and important clue" for establishing the patentability of claimed techniques, although it is not the only available test. See Bilski v. Kappos, 130 S. Ct. 3218, 3227 (2010).

[97] The Court referred explicitly to the precedent Prometheus v Mayo, where the "machine-or-transformation" test was strictly applied. See Prometheus Labs, Inc v Mayo Collaborative Services 581 F 3d 1336 (Fed Cir 2009).

[98] Myriad I, cit., at 237 (quoting Bilski, 545 F.3d at 962–63).

[99] Myriad I, cit. at 185.

New York is to have placed the gene patent controversy at the forefront of the science policy agenda reopening a debate over civil liberties issues in relation to genetic research.

5.4.2 The Federal Circuit's Decision: "Myriad II"

Considering the magnitude and long-term potential impact of the District's Court decision, it was entirely reasonable for the defendants to pursue their appeal. Consequently, on June 16, 2010, Myriad and its partners filed their notice of appeal of the district court decision with the Federal Circuit.[100]

In particular, Myriad challenged two district court's decisions: (i) the grant of a summary judgment that all of the challenged claims are drawn to non-patentable subject matter under 35 U.S.C. § 101; (ii) the district court's rejection of Myriad's motion to dismiss for lack of standing and subject matter jurisdiction.

The Federal Circuit affirmed in part and reversed in part.[101]

On the issue of jurisdiction, the Federal Circuit observed that the district court incorrectly held that all the plaintiffs had the standing to sue, concluding that just one plaintiff, Dr. Harry Ostrer, has standing to challenge the validity of Myriad's patents.[102]

On the merits, the Federal Circuit reversed the district court's decision that Myriad's composition claims to "isolated" DNA molecules cover patent-ineligible products of nature under § 101 of the patent act since the molecules as claimed do not exist in nature.[103] Demonstrating a scientific understanding of cell biology, the court observed that "Isolated DNA has been cleaved (i.e., had covalent bonds in its backbone chemically severed) or synthesized to consist of just a fraction of a naturally occurring DNA molecule."[104] Accordingly, "BRCA1 and BRCA2 in their isolated state are not the same molecules as DNA as it exists in the body; human intervention in cleaving or synthesizing a portion of a native chromosomal DNA imparts on that isolated DNA a distinctive chemical identity from that possessed by native DNA."[105]

Two of the three judges on the Federal Circuit's panel, Judges Lourie and Moore, agreed that isolated DNA was patentable, whereas Judge Bryson opined to the contrary.

Writing for the majority, Judge Lourie held that "isolated DNAs, not just cDNAs have a markedly different chemical structure compared to native DNAs"[106] and

[100] See Notice of Appeal, Ass'n for Molecular Pathology, 702 F. Supp. 2d 181 (No. 09 Civ. 4515).

[101] Ass'n for Molecular Pathology, 653 F.3d 1329 (Fed. Cir. 2011) at 1333–34.

[102] Id., at 1348.

[103] Myriad II, 653 F.3d 1329, 1352 (Fed. Cir. 2011).

[104] Id. 1352–53.

[105] Id.

[106] Id., at 1353.

therefore it can be considered a "distinct chemical entity" differentiated from their equivalent DNAs in nature.[107] Referring to the Supreme Court decisions in Diamond v Chakrabarty[108] and Funk Brothers Seed v Kalo Inoculant,[109] he held that:

> The distinction, therefore, between a product of nature and a human-made invention for purposes of § 101 turns on a change in the claimed composition's identity compared with what exists in nature. Specifically, the Supreme Court has drawn a line between compositions that, even if combined or altered in a manner not found in nature, have similar characteristics as in nature, and compositions that human intervention has given "markedly different," or "distinctive," characteristics. [...]. Applying this test to the isolated DNAs in this case, we conclude that the challenged claims are drawn to patentable subject matter because the claims cover molecules that are markedly different – have a distinctive chemical identity and nature – from molecules that exist in nature.[110]

Judge Lourie also censured the district court for having considered DNA as a "physical embodiment of information" and for ruling the functional characteristics more significant than the structural ones:

> Plaintiffs argue that because the claimed isolated DNAs retain the same nucleotide sequence as native DNAs, they do not have any "markedly different" characteristics. This approach, however, looks not at whether isolated DNAs are markedly different – have a distinctive characteristic – from naturally occurring DNAs, as the Supreme Court has directed, but at one similarity: the information content contained in isolated and native DNA's nucleotide sequence. Adopting this approach, the district court disparaged the patent eligibility of isolated DNA molecules because their genetic function is to transmit information. We disagree, as it is the distinctive nature of DNA molecules as isolated compositions of matter that determines their patent eligibility rather than their physiological use or benefit. Uses of chemical substances may be relevant to the non-obviousness of these substances or to method claims embodying those uses, but the patent eligibility of an isolated DNA is not negated because it has similar informational properties to a different, more complex natural material that embodies it. The claimed isolated DNA molecules are distinct from their natural existence as portions of larger entities, and their informational content is irrelevant to that fact. We recognize that biologists may think of molecules in terms of their uses, but genes are in fact materials having a chemical nature and, as such, are best described in patents by their structures rather than their functions.[111]

The Federal Circuit also reversed the district court's decision that Myriad's method claim to screening possible cancer therapeutics including changes in cell growth rates is essentially directed to a patent-ineligible scientific principle.

The Federal Circuit did, however, affirm the court's decision that Myriad's method claims directed to "comparing" or "analyzing" DNA sequences are patent ineligible; such claims include no transformative steps and cover only patent-ineligible abstract, mental steps. On this point the Court stated that:

> [...] Myriad's claims to "comparing" or "analyzing" two gene sequences fall outside the scope of § 101 because they claim only abstract mental processes. [...] The claims recite,

[107] Id., at 1351–52.

[108] Diamond v Chakrabarty, 447 US 303, 309 (1980).

[109] Funk Brothers Seed Co v Kalo Inoculant Co, 333 US 127 (1948).

[110] Myriad II, at 1351.

[111] Id. at 1353.

> for example, a "method for screening a tumor sample," by "comparing" a first BRCA1 sequence from a tumor sample and a second BRCA1 sequence from a non-tumor sample, wherein a difference in sequence indicates an alteration in the tumor sample. [...] This claim thus recites nothing more than the abstract mental steps necessary to compare two different nucleotide sequences: look at the first position in a first sequence; determine the nucleotide sequence at that first position; look at the first position in a second sequence; determine the nucleotide sequence at that first position; determine if the nucleotide at the first position in the first sequence and the first position in the second sequence are the same or different, wherein the latter indicates an alternation; and repeat for the next position.[112]

Following the federal court's ruling, on December 7, 2011 the plaintiffs in *Ass'n for Molecular Pathology v. USPTO* filed their petition for a writ of certiorari with the U.S. Supreme Court to review the decision.[113] The petition presented two questions. The first question addresses the limits of patentable subject matter and asks the Court to decide whether human genes are patentable. The second question focuses on plaintiffs' standing to sue. Specifically, the petition asks: "Did the court of appeals err in adopting a new and inflexible rule, contrary to normal standing rules and this Court's decision in *MedImmune, Inc. v. Genentech, Inc.*, 549 U.S. 118 (2007).

5.4.3 "Myriad III" and the Final Decision of the US. Supreme Court

The Supreme Court granted the writ of certiorari[114] filed by the plaintiffs and sent the case back to the US Court of Appeals for the Federal Circuit for reconsideration in light of the Mayo Collaborative Services v. Prometheus decision and its potential to influence or impact also the Myriad case.[115] Consequently, on August 16, 2012, the Federal Circuit issued its new pronouncement reversing - for a second time - the district court's decision that isolated gene sequences are not patentable.[116] At the same time, the Court also partly confirmed the District Court's decision that some method patents directed to "comparing" or "analyzing" gene sequences may not be

[112] Id., at 1356.

[113] See http://www.supremecourt.gov/Circuits/Docketing/Circ13_2010-1406.pdf (last accessed 28 April 2016).

[114] Petition for Writ of Certiorari, Association for Molecular Pathology v. Myriad Genetics, Inc., 653 F. 3d 1329 (Fed Cir. 2011) (No. 11-725) 2011.

[115] Ass'n for Molecular Pathology v. Myriad Genetics, Inc., 132 S. Ct. 1794 (2012) (with reference to the decision in Mayo Collaborative Services v. Prometheus Laboratories, Inc., 132 S. Ct. 1289 (2012)).

[116] Ass'n for Molecular Pathology v. U.S. Patent & Trademark Office, 689 F.3d 1303 (Fed. Cir. 2012)

patentable.[117] Nevertheless, the plaintiffs filed a new petition for a writ of Certiorari[118] and the Supreme Court agreed to once again hear the case limiting the question of whether human genes are patent eligible.[119] On June 13, 2013, the U.S. Supreme Court issued this long-awaited decision invalidating, *de facto*, the patents on BRCA 1 and BRCA 2 and concluding that isolated genomic DNA is not eligible for patenting under Section 101 of the US patent statute.[120] The Court's reasoning essentially rests on the difference between products as they are found in nature as opposed to those that have been transformed or altered into something man-made. Mentioning the Supreme Court's prior decision in Diamond v. Chakrabarty, the judges argued that: "Myriad recognizes that our decision in Chakrabarty is central to this inquiry. [...] In Chakrabarty, scientists added four plasmids to a bacterium, which enabled it to break down various components of crude oil." At the same time, the Court also recognized that the Chakrabarty bacterium was new "with markedly different characteristics from any found in nature." The Court finally concluded that, "Myriad did not create anything", namely "it found an important and useful gene, but separating that gene from its surrounding genetic material is not an act of invention." As a consequence, these "naturally occurring, isolated DNA segments" were ruled to be patent ineligible subject matter.

This landmark decision represents a substantial shift in patent law and overturns current Patent Offices policy. However, the Court left the possibility open to patent artificially created DNA sequences, such as cDNA, because they do not occur naturally. In other words, DNA that has been modified from its naturally occurring form will still be subject to patent monopolies. On this point, the Court stated that:

> cDNA is not a "product of nature," so it is patent eligible under §101. cDNA does not present the same obstacles to patentability as naturally occurring, isolated DNA segments. Its creation results in an exons-only molecule, which is not naturally occurring. Its order of the exons may be dictated by nature, but the lab technician unquestionably creates something new when introns are removed from a DNA sequence to make cDNA.[121]

Even if the full and practical consequences of this decision remain to be seen, some early commentators argued that it could increase "the uncertainty regarding the availability of effective patent protection in important areas of biotechnology

---

[117] Id. On this point, the Court stated the following: "We turn next to Myriad's challenged method claims. This court in its now-vacated decision of July 29, 2011, had held method claims 1 of the '999,'001, and '441 patents, as well as method claims 1 and 2 of the '857 patent – all of which consist of analyzing and comparing certain DNA sequences – not to be patent-eligible subject matter on the ground that they claim only abstract mental processes. In light of the Supreme Court's decision in Mayo, we reaffirm that prior holding. The Court made clear that such diagnostic methods in that case essentially claim natural laws that are not eligible for patent."

[118] 689 F.3d 1303 (Fed. Cir. 2012), petition for cert. filed (U.S. Sept. 25, 2012).

[119] Ass'n for Molecular Pathology v. Myriad Genetics, et al. (USSC Docket 12-398) (Certiorari granted November 30, 2012).

[120] Association for Molecular Pathology v Myriad Genetics, Inc., 133 S. Ct. 2107, 186 L. Ed. 2d. 124 (2013) [Myriad III].

[121] Id.

and pharmaceutical research".[122] However – at the moment – the only evident effect of this decision is that it could affect the validity of granted patents and make it harder to obtain patents protecting newly isolated products of nature and other biotechnology - based inventions. Understanding the implications of the Supreme Court's decision on the biotech field will require further analysis and consideration also in terms of its influence at global level. In addition to its domestic impact, the case can in fact constitute an important international legal precedent that courts in other countries can look to when evaluating similar questions.

In order to mitigate the uncertainties coming from the Supreme Court's decisions in Mayo and Myriad, the United States Patent and Trademark Office (USPTO) is now working on a new guidance on subject matter eligibility. In particular, on the 16 of December 2014 the USPTO issued a new guidance - followed by two updates in July 2015 and May 2016 - describing an innovative eligibility test.[123] The Guidance has the purpose of assisting USPTO staff in examination and post-grant proceedings to define whether claimed subject matter is eligible under 35 U.S.C. 101.

5.5 Possible Alternatives to Private Ownership of Genetic Resources

Controversies that surround human genetic resources reveal that the main concern at present is how to identify and measure the uncertain legal status of new immaterial goods, namely of genetic information.

The proliferation of patents, and especially of gene patents, has received considerable scholarly attention on measures to avoid or mitigate the emergence of patent thickets and anticommons effects.[124] Working through an analysis of the various statutory, regulatory and judicial rules involved in governing immaterial information goods, we would like to identify the most critical points against a strict proprietary regime. In particular, from this analysis it follows that one of the most

[122] See e.g. Christopher M. Holman, In Myriad the Supreme Court Has, Once Again, Increased the Uncertainty of U.S. Patent Law, 32 Biotech. L. Rep. 1, 1 (2013); Arti K. Rai, Biomedical Patents at the Supreme Court: A Path Forward, 66 Stan. L. Rev. Online 111 (2013). See also Daniel L. Burk, Are Human Genes Patentable? 44 Int'l Rev. Intell. Prop. & Competition L. 747 (2013) (arguing that the decision leaves the law in this area far more confused and uncertain than before).

[123] See United States Patent and Trademark Office 37 CFR Part 1 [Docket No. PTO–P–2014–0058] 2014 Interim Guidance on Patent Subject Matter Eligibility, Federal Register Vol. 79, N. 241 (16 December 2014); United States Patent and Trademark Office 37 CFR Part 1 [Docket No. PTO–P–2015–0034] July 2015 Update on Patent Subject Matter Eligibility, Federal Register Vol. 80, N. 146 (30 July 2015); United States Patent and Trademark Office 37 CFR Part 1 [Docket No. PTO–P–2016–0003] May 2016 Update on Patent Subject Matter Eligibility, Federal Register Vol. 81, N. 88 (6 May 2016).

[124] For a general discussion on the problem of these two phenomena, see Daniel L. Burk and Mark A. Lemley, The Patent Crisis and How the Courts Can Solve It 76 (2009); Heller, The Tragedy of the Anticommons: Property in the Transition from Marx to Markets, cit., at 670; Carl Shapiro, Navigating the Patent Thicket: Cross Licenses, Patent Pools, and Standard Setting, 1 Innovation Policy and The Economy 119 (Jaffe et al. 2001).

challenging aspects of litigation in this area involves the determination of the boundary line between the "domain of property" and the "domain of liberty".[125]

The appropriation and commercialization of immaterial goods is possible. However, it becomes obvious that the current strong property rights regime is based on a legally untenable ground: in fact, its implementation totally depends on the design and conservation of the artificial scarcity of immaterial good which is supported and maintained by a set of questionable assumptions.[126] The considerable increases in patent protections have not converted comparable increases in innovation. Furthermore – as suggested by some scholars – there is little historical evidence that supports the argument that intellectual property monopolies efficiently increase innovation and knowledge transfer activity.[127] On the contrary, too much ownership of intellectual property can have the effect of decreasing rather than increasing innovation.[128]

The dilemma in the governance of immaterial goods suggests there is a fundamental tension between the security of property and the exercise of natural liberty. Genetic information is a public good and must be freely available to other researchers who want to use and test it in similar process. As bioscience is being transformed into an information science,[129] those who want to do research must have free access to this information. It implies that users of naturally occurring genetic resources can not appropriate the value of genetic information. The scope of the patent system has expanded its boundaries to protect matters whose protection is questionable. At the same time, biological discovery has become a "work of low inventorship", and much more a work of "mere cartography".[130] The direct consequence of this new phenomenon is that courts are more often dealing with an increasing number of legal actions against forms of privatization of knowledge that were previously public common goods or consisting in mere reformulation of natural phenomena. The growing advances in the biosciences and medical technology led – as we have seen – to an increasing number of new controversies and lawsuits in this area. This is an indirect indication that the privatization of product of nature is becoming a

---

[125] See Yochai Benkler, Constitutional Bounds of Database Protection: The Role of Judicial Review in the Creation and Definition of Private Rights in Information", 15 Berkeley Tech. L.J. 535, 557 (2000); Giorgio Resta, Nuovi Beni Immateriali e Numerus Clausus dei Diritti Esclusivi, Diritti Esclusivi e Nuovi Beni Immateriali 3, 68 (Giorgio Resta, ed. 2011).

[126] See generally Michele Boldrin and David K. Levine, Against Intellectual Monopoly (2008).

[127] James Bessen and Michael J. Meurer, Patent Failure: How Judges, Bureaucrats, and Lawyers Put Innovators at Risk 46–71 (2008); Boldrin, Levine, Against Intellectual Monopoly, cit.;. Michael A. Heller, The Gridlock Economy: How Too Much Ownership Wrecks Markets, Stops Innovation, and Costs Lives (2008); Burk and Lemley, The Patent Crisis and How the Courts Can Solve It, cit., at 95–100.

[128] Murray and Stern, Do Formal Intellectual Property Rights Hinder the Free Flow of Scientific Knowledge? An Empirical Test of the Anti-Commons Hypothesis, cit.; John P. Walsh et al., Working Through the Patent Problem, Science, No. 299, 2003, 1021.

[129] Hess and Ostrom, A Framework for Analysing the Microbiological Commons, cit., at 335.

[130] Oskar Liivak, Maintaining Competition in Copying: Narrowing the Scope of Gene Patents, 41 U.C. Davis Law Review 177, 185 (2007).

very sensitive and critical issue with cross-cutting implications since it negatively impacts society in many meaningful manners.

The ways in which society, governments and industry can deal with health-related issues vary strongly from one scenario to the other and reflects their different policy orientations. However, an important aspect of the current policy is that – despite some recent improvements – is still largely dominated by the extreme views. It is however an occasion for people to develop discussion and engage in thoughtful discourse about the pros and cons of patenting genes and the ramifications of private control over common information.[131] Many of these trends have begun to merge as it becomes obvious that what is needed is a major rethinking of the current processes related to the ownership of genetic material and information: a recasting of "the basic patent paradigm that would give much greater weight to the provision of public goods and "access to knowledge" in general, at the expense of private incentives to innovate".[132] That means that in this situation, it is necessary to reconsider and expand many of the issues occurring in the world of patenting life forms. In order to provide an equal, efficient and sustainable use of genetic information, it is possible to define four different scenarios that could potentially arise in response to different interest groups attempting to influence national and international policy-making in this area.[133] The first scenario assumes a more stringent set of worldwide patent standards under an international treaty, such as the WIPO Substantive Patent Law Treaty with the aim of finding commonalities between national and regional substantive patent law.[134] This is a position supported by many transnational corporations.[135] A second possible scenario foresees the development of a diversified scheme in which emerging or unindustrialized countries progressively redesign the current patent system as needed to fit it to their requirements and needs. A third scenario assumes a radical change toward second-tier regimes involving a more general application of a license of rights regime in cumulative innovation fields. This approach should specifically address the problems caused by cumulative and sequential innovation. Finally, the fourth scenario assumes a complete recasting of the global patent paradigm providing much better support and weight distribution to

---

[131] Geertrui Van Overwalle, et al., Models for Facilitating Access to Patents on Genetic Invention, 7 Nature Review Genetics 143 (2006); Geertrui Van Overwalle, Turning Patent Swords into Shares, 330 Science 1630, 1631 (2010).

[132] See Jerome Reichman and Rochelle C. Dreyfuss, Harmonization Without Consensus: Critical Reflections on Drafting a Substantive Patent Law Treaty, 57 Duke L. J. 85, 105 (2007); European Patent Office, Scenarios For The Future – How Might IP Regimes Evolve by 2025? What Global Legitimacy Might Such Regimes Have? Munich, European Patent Organization, 2007, at 72.

[133] European Patent Office, Scenarios For The Future - How Might IP Regimes Evolve by 2025? What Global Legitimacy Might Such Regimes Have? cit.

[134] WIPO, Substantive Patent Law Harmonization, available at <www.wipo.int/patent/law/en/harmonization.htm>; Draft Substantive Patent Law Treaty, WIPO Standing Committee On The Law Of Patents, Tenth Session, Geneva 10–14 May 2004, available at <www.wipo.int/edocs/mdocs/scp/en/scp_10/scp_10_2.pdf>.

[135] European Patent Office, Scenarios For The Future – How Might IP Regimes Evolve by 2025? What Global Legitimacy Might Such Regimes Have? cit.

the provision of public goods and "access to knowledge" in general, at the expense of the exclusive benefits of some intellectual property rights.[136] Within this latter scenario, at least two alternative approaches are possible: one that focuses on the quasi-public goods properties of genetic information and one that focuses on the quasi-private goods properties of scientific data.[137] The quasi-public goods approach can be used when scientific innovations are created with public funding. In this case, scientific information has already public good characteristics that make it perfectly suitable for open availability because taxpayer has formerly paid for its production and use.[138] The quasi-private goods approach can instead be helpful when investigators do not agree to fully and openly share their scientific findings, but they are however interested to disclose their data – under certain conditions – with others researchers.[139]

5.6 Changing the Landscape for Biotechnology

The feature which has emerged above all others from the cases examined in this part of the book concerns the question of how the patent system has expanded its boundaries to protect matters whose protection is questionable invading spaces already occupied by others rights. The analysis also highlights how this particular situation can harm innovation and knowledge sharing, public health and access to medicines by making the genes of our bodies privately owned.

Opponents of gene patents argue that this praxis violates the freedom of speech, expression and communication – common to all Western liberal democracies –

---

136 See Reichman and Dreyfuss, Harmonization Without Consensus: Critical Reflections on Drafting a Substantive Patent Law Treaty, cit.

137 Quasi-public goods are goods that are essentially public in nature, but do not reveal fully the features of non-excludability and non-rivalry. On the other hand, the quasi-private goods are characterized by non-rivalry combined with the possibility of exclusion. See Robert Cooter and Thomas Ulen, Law and Economics, 42, 106, 3d. ed. (2000) (defining public and private goods); Inge Kaul et al., Defining Global Public Goods, Global Public Goods: International Cooperation in the twenty-first century 2 (Inge Kaul et al., Eds., 1999). See also Michael Callon, Is Science a Public Good?, 19 Science, Technology, & Human Values, 395, 400 (1994) (observing that "the qualification of science as a quasi-public good rather than as a full-fledged public good derives essentially from the fact that it is to a certain degree appropriable – whereas in standard theory a true public good has to be completely inappropriable.").

138 See Jerome Reichman and Paul Uhlir, A Contractually Reconstructed Research Commons for Scientific Data in a Highly Protectionist Intellectual Property Environment, 66 Law & Contemp. Probs. 315, 326, (2003) (arguing that the taxpayer has already paid once for the production of these data and should not pay twice). For illustrative examples of this approach, see Jerome H. Reichman et al, Governing digitally integrated genetic resources, data, and literature: global intellectual property strategies for a redesigned microbial research commons 437 (2016) (illustrating concrete and functioning examples of "open knowledge" initiatives in the field of genetic research).

139 See Geertrui van Overwalle, Exclusive Ownership versus Open Commons: The Case of Gene Patents, 4 WIPO Journal. 139, 154 (2013) (observing that resources can be "managed under symmetric access and use rules and where access and use cannot be refused, be it for fee or for free").

because of their potential to restrict the individual's freedom of expression.[140] From what has been observed, it is evident that genetic materials are different from other things that are patented, because they are not proper inventions, and other researchers cannot invent alternative genes. As recently argued by the American Civil Liberties Union "even if patent-holders publish information about the genes they have identified, there is nothing to invent around – the genetic material contained in the gene is the information. Because this information is the foundation for future diagnostic tests and potential treatments, tying it up as intellectual property can inhibit, rather than stimulate, advances in biomedical research".[141]

These new key legal questions have started to be challenged more frequently also in courts in different countries. In particular, the effects and consequences of these controversial judgments have been intensively discussed both in academia and policy circles. Courts and scholars have reopened and fueled the debate over the benefits and risks associated with patent protection regarding diagnostic methods, natural compounds and other scientific research techniques. For the most part, these discussions are focused on patent applications with the aim to determine the patentability of a particular invention related to human DNA sequences, stem cells developed in vitro or other natural resources. A key example is the discussed controversy surrounding Myriad Genetic's BRCA patents involving a human gene associated with breast cancer.[142] But, on the same footing is also the so called "Brüstle case" recently decided by the European Court of Justice and linked to a patent concerning the production of neural precursor cells, (used for the treatment of neurological diseases) derived from human embryonic stem cells.[143]

The main causes of this new complexity within the patent system, when applied to the genetic materials, are due to the indiscriminate granting of patents without proper regard for the real value of the invention. In addition, new technologies have completely changed how discoveries are made in genetics and genomic research.[144] These disputed patents are the results of transnational corporation strategies to ensure extensive gene patent portfolios regardless of their real function. The outcome of this methodological approach is – as already pointed out – that gene

[140] Complaint at 19, 22–25, Ass'n for Molecular Pathology v. U.S. Patent & Trademark Office, 702 F. Supp. 2d 181 (S.D.N.Y. 2010) (No. 09 Civ. 4515).

[141] American Civil Liberties Union, "Legal Challenge to Human Gene Patents", (2009) available on the Internet at <www.aclu.org/pdfs/freespeech/brca_qanda.pdf> (last accessed on 1 March 2015).

[142] See infra § 4.7.

[143] Oliver Brüstle v Greenpeace eV (C-34/10) [2012] 1 C.M.L.R. 41. For a more detailed analysis, see e.g. Enrico Bonadio, Biotech patents and morality after Brüstle, 34 Eur. Intell. Prop. Rev. 433 (2012); Aurora Plomer, After Brüstle: EU accession to the ECHR and the future of European patent law, 2 Queen Mary J. of Intell. Prop. 110 (2012);

[144] See Rebecca S. Eisemberg, Patents on DNA Sequences: Molecules and Information, in The Commodification of Information (N. Elkin-Koren & N.W. Netanel, eds., 2002) at 416.

discovery has become a "work of low inventorship", much more a work of "mere cartography".[145]

The current patent trends for global technological innovations seem both inefficient and unsustainable. Monopolies or oligopolies in this sector may threaten not only the free exchange of information in the scientific community, but they may also have critical impacts in the area of healthcare and scientific research. Empirical studies support the assumption that patenting reduces rather than increases global technology diffusion.[146]

As highlighted by some observers "royalty costs now influence the direction of research in basic diseases, and often even the testing for diseases. Such barriers to medical testing and research are not in the public interest. Do you want to be told by your doctor, "Oh, nobody studies your disease anymore because the owner of the gene/enzyme/correlation has made it too expensive to do research?"[147] Genomics (as well as other technological advances) are pushing the IP system into unexplored areas, challenging the accepted rules of the game. This state of affairs suggests the need to establish new guidelines recognizing the changed landscape and the crucial role played by science and technology in modern society. Without a radical recasting of the system, no significant progress will be possible. On the contrary, if the present condition persists, it could actually hurt innovation, rather than help it. As suggested by other authors, patent law "should be assessed from a human right's perspective" also introducing certain limits on patentable subject matter in order to safeguard the rights of human being.[148]

As we have extensively discussed, the question of whether patents should be granted on human DNA is a delicate and highly controversial issue with many unresolved aspects especially on the interaction between human rights and intellectual property. The public debate is particularly harsh and divisive. As a consequence also policy debate appears increasingly polarized and adversarial. In this heated ideological environment, "the outermost positions have become disconnected from what the available evidence actually says", even if "there are grains of truth to many of the extreme assertions." [149] The rhetoric surrounding human gene patents could be easily summarized again in Michael Crichton's frequently cited statement, in which he explicitly stated:

[145] See Oskar Liivak, Maintaining Competition in Copying: Narrowing the Scope of Gene Patents, 41. U.C. Davis L. Rev. 177, 185 (2007).

[146] See e.g. Fiona Murray & Scott Stern, Do Formal Intellectual Property Rights Hinder the Free Flow of Scientific Knowledge? An Empirical Test of the Anti-Commons Hypothesis, 63 J. Econ. Behav. & Org. 648 (2007); John P. Walsh, Ashish Arora & Wesley M. Cohen, Working Through the Patent Problem, 299 Science 1021 (2003).

[147] See Michael Crichton, This Essay Breaks the Law, N.Y. Times, Mar. 19, 2006, at 13.

[148] See Geertrui Van Overwalle, Human rights' limitations in patent law, in Intellectual Property And Human Rights. A Paradox 236, 263 (Willem Grosheide ed., 2010).

[149] See Timothy Caulfield, Reflections on the Gene Patent War: The Myriad Battle, Sputnik and Beyond, 57 Clinical Chemistry 977 (2011).

> You, or someone you love, may die because of a gene patent that should never have been granted in the first place […]. Gene patents are now used to halt research, prevent medical testing and keep vital information from you and your doctor. Gene patents slow the pace of medical advance on deadly diseases. And they raise costs exorbitantly […]. Because the holder of the gene patent can charge whatever he wants, and does.... The gene may exist in your body, but it's now private property.[150]

Similar statements exemplify the common theme that runs through discussions of contemporary science policy developments. The above quote essentially describes how the policy attention can be easily dominated by the extreme views. However, Crichton's provocative statement provides also a good overview of what is at stake. It is an occasion for people to develop discussion and the opportunity to engage in thoughtful discourse about the pros and cons of patenting genes and the ramifications of private control over a human gene.[151]

Many of these trends have begun to merge as it becomes obvious that what is needed is a major rethinking of the current processes related to the ownership of genetic material and information: a recasting of "the basic patent paradigm that would give much greater weight to the provision of public goods and "access to knowledge" in general, at the expense of private incentives to innovate".[152] Also for these reasons, intellectual property rights should be considered not as an absolute right, but as a bundle of rights with some specific social limits.[153]

References

Adelman, David E. 2005. A fallacy of the commons in biotech patent policy. *Berkeley Technology Law Journal* 20: 985.

Adelman, David E., and Kathryn L. DeAngelis. 2007. Patent metrics: The mismeasure of innovation in the biotech patent debate. *Texas Law Review* 85: 1677.

Allison, Malorye. 2011. Myriad decision reassures biotechs but diagnostics still murky. *Nature Biotechnology* 29: 771.

Amani, Bita. 2009. *State agency and the patenting of life in international law: Merchants and missionaries in a global society*. Farnham/Burlington: Ashgate.

[150] See Michael Crichton, Op-Ed., Patenting Life, N.Y. Times, Feb. 13, 2007, at A23, available at <http://www.nytimes.com/2007/02/13/opinion/13crichton.ht l> (last accessed 28 April 2016).

[151] For some possible and practicable solutions, see e.g. Geertrui Van Overwalle et al., Models for Facilitating Access to Patents on Genetic Invention, 7 Nature Review Genetics 143 (2006); Geertrui Van Overwalle, Turning Patent Swords into Shares, cit.

[152] See Jerome H. Reichman & Rochelle Cooper Dreyfuss, Harmonization Without Consensus: Critical Reflections on Drafting a Substantive Patent Law Treaty, 57 Duke L.J. 85, 105–6 (2007); European Patent Office (EPO), Scenarios For The Future – How Might IP Regimes Evolve by 2025? What Global Legitimacy Might Such Regimes Have? 72 (2007) (In the report, the EPO defines four different scenarios that could potentially arise in response to different interest groups attempting to influence national and international policymaking in this area).

[153] See Josef Kohler, Das Autorrecht, eine zivilistische Abhandlung: Zugleich ein Beitrag zur Lehre vom Eigenthum, vom Miteigenthum, vom Rechtsgeschäft und vom Individualrecht 141 (1880).

Ancarani, Vittorio. 2008. *The politics of the human genome project. Do institutions matter?* Roma: Aracne.

Andrews, Lori B., and Jordan Paradise. 2005. Essay, gene patents: The need for bioethics scrutiny and legal change. *Yale Journal of Health Policy Law & Ethics* 5: 403–404.

Bakshi, Ashish M. 2014. Gene patents at the Supreme Court: Association for molecular pathology v. Myriad genetics. *Journal of Law & the Biosciences* 1: 183.

Balmer, Brian. 1996. Managing mapping in the human genome project. *Social Studies of Science* 26: 531.

Benkler, Yochai. 2006. *The wealth of networks: How social production transforms markets and freedom*. New Haven: Yale University Press.

Bernier, Louise. 2010. *Justice in genetics: Intellectual property and human rights from a cosmopolitan liberal perspective*. Cheltenham/Northampton: Edward Elgar Publishing.

Bessen, James, and Michael J. Meurer. 2008. *Patent failure: How judges, bureaucrats, and lawyers put innovators at risk*. Princeton: Princeton University Press.

Bimber, Bruce. 2003. *Information and American democracy: Technology in the evolution of political power*. Cambridge/New York: Cambridge University Press.

Bin, Roberto. 2006. *La Corte e la Scienza*, in Bio-Tecnologie e Valori Costituzionali. Il Contributo della Giustizia Costituzionale, (Atonio D'Aloia ed.). Torino: Giappichelli.

Bin, Roberto, et al. (eds.). 2011. *Biotech innovations & fundamental rights*. Milan/New York: Springer.

Bohman, James. 2004. Constitution making and democratic innovation: The European union and transnational governance. *European Journal of Political Theory* 3: 315.

Boldrin, Michele, and David K. Levine. 2010. *Against intellectual monopoly*. New York: Cambridge University Press.

Bonadio, Enrico. 2012. Biotech patents and morality after Brüstle. *European Intellectual Property Review* 34: 433.

Boschiero, Nerina (ed.). 2006. *Bioetica e Biotecnologie nel Diritto Internazionale e Comunitario*. Torino: Giappichelli.

Boyle, James. 2003. The second enclosure movement and the construction of the public domain. *Law & Contemporary Problems* 66: 33.

Braman, Sandra (ed.). 2004. *Biotechnology and communication: The meta-technologies of information*. Mahwah: Lawrence Erlbaum Associates.

Braman, Sandra, et al. 2004. Technology. In *The sage handbook of media studies*, ed. John D.H. Downing, 123. Thousand Oaks: Sage Publications.

Bratton, Mark (ed.). 2009. *God, ethics and the human genome: Theological, legal and scientific perspectives*. London: Church House Publishing.

Brownsword, Roger. 2008. *Rights, regulation, and the technological revolution*. Oxford: Oxford University Press.

Brownsword, Roger, and Morag Goodwin. 2012. *Law and technologies of the twenty-first century*. Cambridge: Cambridge University Press.

Burk, Daniel L. 2013a. Anticipating patentable subject matter. *Stanford Law Review Online* 65: 109.

Burk, Daniel L. 2013b. Are human genes patentable? *International Review of Intellectual Property and Competition Law* 44: 747.

Burk, Daniel L. 2013c. Edifying thoughts of a patent watcher: The nature of DNA. *UCLA Law Review Discourse* 60: 92.

Burk, Daniel L., and Mark A. Lemley. 2009. *The patent crisis and how the courts can solve it*. Chicago: University of Chicago Press.

Callon, Michael. 1994. Is science a public good? *Science, Technology & Human Values* 19: 395.

Callon, Michel, Pierre Lascoumes, and Yannick Barthe. 2009. *Acting in an uncertain world: An essay on technical democracy*. Cambridge, MA: The MIT Press.

Caulfield, Timothy, et al. 2007. Myriad and the mass media: The covering of a gene patent controversy. *Genetics in Medicine* 9: 850.

Center for Responsible Genetics Consumer Genetic Privacy Manual. 2010. Available at http://www.councilforresponsiblegenetics.org/geneticprivacy/)

Chandra, Rajshree. 2012. *Knowledge as property issues in the moral grounding of intellectual property rights*. New Delhi: Oxford University Press.
Chandrasekharan, Subhashini, et al. 2009. Proprietary science, open science and the role of patent disclosure: The case of zinc-finger proteins. *Nature Biotechnology* 27: 140.
Chapman, Audrey R. 2009. Towards an understanding of the right to enjoy the benefits from scientific progress and its applications. *Journal of Human Rights* 8: 1.
Claude, Richard Pierre. 2002. *Pierre science in the service of human rights*. Philadelphia: University of Pennsylvania Press.
Cook-Deegan, Robert, et al. 2009. The dangers of diagnostic monopolies. *Nature* 458: 405.
Cooter, Robert, and Thomas Ulen. 2000. *Law and economics*, 3rd ed. Reading: Addison Wesley.
Courtney, Aidan. 2013. Dignity, plurality and patentability: The unfinished story of Brustle v Greenpeace. *European Law Review* 38: 92.
Crichton, Michael. 2007, February 13. Patenting life. *The New York Times*, A23
D'Antonio, Virgilio. 2004. *Invenzioni Biotecnologiche e Modelli Giuridici: Europa e Stati Uniti*. Napoli: Jovene.
David, Paul A. 2002. The political economy of public science: A contribution to the regulation of science and technology. In *The regulation of science and technology*, ed. Smith Helen Lawton, 33. London: Palgrave Publishers.
David, Paul A. 2003. The economic logic of "Open Science" and the balance between private property rights and the public domain in scientific data and information: A primer. In *The role of scientific and technical data and information in the public domain*, ed. Julie M. Esanu and Paul F. Uhlir, 19. Washington, DC: National Academy Press.
David, Pail, and Dominique Foray. 1995. Accessing and expanding the science and technology knowledge base. *Science Technology Industry Review* 16: 13.
Den Exter, André. 2010. Personalized medicine and access to genetic technologies. *Revista de Derecho y Genoma Humano* 33: 49.
Devlin, Patrick. 1965. *The enforcement of morals*. Oxford: Oxford University Press.
Doll, John. 1998. The patenting of DNA. *Science* 280: 689.
Donders, Yvonne. 2011. The right to enjoy the benefits of scientific progress: In search of state obligations in relation to health. *Medicine Health Care & Philosophy* 14: 371.
Dreyfuss, Rochelle C. 2010. Does IP need IP? Accomodating intellectual production outside the intellectual paradigm. *Cardozo Law Review* 31: 1437.
Dreyfuss, Rochelle C. 2013. The patentability of genetic diagnostics in U. S. Law and Policy. In *Pharmaceutical innovation, competition and patent law: A trilateral perspective*, ed. Josef Drexl and Nari Leei, 7. Cheltenham/Northampton: Edward Elgar Publishing.
Dreyfuss, Rochelle C., and César Rodríguez-Garavito (eds.). 2014. *Balancing wealth and health: The battle over intellectual property and access to medicines in Latin America*. Oxford: Oxford University Press.
Eisenberg, R.S. 1987. Proprietary rights and the norms of science in biotechnology research. *Yale Law Journal* 97: 177.
Eisenberg, Rebecca S. 1989. Patents and the progress of science: Exclusive rights and experimental use. *University of Chicago Law Review* 56: 1017.
Eisenberg, Rebecca S. 1992. Genes, patents, and product development. *Science* 257: 903.
Feenberg, Andrew. 1999. *Questioning technology*. New York: Routledge.
Feldman, Robin. 2009a. *The role of science in law*. New York: Oxford University Press.
Feldman, Robin. 2009b. Historic perspectives on law & science. *Stanford Technology Law Review* 12: 1.
Frischmann, Brett M., et al. (eds.). 2014. *Governing knowledge commons*. Oxford/New York: Oxford University Press.
Gaisser, Sibylle, et al. 2009. The phantom menace of gene patents. *Nature* 458: 407.
Geiger, Christophe. 2006. Constitutionalising' intellectual property Law? The influence of fundamental rights on intellectual property in the European Union. *International Review of Intellectual Property and Competition Law* 37: 371.

Geiger, Christophe (ed.). 2015. *Research handbook on human rights and intellectual property*. Cheltenham: Edward Elgar Publishing.
Ghosh, Shubba. 2012. *Identity, invention and the culture of personalized medicine patenting*. New York: Cambridge University Press.
Ghosh, Samantak. 2014. The taking of human biological products. *California Law Review* 102: 511.
Giordano, Simona, et al. (eds.). 2012. *Scientific freedom*. London: Bloomsbury Publishing.
Girotto, Sabina. 2010. *Il Trattamento dei Dati Biometrici*, in Trattato di Biodiritto Vol. I 1237 (Stefano Rodotà & Mariachiara Tallacchini eds.) Milano: Giuffè.
Gitter, Donna M. 2001. International conflicts over patenting human DNA sequences in the United States and the European Union: An argument for compulsory licensing and a fair-use exemption. *New York University Law Review* 76: 1623.
Gloppen, Siri, and Mindy Jane Roseman. 2011. Introduction: Can litigation bring justice to health? In *Litigating health rights: Can courts bring more justice to health*?, ed. Alicia Ely Yamin and Siri Gloppen. Cambridge: Harvard University Press.
Godt, Christine. 2014. Intellectual property and European fundamental rights, In *Constitutionalization of European private law: XXII/2*. ed. Hans Micklitz, 211. Oxford: Oxford University Press.
Goggin, L. Malcom (ed.). 1986. Governing science and technology: Reconciling science and technology and democracy. In *Governing science and technology in a democracy*.ed. Malcom Goggin. Knoxville: University of Tennessee Press.
Gold, Richard E. 2013. Patents and human rights: A heterodox analysis. *Journal Law Medicine & Ethics* 41: 185.
Gold, Richard E., and Julia Carbone. 2010. Myriad genetics: In the eye of the policy storm. *Genetics in Medicine* 12: S39.
Greenfield, Debra. 2009. Intangible or embodied information: The non-statutory nature of human genetic material. *Santa Clara Computer & High Technology Law Journal* 25: 467.
Grodin, Michael (ed.). 2013. *Health and human rights in a changing world*, 3rd ed. New York: Routledge.
Grosheide, Willem (ed.). 2010. *Intellectual property and human rights. A paradox*. Cheltenham/ Northampton: Edward Elgar.
Guellec, Dominique, and Bruno van Pottelsberghe de la Potterie. 2007. *The economic of the European patent system: IP policy for innovation and competition*. Oxford/New York: Oxford University Press.
Hanson, Mark J. 1997. Religious voices in biotechnology: The case of gene patenting. *Hastings Center Report* 27: 1.
Hardin, Garret. 1968. The tragedy of the commons. *Science* 162: 1243.
Haunss, Sebastian. 2013. *Conflicts in the knowledge society. The contentious politics of intellectual property*. Cambridge: Cambridge University Press.
Helfer, Laurence R., and Graeme W. Austin. 2011. *Human rights and intellectual property: Mapping the global interface*. Cambridge: Cambridge University Press.
Heller, Michael A. 1998. The tragedy of the anticommons: Property in the transition from Marx to markets. *Harvard Law Review* 111: 621.
Heller, Michael A. 2008. *The gridlock economy: How too much ownership wrecks markets, stops innovation, and costs lives*. New York: Basic Books.
Heller, Michael A., and Rebecca S. Eisenberg. 1998. Can patents deter innovation? The anticommons in biomedical research. *Science* 280: 698.
Hess, Charlotte, and Elinor Ostrom (eds.). 2006. *Understanding knowledge as a commons: From theory to practice*. Cambridge, MA: MIT Press.
Hestermeyer, Holger P. 2007. *Human rights and the WTO: The case of patents and access to medicines*. Oxford: Oxford University Press.
Holman, Christopher M. 2008. Trends in human gene patent litigation. *Science* 322: 198.

Holman, Christopher M. 2013. In myriad the supreme court has, once again, increased the uncertainty of U.S. patent law. *Biotechnology Law Report* 32: 1.

Holman, Molly A., and Stephen R. Munzer. 2000. Intellectual property rights in genes and gene fragments: A registration solution for expressed sequence tags. *Iowa Law Review* 85: 735.

Irwin, Alan. 2001. Constructing the scientific citizen: Science and democracy in the biosciences. *Public Understanding of Science* 10: 1.

Jackson, Jonah D. 2011. Something like the sun: Why even "Isolated and Purified" genes are still products of nature. *Texas Law Review* 89: 1453.

Jasanoff, Sheila. 1995. *Science at the bar. Law, science and technology in America*. Cambridge, MA: Harvard University Press.

Jasanoff, Sheila. 2004. Science and citizenship: A new synergy. *Science and Public Policy* 90.

Jasanoff, Sheila. 2005. *Designs on nature: Science and democracy in Europe and the United States*. Princeton: Princeton University Press.

Jasanoff, Sheila. 2011a. Constitutional moments in governing science and technology. *Science and Engineering Ethics* 17: 621.

Jasanoff, Sheila (ed.). 2011b. *Reframing rights: Bioconstitutionalism in the genetic age*. Cambridge, MA: MIT Press.

Jensen, Kyle, and Fiona Murray. 2005. Intellectual property landscape of the human genome. *Science* 310: 239.

Jørgensen, Rikke Frank. 2006. *Human rights in the global information society*. Cambridge, MA: MIT Press.

Kauble, Krysta. 2011. Patenting everything under the sun: Invoking the first amendment to limit the use of gene patents. *UCLA Law Review* 58: 1123.

Kaul, Inge et al. 1999. Defining global public goods. In *Global public goods; International cooperation in the 21st century*, ed. Inge Kaul et al., 2. New York: Oxford University Press.

Kaye, Jane, et al. 2007. Patents and translational research in genomics. *Nature Biotechnology* 25: 739.

Kevles, Daniel J. 2013. *Can they patent your genes*? The New York Review of Books, March 7.

Kevles, Daniel J., and Ari Berkowitz. 2001. The gene patenting controversy: A convergence of law, economic interests, and ethics. *Brooklyn Law Review* 67: 233.

Kleinman, Daniel Lee. 2000. Democratizations of science and technology. In *Science, technology, and democracy*, ed. Daniel Lee Kleinmann, 139. Albany: State University of New York Press.

Krimsky, Sheldon. 1982. *Genetic alchemy: The social history of the recombinant DNA controversy*. Cambridge, MA: MIT University Press.

Krimsky, Sheldon, and Peter Shorett (eds.). 2005. *Rights and liberties in the biotech age: Why we need a genetic bill of rights*. Lanham: Rowman & Littlefield Publishers.

Kur, Annette, and Marianne Levin. 2011. *Intellectual property rights in a fair world trade system: Proposals for reform of TRIPS*. Cheltenham: Edward Elgar.

Laurie, Graeme. 2004. *Genetic privacy. A challenge to medico-legal norms*. Cambridge: Cambridge University Press.

Lawton Smith, Helen (ed.). 2002. *The regulation of science and technology*. New York: Palgrave Publishers.

Leenes, Ronald E., et al. (eds.). 2008. *Constitutional rights and new technologies. A comparative study*. The Hague: T.M.C. Asser Press.

Liivak, Oskar. 2007. Maintaining competition in copying: Narrowing the scope of gene patents. *U.C. Davis Law Review* 41: 177.

Marks, Stephen. 2010. *Out of obscurity: The right to benefit from advances in science and technology and its implications for global health*. In Proceedings of the 3rd conference on law, science, and technology: Health and science: Human rights and legal issues. Taipei: Academia Sinica.

Matthijs, Gert. 2011. Gene and genetic diagnostic method patent claims: A comparison under current European and US patent law. *European Journal of Human Genetics* 19: 1.

Michaels, Dennis. 1999. Bioprospecting agreements: Forging a comprehensive strategy for managing genetic resources on public lands. *Environs: Environmental Law & Policy Journal* 22: 3.

Mills, Oliver. 2010. *Biotechnological inventions. Moral restraints and patent law*. Farnham/Burlington: Ashgate.
Minssen, Timo, and David Nilson. 2011. Standing on shaky ground: US patent-eligibility of isolated DNA and genetic diagnostics after AMP v USPTO – part I. *Queen Mary Journal of Intellectual Property* 1: 223.
Minssen, Timo, and David Nilson. 2012a. Standing on shaky ground: US patent-eligibility of isolated DNA and genetic diagnostics after AMP v USPTO – part III. *Queen Mary Journal of Intellectual Property* 1: 225.
Minssen, Timo, and David Nilson. 2012b. Standing on shaky ground: US patent-eligibility of isolated DNA and genetic diagnostics after AMP v USPTO – part II. *Queen Mary Journal of Intellectual Property* 1: 136.
Moir, Hazel V.J. 2013. *Patent policy and innovation. Do legal rules deliver effective economic outcomes?* Cheltenham: Edward Elgar Publishing.
Moore, Adam D. 2003. Intellectual property, innovation, and social progress: The case against incentive based arguments. *Hamline Law Review* 26: 601.
Moore, Jocob D. 2011. The forgotten victim in the human gene patenting debate: Pharmaceutical companies. *Florida Law Review* 63: 1277.
Murphy, Thérèse (ed.). 2009. *New technologies and human rights*. Oxford/New York: Oxford University Press.
Murray, Fiona, and Scott Stern. 2007. Do formal intellectual property rights hinder the free flow of scientific knowledge? An empirical test of the anti-commons hypothesis. *Journal of Economic Behavior and Organization* 63: 648.
Murray, Kali, and Esther van Zimmeren. 2011. Dynamic patent governance in Europe and the United States: The Myriad example. *Cardozo Journal of International & Comparative Law* 19: 287.
Ostrom, Elinor. 1990. *Governing the commons: The evolution of institutions for collective action*. Cambridge: Cambridge University Press.
Ouellette, Lisa Larrimore. 2010. Access to bio-knowledge: From gene patents to biomedical materials. Stanford Technology Law Review N1.
Paradise, Jordan, et al. 2005. Patents on human genes: An analysis of scope and claims. *Science* 307: 1566.
Parkinson, John (ed.). 2009. *Expressed sequence tags (ESTs). Generation and analysis*. New York: Humana Press.
Pascuzzi, Giovanni, Izzo, and Matteo Umberto e Macilotti (eds.). 2013. *Comparative issues in the governance of research biobanks: Property, privacy, intellectual property and the role of technology*. Berlin/New York: Springer.
Pauwels, Caroline, et al. (eds.). 2009. *Rethinking European media and communications policy*. Brussels: VUB Press.
Pestre, Dominique. 2008. Challenges for the democratic management of technoscience: Governance, participation and the political today. *Science as Culture* 17: 101.
Pierce, Brandon L. 2009. The impact of patents on the development of genome-based clinical diagnostics: An analysis of case studies. *Genetics in Medicine* 11: 202.
Pizzoferrato, Alberto. 2002. *Brevetto per Invenzioni e Biotecnologie*. Padova: Cedam.
Plomer, Aurora. 2005. *The law and ethics of medical research: International bioethics and human rights*. London: Cavendish Publishing.
Plomer, Aurora. 2012. After Brüstle: EU accession to the ECHR and the future of European patent law. *Queen Mary Journal of Intellectual Property* 2: 110.
Plomer, Aurora. 2013. The human rights paradox: Intellectual property rights and rights of access to science. *Human Rights Quarterly* 35: 143.
Plomer, Aurora. 2015. *Patents, human rights and access to science*. Cheltenham: Edward Elgar.
Plomer, Aurora, and Paul Torremans (eds.). 2009. *Embryonic stem cell patents. European law and ethics*. Oxford: Oxford University Press.
Plomer, Aurora, et al. 2008. Challenges to human embryonic stem cell patents. *Cell Stem Cell* 2: 13.

Rai, Arti K. 1999. Regulating scientific research: Intellectual property rights and the norms of science. *Northwestern University Law* 94: 77.

Rai, Arti K. 2013. Biomedical patents at the supreme court: A path forward. *Stanford Law Review Online* 66: 111.

Rai, Arti K. 2014. Diagnostic patents at the supreme court. *Marquette Intellectual Property Law Review* 18: 1.

Rai, Arti K., and Rebecca S. Eisenberg. 2003. Bayh-Dole reform and the progress of biomedicine. *Law Contemporary Problms* 66: 289.

Reichman, Jerome H., and Paul A. Uhlir. 2003. Contractually reconstructed research commons for scientific data in a highly protectionist intellectual property environment. *Law and Contemporary Problems* 66: 315.

Reichman, Jerome H., and Rochelle C. Dreyfuss. 2007. Harmonization without consensus: Critical reflections on drafting a substantive patent law treaty. *Duke Law Journal* 57: 85.

Reichman, Jerome H., et al. 2016. *Governing digitally integrated genetic resources, data, and literature: Global intellectual property strategies for a redesigned microbial research commons.* New York: Cambridge University Press.

Resnik, David B. 2001. DNA patents and human dignity. *Journal of Law Medicine & Ethics* 29: 152.

Resnik, David B. 2004. *Owning the genome. A moral analysis of DNA patenting.* Albany: SUNY Press.

Resta, Giorgio. 2009. Proprietà Intellettuale e Diritti Fondamentali: Una Relazione Ambigua. In *Persona, Derecho y Libertad: Nuevas Perspectivas. Escritos en Homenaje al Profesor Carlos Fernández Sessarego*, ed. Carlos Alberto Calderón Puertas, et al., 787. Lima: Motivensa Editora Jurídica.

Resta, Giorgio. 2011. Nuovi Beni Immateriali e Numerus Clausus dei Diritti Esclusivi. In *Diritti Esclusivi e Nuovi Beni Immateriali 3*, ed. Giorgio Resta, 68. Torino: Utet.

Resta, Giorgio. 2011. The case against the privatization of knowledge: Some thoughts on the Myriad genetics controversy. In *Biotech innovations & fundamental rights*, ed. Roberto Bin, et al. Milan; New York: Springer.

Rimmer, Matthew. 2008. *Intellectual property and biotechnology. Biological inventions.* Cheltenham: Edward Elgar.

Rimmer, Matthew, and Alison McLennan. 2012. *Intellectual property and emerging technologies: The new biology.* Cheltenham: Edward Elgar Publishing.

Robinson, Douglas, and Nina Medlock. 2005. Diamond v. Chakrabarty: A retrospective on 25 years of biotech patents. *Intellectual Property & Technology Journal* 17: 12.

Roffe, Pedro, and Maximiliano Santa Cruz. 2007. *Intellectual property rights and sustainable development: A survey of major issues.* Santiago: United Nations Publication.

Saladino, Tina. 2011. Seeing the forest through the trees: Gene patents & the reality of the commons. *Bekeley Technology Law Journal* 26: 301.

Samuelson, Pamela. 2003. Mapping the digital public domain: Threats and opportunities. *Law and Contemporary Problems* 66: 147.

Santosusso, Amedeo. 2011. *Diritto, Scienza e Nuove Tecnologie.* Padova: Cedam.

Santosuosso, Amedeo, et al. 2007. What constitutional protection for freedom of scientific research? *Journal of Medical Ethics* 33: 342.

Sarnoff, Joshua D. 2011. Patent eligible medical and biotechnology inventions after Bilski, Prometheus and Myriad. *Texas Intellectual Property Law Journal* 19: 393.

Schuster, Martina Ines. 2012. The Court of Justice of the European Union's ruling on the patentability of human embryonic stem-cell-related inventions (case C-34/10). *International Review of Intellectual Property and Competition Law* 43: 626.

Shaver, Lea. 2010. The right to science and culture. *Wisconsin Law Review* 2010: 121.

Shiva, Vandana. 1997. *Biopiracy: The plunder of nature and knowledge.* New York: South End Press.

Sinjela, Mpazi (ed.). 2007. *Human rights and intellectual property rights: Tensions and convergences.* Leiden: Martinus Nijhoff Publishers.

Soini, Sirpa, et al. 2008. Patenting and licensing in genetic testing: Ethical, legal and social issues. *European Journal of Human Genetics* 16: S10.
Spinello, Richard A., and Maria Bottis. 2009. *A defense of intellectual property rights*. Cheltenham/ Northampton: Edward Elgar.
Stazi, Andrea. 2015. *Biotechnological inventions and patentability of life: The US and European experience*. Cheltenham: Edward Elgar.
Stemerding, Dirk. 1993. How to deal with the implications of human genome research? On the bounds of a politics of regulation. In *Ethics of human genome analysis. European perspectives*, eds. Hille Haker, Richard Hearn and Klaus Steigleder, 217. Tübingen: Attempto Verlag.
Sterckx, Sirid, and Julian Cockbain. 2012. *Exclusions from patentability: How far has the European patent office eroded boundaries?* Cambridge: Cambridge University Press.
Straus, Joseph, et al. 2004. *Genetic inventions and patent law, an empirical survey of selected German R&D institutions*. Munich: Verlag Medien Design.
Tallacchini, Mariachiara. 2003. La Trappola e il Topo: La Brevettabilità della Materia Vivente. In *Le tecniche della Biologia e gli Arnesi del Diritto*, ed. Amedeo Santosuosso, 203. Pavia: Ibis.
Tallacchini, Mariachiara. 2013. Human tissues in the 'Public Space': Beyond the property/privacy dichotomy. In *Comparative issues in the governance of research biobanks: Property, privacy, intellectual property and the role of technology*, ed. Giovanni Pascuzzi, Umberto Izzo, Matteo Macilotti. Berlin/New York: Springer.
Torremans, Paul L.C. (ed.). 2008. *Intellectual property and human rights*. Alphen aan den Rijn: Kluwer Law International.
Ullrich, Hans. 2004. Harmony and unity of European intellectual property protection. In *Intellectual property in the new millennium*, ed. David Vaver and Lionel Bently, 20. Cambridge/ New York: Cambridge University Press.
Vallas, Steven P., Daniel Lee Kleinman, and Dina Biscotti. 2011. Political structures and the making of U.S. biotechnology. In *State of innovation: The U.S. government's role in technology development*, ed. Block Fred and Keller Matthew, 57. Boulder: Paradigm Publishers.
Van Overwalle, Geertrui (ed.). 2009. *Gene patents and collaborative licensing models. Patent pools, clearinghouses, open source models and liability regimes*. Cambridge: Cambridge University Press.
van Overwalle, Geertrui. 2013. Exclusive ownership versus open commons: The case of gene patents. *WIPO Journal* 4: 139.
Van Overwalle, Geertrui, et al. 2006. Models for facilitating access to patents on genetic inventions. *Nature Reviews Genetics* 7: 143.
Varju, Marton. 2014. *European union human rights law: The dynamics of interpretation and context*. Cheltenham: Edward Elgar Publishing.
Verbeure, Birgit, et al. 2006. Analysing DNA patents in relation with diagnostic genetic testing. *European Journal of Human Genetics* 14: 26.
Vila De Azevedo Cunha, Mario, et al. (eds.). 2013. *New technologies and human rights*. Farnham: Ashgate Publishing.
Warren-Jones, Amanda. 2001. *Patenting rDNA. Human and animal biotechnology in the United Kingdom and Europe*. Witney: Lawtext Pub.
Weeramantry, Christopher Gregory (ed.). 1990. *Human rights and scientific and technological development*. Tokyo: United Nations University Press.
Wright, Susan. 1994. *Molecular politics: Developing American and British regulatory policy for genetic engineering*. Chicago: University of Chicago Press.
Young, Katharine G., and Julieta Lemaitre. 2013. The comparative fortunes of the right to health: Two tales of justiciability in Colombia and South Africa. *Harvest Human Rights Journal* 26: 179.

Final Remarks

This book presents a distinctive approach to the study of individual rights in the modern society, focusing on the role of exclusive rights in establishing a severe erosion of traditional civil liberties and other fundamental individual legal rights. Scientific and technological innovations have increased tension between rights protection, information ownership and intellectual freedom. We have also observed a sort of convergence and mutual interaction between issues relating to digital technologies and issues relating the organic world, including the human body. In this context the study has taken into consideration biological and digital information controversies relating to breaches of individual rights, restrictions of personal freedom and incidents of misappropriation of natural resources. We have also seen how both biosciences and digital technologies are considered to be 'meta' technologies of information, meaning that they have both an informational nature and are significant not just in their own right, but also because of the effect that they can have on a whole range of other sectors. Both these technologies have changed the nature of society expanding "the degrees of freedom with which humans can act in the social and material worlds".[1] In addition, their informational nature is transforming the way we deal with information resources: in particular, meta-technologies through their ability to "codify and collate diverse and complex knowledge resources", have made the enclosure of the available knowledge and information assets "more feasible, and by doing so have enabled a concentration of important knowledge resources".[2]

The specific dimensions along which these informational meta-technologies differ from industrial technologies constitute the promise and the challenge of the

[1] Sandra Braman, Informational Meta-Technologies and International Relations: The Case of Biotechnologies 91, 92, in Information technologies and global politics: The changing scope of power and governance (James N. Rosenau and J.P. Singh, eds. 2002).

[2] See Christopher May, Justifying Enclosure? Intellectual Property and Meta-Technologies, in Biotechnology and Communication: The Meta-Technologies of Information 119, 137 (2004).

N. Lucchi, *The Impact of Science and Technology on the Rights of the Individual*, Law, Governance and Technology Series 26,
DOI 10.1007/978-3-319-30439-7

"informational society".[3] Indeed, protection, production, circulation and consumption of information assets are now key aspects of social production and power. This informational shift occurred in both the biological and communicative fields. On the one hand, information and digital communication systems do not involve anymore tangible copies. In addition, the Internet allows information to be widely disseminated and readily accessed at incredible speed with extremely low expense connecting directly the source and the end user without intermediation.[4] This new flexibility offered by digital media allows people to easily copy, modify, and shift them in time and space. Then, the newly acquired independence from the carriers secured by digitalization allows users to manipulate the information with the consequence that the "originality" of a work is threatened to be lost.[5]

On the other hand, also in the field of biotechnology there is a heated debate about its informational shift. The physical, material elements of living organisms and information "are now routinely treated as an isomorphism"[6] to the extent that genomics has "literally" become an information science.[7] This informational shift within biotechnology has allowed to consider the genetic material as a simple combination of various chemicals seeing this collection of information "as a type of commodity to be produced, owned, traded, and consumed like other goods".[8]

Starting from this premise, the book has offered a critical and comparative analysis of the impact of science and technology on individual rights and the public interest. It has also provided a map of the changing nature of law in the face of emerging controversies in science and technology, investigating the problematic status of the intellectual assets in the information age. In this framework, the study has tried to trace provocative parallels and analogies between the regulative rules of technologies for the biological and communicative fields looking at these issues in the perspective of European and North American jurisdictions. The red thread connecting these two apparently distinct domains is represented by the expansive intellectual property protection and enforcement measures incorporated in recent legislations. The growth of regulatory parameters such as protection of intellectual property rights, can severely affect the properties of both these meta-technologies "by altering the conditions in which they appear"[9] and also establishing restrictions on the

[3] See Manuel Castells, The Rise of the Network Society: The Information Age, Economy, Society and Culture 21, note 31 (2d. ed. 2000) (proposing an analytical distinction between the notions of "information society" and "informational society".

[4] See Nicola Lucchi, Digital Media and Intellectual Property, cit. at 160.

[5] Id.

[6] See Leah A. Lievrouw, Biotechnology, Intellectual Property, and the Prospects for Scientific Communication, in Biotechnology and Communication: The Meta-Technologies of Information 145, 160 (2004).

[7] Id.

[8] Id.

[9] See Sandra Braman, The Meta-Technologies of Information, in Biotechnology and Communication: The Meta-Technologies of Information, cit., at 27.

ownership of socially useful information and knowledge.[10] We have also seen that a more fundamental critique to the increasingly expansive reach of intellectual property protection and its possible adverse effects on the rights to freedom of expression and the right to enjoy the benefits of scientific progress and their applications, has been also put forward by Special Rapporteurs appointed by the United Nations Human Rights Council.[11]

The use of powerful information and communications technologies in both the organic and digital worlds has contributed to an expansion of the existing possibilities for the commodification of human and genetic information.[12] Other shared features of this regulatory environment include legal moralism in the process of legislation on ethical issues, the lack of specialist knowledge and experience of policymakers in the areas in which they are called to regulate and excessive lobbying pressure of interest groups. In addition – as we have observed – the regulatory framework of technologies for the biological and communicative realms are often undermined by a lack of coherence between national and international policies and without a weighted contextualization within the broader framework of human rights law.[13]

In this particular dimension, intellectual property rights – specifically patents and copyright – play a key role in making information knowledge accessible. Having in mind this perspective, we have discussed the legal issues raised by the problem of ownership of genetic and digital information. From the analyses and comparisons conducted in this study, it has clearly emerged that copyright and patent law are much less "rights granted in order to incentivize creative and innovative conduct" designed "to further public access to a richer and more diverse array of creative products".[14] On the contrary, they are increasingly used as instruments to control information, property and access. Such a drift, inevitably causes a conflict of rules involving an obvious tension between competing principles. The framework discussed in the above pages, provides also a consistent and explicit representation of

[10] See Christopher May, Justifying Enclosure? Intellectual Property and Meta-Technologies, cit. at 130.

[11] See United Nations General Assembly, Human Rights Council, Report of the Special Rapporteur in the Field of Cultural Rights: The Right to Enjoy the Benefits of Scientific Progress and its Applications, Farida Shaheed, U.N. Doc. UA/HRC/20/26 (14 May 2012) at 15; United Nations General Assembly, Human Rights Council, Report of the Special Rapporteur in the Field of Cultural Rights: Copyright policy and the right to science and culture, Farida Shaheed, U.N. Doc. A/HRC/28/57 (24 Dec. 2014); United Nations General Assembly, Human Rights Council, Report of the Special Rapporteur in the Field of Cultural Rights: Patent policy and the right to science and culture, Farida Shaheed, U.N. Doc. A/70/279 (4 Aug. 2015); United Nations General Assembly, Human Rights Council, Commission on Human Rights, Report by the Special Rapporteur on the Promotion and Protection of the Right to Freedom of Opinion and Expression, Frank La Rue, U.N. Doc. A/HRC/17/27 (16 May 2011).

[12] Id. at 119.

[13] As a consequence, human rights are often invoked under different circumstances to limit the impact of intellectual property rights.

[14] See Graeme B. Dinwoodie & Mark D. Janis, Trademarks and Unfair Competition: Law and Policy 10–11 (2004)

current legal approaches in light of changes in the contemporary society. In the field of scientific innovation, it is noteworthy that these effects tend to be more complicated because of complementary interaction of legal moralism. Judges and legislators are frequently influenced in their decisions by many elements: legal moralism is perhaps one of the most underhanded. At the same time, in the specific context of technology-based innovations, transnational corporation are able to exert enormous influence on legislators to maximizing their global interests. As already argued by other authors "the law today not only interprets the social impacts of science and technology but also constructs the very environment in which science and technology come to have meaning, utility, and force".[15] As a consequence, the interaction between the highly specialized fields of "law and science" and "law and technology" inevitably results in confusion and misunderstanding.

In order to overcome these threats and address these challenges, we attempted to propose some new global intellectual property strategies for informational or knowledge-based assets.

As far as concerns the biological domain, we explored (§ 5.5) diverse sharing strategies supporting the idea of a complete recasting of the global patent paradigm providing much better support mechanisms and weight distribution to the provision of public goods and "access to knowledge" in general, at the expense of the exclusive benefits of some intellectual property rights.[16] In this respect, at least two alternative approaches are possible: one that focuses on the quasi-public goods properties of genetic information[17] and one that focuses on the quasi-private goods properties of scientific data.[18] The quasi-public goods approach can be used – for example – when scientific innovations are created with public funding. In this case indeed scientific information has already public good features that make it perfectly suitable for open availability because taxpayer has formerly paid for its production and use.[19] The quasi-private goods approach can instead be helpful when investigators

[15] See Sheila Jasanoff, Science at the Bar. Law, Science and Technology in America 16 (1995).

[16] See Reichman and Dreyfuss, Harmonization Without Consensus: Critical Reflections on Drafting a Substantive Patent Law Treaty, cit.

[17] On this, see Nicola Lucchi, Understanding Genetic Information as a Commons: From Bioprospecting to Personalized Medicine. 7 Int. J. Commons 313 (2013).

[18] Quasi-public goods are goods that are essentially public in nature, but do not reveal fully the features of non-excludability and non-rivalry. On the other hand, the quasi-private goods are characterized by non-rivalry combined with the possibility of exclusion. See Robert Cooter and Thomas Ulen, Law and Economics, 42, 106, 3d. ed. (2000) (defining public and private goods); Inge Kaul et al., Defining Global Public Goods, Global Public Goods: International Cooperation in the 21st Century 2 (Inge Kaul et al., Eds., 1999). See also Michael Callon, Is Science a Public Good?, 19 Science, Technology, & Human Values, 395, 400 (1994) (observing that "the qualification of science as a quasi-public good rather than as a full-fledged public good derives essentially from the fact that it is to a certain degree appropriable—whereas in standard theory a true public good has to be completely inappropriable.").

[19] See Jerome Reichman and Paul Uhlir, A Contractually Reconstructed Research Commons for Scientific Data in a Highly Protectionist Intellectual Property Environment, 66 Law & Contemp. Probs. 315, 326, (2003) (arguing that the taxpayer has already paid once for the production of these data and should not pay twice). For an analytical discussion and some examples of this approach,

do not agree to fully and openly share their scientific findings, but they are however interested to disclose their data – under certain conditions – with others researchers.[20]

As far as communication technology is concerned, we stressed the importance of fundamental rights as an institutional safeguard against the expansionary tendency of market powers (§ 3.6). We have also seen the fundamental role played by Courts in shaping and adapting the frontiers of fundamental legal rights in the context of communication technologies. The pervasiveness of digital platforms begs also the question of whether an elaboration of new rights and constitutional liberties is required, or whether existing legal instruments can be adjusted to meet the demands of a new reality. This point opens the topical and recurrent debate about the necessity of a specific Internet bill of rights. Following this emerging doctrinal discussion, we have considered a series of initiatives taking place in different countries highlighting the importance of developing a more proactive stance towards integrating rights and freedoms on the Internet, with the objective of providing them with a comprehensive set of principles and obligations comparable to those provided for constitutional rights.[21]

To facilitate the adaptation of copyright and patent law to changed economic, technical and social circumstances, it could be necessary to move away from a rigid system of regulation and introduce flexibilization mechanisms in the form of "open" concepts and general clauses. It is also necessary to rethink the scope and extent of patent and copyright law. As a general rule, the core policies to address this issue involve the strengthening of legal restrictions to prevent harm to the rights of individuals and a comprehensive reform of the system of exclusive rights. Among these improvements should be mentioned the introduction of new and appropriate limitations and exceptions such as subject matter exclusions from patentability, broader use of compulsory licenses and more robust and flexible exceptions and limitations in order to respond to the rapid social, economic, and technological change. In particular, when looking at the regulatory aspects of science and technology, it appears necessary to reconsider the idea of a single and rigid form of intellectual property protection applicable across distinctive and sensitive information assets that may require different level of access or control and that are the result of different technologies or scientific production processes. On this ground, Government's response seems still inadequate not only because the effectiveness of the use of these policy

see Jerome H. Reichman et al, Governing digitally integrated genetic resources, data, and literature: global intellectual property strategies for a redesigned microbial research commons 437 (2016) (illustrating concrete and functioning examples of "open knowledge" initiatives in the field of genetic research).

[20] See Geertrui van Overwalle, Exclusive Ownership versus Open Commons: The Case of Gene Patents, 4 WIPO Journal. 139, 154 (2013) (observing that resources can be "managed under symmetric access and use rules and where access and use cannot be refused, be it for fee or for free").

[21] See See Lex Gill et al, Towards Digital Constitutionalism? Mapping Attempts to Craft an Internet Bill of Rights, Berkman Center Research Publication No. 2015–15 (2015) available at http://ssrn.com/abstract=2687120.

tools varies considerably from country to country, but also because their use is often restricted.[22]

With the further advances of the knowledge economy and rapid technological progress, these situations of conflicts are set to increase in number and size as well as to become more common in different fields of science and different communities and it will oblige the IP system to adapt and comply also with human rights standards.[23]

In a comparative perspective, the case law concerning the evolution of legal interests involved in the protection of individual rights indicates that – in several situations – the safeguard of the citizen's "negative" freedom has progressively extended to include the protection of collective interests that could benefit from that right.[24] Thus, ultimately, the public interest may indeed be embodied within the right of every member of the community.[25] Also the freedom of expression has been involved in this process modifying into a general interest in information. In turn, this transformation has become an actual "right to information", which requires the intervention of public institutions, at least to provide a guarantee of information pluralism.[26] To respond to the demands of distributive justice, countries should take steps to ensure that intellectual property rights promote and safeguard benefit-sharing, that it to say that the benefits from scientific research or technology development should enhance all sectors of society, not just private corporations.[27]

Finally, if there is an issue that in recent years has brought to the attention of legal scholars and legal theorists around the world, its name is circulation of legal models and cross-fertilization of legal approaches. With increasing frequency, judges operating in different and distant legal systems are used to borrowing from each other standards of judgment, argumentative structures, ways to address, and resolve cases substantially similar.

All the legal controversies taken in this study – in addition to having a national impact – can also create persuasive legal precedent that courts in other countries can look to when evaluating similar questions. Science and technology are naturally and essentially based on open and collaborative standards. They are international because scientific facts and principles are universal. As a consequence, also their

---

[22] See Laurence R. Helfer, Mapping the Interface between Human Rights and Intellectual Property, in Research Handbook on Human Rights and Intellectual Property 6, 13 (Christophe Geiger ed., 2015).

[23] See Dominique Guellec & Bruno van Pottelsberghe de la Potterie, The Economics of the European Patent System: IP Policy for Innovation and Competition 125 (2007). Se also generally, Research Handbook on Human Rights and Intellectual Property (Christophe Geiger ed., 2015).

[24] See Roberto Bin, Freedom of Scientific Research in the Field of Genetics, in Biotech Innovations & Fundamental Rights 131, 143 (R. Bin et al., eds. 2011) (The author exemplifies this point by reference to the "negative" right of the freedom of teaching "has fused with a general interest in education, and this has subsequently been translated into a right of each and every one of us to have access to teaching and the benefits of education").

[25] Id.

[26] For a thorough reference to the relationship between freedom of information and the right to be informed, see Eric Barendt, Freedom of Speech, 2nd ed., 108, 112 (2005).

[27] See David B. Resnik, Owning the Genome: A Moral Analysis of DNA Patenting 81 (2004).

regulation must be based on the same characteristics. Science and technology are unanimously considered critical inputs for economic development and growth. Advances in scientific and technological knowledge made possible incredible improvements in the quality of life in both developed and developing countries. Also in the future, the capacity of countries to access, understand, regulate, and efficiently use scientific and technological knowledge will progressively be the determinant of material well-being and quality of life. Obtaining benefits from science and technology depends also on public policies and legal instruments that provide the appropriate enabling environment as well as from the level and quality of the information and communication technologies infrastructure that permit the flow and dissemination of knowledge and information. The absence of an appropriate and well balanced new legal framework constitutes the most serious obstacle to this development.

References

Barendt, E.M. 2005. *Eric freedom of speech*, 2nd ed. Oxford: Oxford University Press.

Bin, Roberto. 2011. Freedom of scientific research in the field of genetics. In *Biotech innovations & fundamental rights*, 131. Milan, New York: Springer.

Braman, Sandra. 2002. Informational meta-technologies and international relations: The case of biotechnologies 91. In *Information technologies and global politics: The changing scope of power and governance*, ed. J.N. Rosenau and J.P. Singh. Albany: State University of New York Press.

Braman, Sandra (ed.). 2004. *Biotechnology and communication: The meta-technologies of information*. Mahwah: Lawrence Erlbaum Associates.

Callon, Michael. 1994. Is science a public good? *Science, Technology, & Human Values, 19*, 395.

Castells, Manuel. 2000. *The rise of the network society: The information age, economy, society and culture*, 2nd ed. Malden: Wiley-Blackwell.

Cooter, Roberti, and Thomas Ulen. 2000. *Law and economics*, 3rd ed. Reading: Addison Wesley.

Dinwoodie, Graeme B., and Mark D. Janis. 2007. *Trademarks and unfair competition: Law and policy*. New York: Aspen Publishers.

Guellec, Dominique, and Bruno van Pottelsberghe de la Potterie. 2007. The economic of the european patent system: IP policy for innovation and competition. Oxford: Oxford University Press.

Haunss, Sebastian. 2013. *Conflicts in the knowledge society. The contentious politics of intellectual property*. Cambridge: Cambridge University Press.

Helfer, L.R. 2015. Mapping the interface between human rights and intellectual property. In *Research handbook on human rights and intellectual property 6*, ed. Geiger Christophe. Cheltenham: Edward Elgar Publishing.

Jasanoff, Sheila. 1995. *Science at the bar. Law, science and technology in America*. Cambridge: Harvard University Press.

Kaul, Inge, et al. 1999. Defining global public goods. In *Global Public Goods; International Cooperation in the 21st Century 2*, ed. Kaul Inge et al. Oxford: Oxford University Press.

Lievrouw Leah, A. 2004. Biotechnology, intellectual property, and the prospects for scientific communication. In *Biotechnology and communication: The meta-technologies of information 145*. Mahwah: Routledge.

Lucchi, Nicola. 2006. *Digital media and intellectual property*. Berlin, New York: Springer.

Lucchi, Nicola. 2013. Understanding genetic information as a commons: from bioprospecting to personalized medicine. *International Journal of the Commons 7*: 313.

May, Christopher. 2004. Justifying enclosure? Intellectual property and meta-technologies. In *Biotechnology and communication: The meta-technologies of information 119*. Mahwah: Routledge.

Reichman, Jerome H., and Paul Uhlir. 2003. A contractually reconstructed research commons for scientific data in a highly protectionist intellectual property environment. *Law and Contemporary Problems, 66*: 315.

Reichman, Jerome H., and Rochelle C. Dreyfuss. 2007. *Harmonization without consensus: Critical reflections on drafting a substantive patent law treaty, Duke Law Journal, 57*: 85.

Reichman, Jerome H., et al. 2016. *Governing digitally integrated genetic resources, data, and literature: global intellectual property strategies for a redesigned microbial research commons.* New York: Cambridge University Press.

Resnik, David B. 2004. *Owning the genome. A moral analysis of DNA patenting*. Albany: SUNY Press.

van Overwalle, Geertrui. 2013. *Exclusive ownership versus open commons: The case of gene patents. WIPO Journal, 4*, 139.

Index

N. Lucchi, *The Impact of Science and Technology on the Rights of the Individual*, Law, Governance and Technology Series 26,
DOI 10.1007/978-3-319-30439-7